Volume VI

Medievalism
A Critical History

MEDIEVALISM

ISSN 2043–8230

Series Editors
Karl Fugelso
Chris Jones

Medievalism aims to provide a forum for monographs and collections devoted to the burgeoning and highly dynamic multi-disciplinary field of medievalism studies: that is, work investigating the influence and appearance of 'the medieval' in the society and culture of later ages. Titles within the series will investigate the post-medieval construction and manifestations of the Middle Ages – attitudes towards, and uses and meanings of, 'the medieval' – in all fields of culture, from politics and international relations, literature, history, architecture, and ceremonial ritual to film and the visual arts. It welcomes a wide range of topics, from historiographical subjects to revivalism, with the emphasis always firmly on what the idea of 'the medieval' has variously meant and continues to mean; it is founded on the belief that scholars interested in the Middle Ages can and should communicate their research both beyond and within the academic community of medievalists, and on the continuing relevance and presence of 'the medieval' in the contemporary world.

New proposals are welcomed. They may be sent directly to the editors or the publishers at the addresses given below.

Professor Karl Fugelso
Art Department
Towson University
3103 Center for the Arts
900 York Road
wson, MD 21252–0001

Dr Chris Jones
School of English
University of St Andrews
St Andrews
Fife KY16 9AL
UK

Boydell & Brewer Ltd
PO Box 9
Woodbridge
Suffolk IP12 3DF
UK

Previous volumes in this series are printed at the back of this book

This time at last: For Anke, with love

Contents

Illustrations

The author and publishers are grateful to all the institutions and individuals listed for permission to reproduce the materials in which they hold copyright. Every effort has been made to trace the copyright holders; apologies are offered for any omission, and the publishers will be pleased to add any necessary acknowledgement in subsequent editions

Preface

This book is a guide to the field which has become known as medievalism studies; it also sketches out a history of medievalism and offers a critique of the practices that have grown up around the study of medievalism, doing so sympathetically and with the aim of furthering future study. Each of these three aims presents a potentially large task and as a result my account does not aim to be a total history, an exhaustive guide or a comprehensive critique. Medievalism is a vast field and it is difficult to imagine comprehensiveness other than in a large collaborative work. A recent French work shows the extent of the problem: *La fabrique du moyen âge* is a collaborative volume limited to the impact of the Middle Ages on nineteenth-century French literature. It nevertheless extends to 1,100 pages written by nearly 70 contributors. Even so, its editors concede that they "pretend neither to exclusivity nor exhaustiveness" and that the work is *not* an encyclopaedia but merely a beginning resource.[1]

A general history of anglophone medievalism is still a desideratum, though large collaborative projects are in progress.[2] It has been remarked before now that medievalism studies as a discipline has consisted of proliferant case studies, usually in essay form in journals (pre-eminently, *Studies in Medievalism* and more recently, in *postmedieval*), but has not been well served by longer studies. I do not pretend to offer that general history here, but I do attempt to offer a meta-commentary on the study of medievalism of a kind which up until now has been lacking. This is necessarily restricted to the cultures I have lived in or visited (chiefly Britain, Australia, and France, and to a lesser extent, Germany and America) and rarely extends beyond those languages that I can read. This book is meant to be exemplary rather than comprehensive, provocative rather than conclusive, agenda-setting rather than argument-settling.

My broad thesis is that what we have come to call "medievalism" – definitions of which I will survey shortly – is as I will propose a feature of post-medieval cultures from the moment of their emergence from the Middle Ages. Indeed, given that any moment of "emergence from a middle age" is somewhat arbitrary, it is the charting of medievalism itself that marks it, or self-creates it. In Britain, for example, it is the concerted conservation of antiquities by John Bale, John Leland, and William Camden

---

[1]   Bernard-Griffiths, Glaudes, and Vibert, "Avertissement," in *La fabrique du moyen âge*, n.p.
[2]   Groom, Parker, and Wagner, eds., *The Oxford Handbook to Victorian Medievalism*; D'Arcens, ed. *The Cambridge Companion to Medievalism*.

that brings into being the historical rupture that marks off the present from a past regarded as qualitatively different: a past that could later be thought of as the *medium aevum*.

In the historical part of my argument, I then proceed to the movement, evident in France, Germany, and Britain in the second half of the eighteenth century, that is variously known as the romantic, the gothic, or the medieval revival. My chief point about this – well known material, after all – is that it was a revival of interest in the primitive broadly conceived; those aspects of the revival that were concerned with the *medieval* have clear outlines only with hindsight. It is easy to locate such figures as Thomas Percy, Thomas Warton, and Richard Hurd as if they were essentially medievalists (I have done this myself); it is important nevertheless to recall that for them the most important category was far less specifically defined. It was simply "the past."

There is no doubt, though, that a category of what would become known as the *medieval* past did emerge as a result of eighteenth-century antiquarian work. Thomas Fosbroke's coinage of the adjective *medieval*, soon after the conclusion of the Napoleonic wars, underlines the emergence of this discrete category; so too does the fact that Fosbroke appears to have been unaware that he was coining a term. For him, in short, the medieval was self-explanatory and coherently bounded, as it had not been for Percy, Warton or even their imaginative heir, Walter Scott; none of these figures worked with a very clear sense of the difference between a medieval period and the early modern period.

What emerged thereafter is what we might now think of as "high medievalism" – first in German and British romanticism, then in Scott's *Ivanhoe* (1819) and its many progeny, including Kenelm Digby's *The Broad Stone of Honour* (1822) and the Eglinton Tournament (1839) and also, very influentially, in French romanticism of the 1830s. Elsewhere in this period, the Viennese artists known as the Nazarenes were returning to medieval models in their painting, as was the Prussian Friedrich Schinkel in his architecture. All these instances can be regarded as reactions against Enlightenment classicism and reason: their monument might be Schinkel's memorial to the Wars of Liberation on the Kreuzberg in Berlin (1817–21), which takes the form of a pinnacled Gothic spire decorated with angelic and allegorical figures, a medievalist and spiritual riposte to Napoleonic neoclassicism.

This very diverse constellation of influences led to the conclusive phase of cultural medievalism in the 1840s. Not coincidentally, the noun *medievalism* itself came into general use in that decade, which witnessed medievalist developments in architecture, literature, opera, religion, and political theory. I treat this as a "long decade" spanning 1839 to 1851, from the rise of Chartism to the Great Exhibition, but the period was equally pivotal on the continent. Architecture witnessed the commencement of Augustus Pugin's Birmingham church, St Chad's, in 1839 and, in the following year, the recommencement of Cologne Cathedral. Prosper Merimée's *Monuments historiques* and Pugin's *Apology for the Revival of Christian Architecture in England* appeared in 1843; in 1844, Viollet-le-Duc's restorations of the Sainte Chapelle and the cathedral of Notre-Dame in Paris commenced, under the auspices of the Commission des Monuments Historiques (established in 1837). In 1845 the Ecclesiological Society in London began advocating the neo-gothic style in church architecture. Pugin and

Barry's Houses of Parliament at Westminster were of course under construction through this decade. John Ruskin published *The Seven Lamps of Architecture* in its first edition in 1849 and an English version of Friedrich von Schlegel's "An Essay on Gothic Architecture" also appeared in that year.

Medievalist literature also flourished. *Der Roland von Berlin* by "Willibald Alexis" (the nearest thing to a canonical medievalist novel in German) appeared in 1840. Edward Bulwer Lytton published his novel of the Wars of the Roses, *The Last of the Barons*, in 1843. Tennyson published his "Morte d'Arthur" (the germ from which *Idylls of the King* grew) in 1842. In 1849, Lady Charlotte Guest published her translation of the *Mabinogion*; J. A. Giles had published an edition of Geoffrey of Monmouth's *Historia regum Britanniae* in 1842. Opera saw Richard Wagner's *Rienzi* (based on Bulwer Lytton's 1835 novel) produced in 1840.

This is also the decade that saw Carlyle's *Past and Present*, his 1843 meditation on the condition of England. Towards the end of the decade, as revolutions broke out across Europe, Dante Gabriel Rossetti, John Everett Millais, and William Holman Hunt established the Pre-Raphaelite Brotherhood in 1848. In the Great Exhibition of 1851, medievalist activity was celebrated by the popularity of Pugin's Mediaeval Court. In all, this "long decade" was marked by social unrest, popular revolution – and medievalism.

What many studies of medievalism propose, at least by implication, is that this moment was one of inauguration; that thereafter, medievalism went from strength to strength and became a canonical feature of many aspects of culture. The assumption is that after Carlyle and Pugin and Ruskin, Schlegel and Merimée and Viollet-le-Duc, medievalism was here to stay. I argue, by contrast, that 1840s medievalism was unique and never to be repeated: this was the first and last time that medievalism achieved something approaching cultural dominance in several different European cultures at once, in the novel, poetry, architecture, opera, and more debatably perhaps, political theory. Thereafter, medievalism in fact declined in all spheres of culture except architecture (in which neo-gothic remained a powerful force in public and ecclesiastical building throughout Europe for most of the rest of the century, and spread to colonies and former colonies of Britain).

It is not the case – of course – that medievalism disappeared. But it is clear in all kinds of ways that its initial impetus rapidly waned. Most of the members of the Pre-Raphaelite Brotherhood quickly moved away from medievalism, for example, while the most dedicated Pre-Raphaelite, William Holman Hunt, had little interest in medievalism in the first place. It is true that some poets, notably the younger William Morris, Tennyson and Algernon Swinburne, did profit from a focus on the myths and legends of the Middle Ages, but novelists largely turned their backs on the distant past that had served Scott so well. Political medievalism as developed by Carlyle (and Ruskin, and Benjamin Disraeli) also declined in the second half of the century.

One factor in what I am proposing as a rapid shift in emphasis was the rise of medieval studies: still another way of looking at the 1840s is to see it as a key decade in the organised *study* of medieval literature, the period when the early scholar Frederic Madden was most active for example, producing the *editiones principes* of *Sir Gawain and the Green Knight* in 1839, Laʒamon's *Brut* in 1847 and the Wycliffite Bible in 1850. The Philological Society, founded in London in 1842, espoused the new philology of such men as Benjamin Thorpe and J. M. Kemble, themselves disciples of Jacob Grimm and Rasmus Rask. In France, the Abbé Migne commenced the monumental *Patrologia latina* in 1844. After 1850, a great deal of the energy that went into the Middle Ages in Britain, Germany, and France was *scholarly*, as the disciplines of history and literary study were formalised. In due course, medieval studies was professionalised with establishment in universities between about 1870 and 1925. Major publication series in Britain, Germany, and France were established early in this period and led to an explosion in the publication of historical, literary, and linguistic texts. By 1925, when the Medieval Academy of America was founded, medieval studies was a standard element of university curricula.

At the same time, non-professional medievalism was declining. As an architectural idiom, for example, neo-gothic came to an end before World War I in Europe, America, Asia, and Australia. Medievalism did of course persist: in one strand, it remained a marker of high art, albeit in ever more occulted forms. The high modernist writers still drew on medieval culture, for example, while modernist architects playfully employed medievalist idioms. Medievalist recreation in its most naked forms, however, lost prestige, coming to be associated with popular entertainment and children's culture.

To oversimplify by way of summary at this point: in the 1840s a convergence of antiquarian activities conferred considerable cultural capital on medievalism; in some spheres, most notably English poetry and European civic architecture, that capital remained highly valued in the second half of the nineteenth century. In all spheres, however, it had declined by the time of World War I. Meanwhile academic departments, especially in the fields of history, art history, and English language and literature, ensured a high value for medieval culture, now defined as the object of academic study. Then as academic medieval studies appeared to decline at the end of the twentieth century, medievalism once more rose, both as the object of popular practices and now as academic study. In the twenty-first century, large sums of money are spent on, and huge audiences attracted to, medievalist popular entertainment on film and television. Thousands of reenactors are drawn to medieval times as the backdrop for their recreations. Academic medievalists now routinely ask whether popular medievalism can do the job of leading people back to medieval studies.

It would be difficult to see organised medieval studies as accounting for the change in taste which saw the end of popular medievalism. Nevertheless, the greatest agon in reception of medieval culture was produced at the beginning of the twentieth century: that between the rigorous investigation of the Middle Ages by scholarly means on the one hand, and imaginative recreation of the period on the other. The tension between the two is felt today, when academic medieval studies and popular medievalism might once again converge. The concerns of this book arise out of that tension, and the sense that it is a very propitious moment to reconsider the rise of medievalism.

Acknowledgements

This book has been in the making for a very long time and along the way I have incurred even more than the usual debts that books bring with them. Many of these debts I hope I have acknowledged (if not exactly repaid) in my notes. I make no apology for the way in which these notes are expansive, as they operate in part as a guide to the deeper thickets of medievalism studies. I would also like to single out several individuals here. Long ago I chose to write an undergraduate dissertation on William Morris alongside my other choices in medieval languages and literatures; Tom Burton, Michael Tolley and Ken Ruthven supported that decision, which has been immensely fruitful. Later, still ignorant of medievalism, I was brought into contact with *Studies in Medievalism* by Leslie Workman and Kathleen Verduin, who kindly invited a contribution on Walter Scott. For several years, I have discussed my concerns about medievalism as a discipline with some acute scholars: from the very earliest days, with Stephanie Trigg and Noel King, later with Ruth Evans, John Ganim, Tom Prendergast, Larry Scanlon, and Carolyn Dinshaw. I am particularly grateful, in the latter stages, for the great generosity of Louise D'Arcens, who has also been a wonderful interlocutor. Medievalism has involved me in a lot of travel; some of the earlier forays were undertaken with Mark Gauntlett (who was also among the first to urge me to publish on this topic and to whom I am forever grateful for the Excaliburgers). I also thank Eckart Bernau, the ideal guide to Guédelon; Iris Bernau and Jonathan Caetano took me to the market at Cabezon de la Sal. I also owe thanks to those who have asked me to write on medievalism and contribute to conferences over the years: especially Bettina Bildhauer, Louise D'Arcens, Steve Ellis, Matthew Fisher, Axel Müller, and Richard Utz and Elizabeth Emery.

For helping with the survey on reenactment, I am especially indebted to Lena Eriksson; as a complete novice, I could not have received more expert or patient guidance. I am of course extremely grateful to the anonymous participants in the survey, and those who helped me organise it: Rebecca Griffiths; Tina Steiner and members of the Beaufort Companye; the Federation of the Wars of the Roses; Carl Sprake and the Companions of the Crow.

With one major exception I have not directly reprinted any earlier material, but I have freely plundered from some of my earlier publications on this topic. In particular, I have drawn on my essay, "From Mediaeval to Mediaevalism: A New Semantic History," *Review of English Studies* 62 (2011): 695–715, and am grateful to the journal's editors (and particularly Elaine Treharne) for permission to re-use. Some parts of the conclusion appeared as "What was Medievalism? Medieval Studies, Medievalism, and Cultural Studies," in *Medieval Cultural Studies*, edited by Ruth Evans, Helen Fulton, and myself (Cardiff: University of Wales Press, 2006), 9–22. I am grateful to my co-editors for permission to re-use this material.

The book was produced in very congenial environments. I probably would not have written it had I not ended up in Manchester, a quintessentially medievalist city, where I found many colleagues ready to help with my interest. I single out Mike Sanders, for conversations on medievalism and the Victorian working classes, and Jeremy Tambling and Daniela Caselli, excellent interlocutors both. Jeremy pointed me to *The Old Curiosity Shop*; Howard Booth to "The Eye of Allah." Yusuf Awad, then a postgraduate student, helped me on questions relating to the crusaders and the Arabic language. Outside Manchester, Heather Glen pointed me to *Mary Barton*. I benefited from the research assistance of Hannah Priest at an early stage, while Thomas Froh's research assistance in the closing stages was invaluable.

I began the writing of the book on a period of research leave in 2009 granted by the University of Manchester. The bulk of it was then written on another period of leave in the autumn and winter of 2012 while I was *Gastwissenschaftler* at the Freie Universität, Berlin. I am enormously grateful to Andrew James Johnston for making that stay possible and for his own intellectual contribution to my project, as well as to Elisabeth Kempf, Maggie Rouse, and Martin Bleisteiner for making my stay so enjoyable and helping out in myriad small ways.

Finally, I must record my gratitude to all involved with this project at Boydell and the Medievalism series, not least for their patience: Karl Fugelso, Caroline Palmer, and the anonymous readers for the press. I leave until last three people whose impact has been enormous, in different ways. In medievalism, I write the things I do in the way I do because of Stephen Knight, and am forever grateful to him – for his generous help along the way and for the expanded view I have inherited from him of the possibilities of medieval studies. Chris Jones asked me if I would write this book at exactly the right time. I hope the result justifies his confidence and is an adequate gift in recompense for his support and encouragement. Finally, the book's dedicatee makes it all possible, and all worthwhile.

Abbreviations

Introduction

THE GHOSTS OF the Middle Ages are unquiet. In the cinema Robin Hood, embodied by Russell Crowe, once more bends his bow in Ridley Scott's film. J. R. R. Tolkien's dwarves, drawn from Old Norse legend, seek the gold stolen by a Beowulfian dragon in *The Hobbit: An Unexpected Journey* (2012) and its sequel, *The Desolation of Smaug* (2013). Turn on the television, where the Wars of the Roses are replayed in the BBC's *The White Queen* (2013) and the cathedral of Kingsbridge rises in *Pillars of the Earth* (2010), a series based on Ken Follett's bestselling novel of the same name (1989); dark-age power struggles are played out in HBO's medievalist fantasy, *Game of Thrones* (2011–) and Channel 4's *Camelot* (2011). Open a newspaper and a journalist will be criticising the medieval practice of torture, somewhere in the world; politicians, promising an end to the medieval practices of this or that Islamic regime; managers of football teams, regretting the application of medieval justice to their players. In Britain, a man walks from Worthing in Sussex to Buckingham Palace to attend the royal wedding of 2011 in full medieval armour with sword and shield.[1] Turn a corner in Melbourne, Manchester, Mumbai and there is a gargoyle, a pointed arch, a crenellated roof, a machicolated wall, ghostly memories of the Middle Ages shadowing modernity.

It is the task of *medievalism studies*, a rising field for the past three decades, to hunt these revenants. The field is, to quote from the definition attributed to T. A. Shippey on the website of the journal *Studies in Medievalism*, "the study of responses to the Middle Ages at all periods since a sense of the mediaeval began to develop."[2] Medievalism studies is usually distinguished from its long-established parent, *medieval studies*, which involves study of the *actual* Middle Ages: the period's literatures, languages, history, architecture, wars, religions and people, from peasants to popes. These are the simplest definitions that can be given of the two related disciplines. Like many simple definitions, they prove to be open to challenge and they will certainly be closely scrutinised and challenged in the course of this book. A first task, then, is to distinguish the disciplines from one another in this fundamental way, with a brief account of them both.

Defining medieval studies is the easier task. The discipline, in its broadest sense, has existed almost since the end of the medieval period itself. The earliest forms

---

[1]   www.lonelyknight.com
[2]   See the *SiM* home page, http://www.medievalism.net/index.hmtl. It is more succinctly described on the *SiM* blog as "manifestations of the middle ages in postmedieval times." http://studiesinmedievalism.blogspot.co.uk/. Both accessed 24 February 2014.

of medieval studies arose because of acts of destruction which both defined the past as medieval and threatened to efface medieval culture. *When* exactly this can be said to have happened depends on *where* one is talking about. In Britain, in the wake of reformation, scholars began collecting medieval manuscripts which were discarded by religious reformers who viewed them as worthless. Antiquarians at Henry VIII's court, John Leland and John Bale, were responsible for the identification and retrieval of medieval literature in the 1540s after the Dissolution of the Monasteries: their activities can be regarded as the beginnings of English medieval literary study.[3] The retrieval of texts in turn provoked the study of medieval languages, which was under way in England before the end of the sixteenth century, when Old English was reconstructed and texts edited by scholars in the circle of Archbishop Matthew Parker.[4]

The British case is not necessarily typical, however, and these early efforts did not lead far, as nascent British medieval studies withered in the course of the sixteenth century, so that the study of Anglo-Saxon had to be refounded at a later date. There were stronger continuities in Catholic countries. The study of medieval history can be traced to the seventeenth century and the establishment in the 1630s of the *Acta sanctorum* project by the Jesuit Jean Bolland. The discipline of palaeography was established by Jean Mabillon later in that century. In France, the question of the origins of Old French was the subject of inquiry in the seventeenth century in the work of Du Cange, and greatly advanced in the eighteenth, in particular by La Curne de Sainte-Palaye, while in Italy medieval history was furthered by Lodovico Muratori.[5]

Medieval studies thus began as a series of retrievals, and was born out of the death of the Middle Ages. The impossible question of when the Middle Ages can be said to have ended can be left aside for the moment; the point here is that the moment of retrieval, and the moment of recognition of a middle age, amount to almost the same thing: it is when such people as Bale and Leland set out to preserve elements of a culture that that culture can be said to belong definitively to the past.

There are sometimes indications that early medieval studies received some official, institutional promotion in medieval studies. Certainly, as Allen Frantzen has shown, the study of Anglo-Saxon received some royal support in the context of reformation because of its apparent indications of the continuity of an English church. British political theory is another sphere in which official interests – particularly parliamentary interests – looked actively to what was thought to be medieval precedent.[6] In France, where the monasteries were a force longer than

---

[3]   See Simpson, *Reform and Cultural Revolution*, ch. 1. William Kuskin, however, sees William Caxton as the more important figure, in his essay, "At Hector's Tomb: Fifteenth-Century Literary History and Shakespeare's *Troilus and Cressida*".

[4]   Frantzen, *Desire for Origins*, 43–44.

[5]   On Bolland, Mabillon, and Muratori see the entries, respectively by Donald Sullivan, Rutherford Aris, and Susan Nicassio in Damico and Zavadil, eds., *Medieval Scholarship: Biographical Studies in the Formation of a Discipline*, 1–14, 15–32, 33–45; on Sainte-Palaye see Gossman, *Medievalism and the Ideologies of the Enlightenment*, esp. pp. 153, 175–211.

[6]   On this see Smith, *The Gothic Bequest*.

in England, medieval history was propelled by Benedictine monks. The Académie des Inscriptions was founded by Louis XIV's finance minister Colbert in 1663 as a very limited body, then re-established and expanded in 1701 as a genuine learned academy which became the major force in eighteenth-century French medieval studies.[7] Such bodies were then well situated when, in the nineteenth century, national pride came to be associated with these kinds of scholarly investigations.

Nevertheless medieval studies has more often been subterranean. To its own disadvantage, medieval culture was generally regarded as opposed to classical culture. In reformed cultures, the Middle Ages had to serve as the barbarous "other," the dark age from which the reformation had liberated a newly renascent culture. The circumstances of the birth of medieval studies ensured that its growth would be stunted. In Britain, medieval studies became the preserve of antiquarians, many of them somewhat outside official canons of learning. One of the greatest of early works in medieval studies in Britain, George Hickes's *Linguarum Veterum Septentrionalium Thesaurus Grammatico-Criticus et Archaeologicus* (1703–05), was produced while its author was in hiding as a result of his refusal to swear allegiance to the monarchs William and Mary and his subsequent outlawry.[8] The most prolific editor of this period, Thomas Hearne, was also a nonjuror who at one stage "was literally locked out of the [Bodleian] library" as a response to his political views.[9]

When such great manuscript collections as the Cotton and Harley libraries passed into the public realm in the 1750s with the opening of the British Museum, scholars once again concerned themselves with medieval texts, creating what was at first a minor antiquarian movement which, in the years of European peace after the Napoleonic wars, slowly developed into a scholarly discipline. Throughout Europe in the second half of the nineteenth century, medieval literature and history were put forward by adherents as meriting the same attention given to classical culture. Gradually medieval studies began to take on quasi-official status. In Britain, for example, the study of medieval history was furthered by a major publishing initiative in 1857, usually known as the Rolls Series (its actual title is "Rerum Britannicarum Medii Aevi Scriptores, or Chronicles and Memorials of Great Britain and Ireland during the Middle Ages"). The study of medieval literature was advanced in the years after 1864, when the Early English Text Society began its series of editions of medieval English texts. The field of medieval history began to be professionalised with the founding of the journal *English Historical Review* in 1886. Parallel developments in other European countries include the refounding, by Georg Waitz in Berlin in 1875, of the major publication series, the *Monumenta Germaniae Historica* (MGH). The same year saw the establishment in Paris of the *Société des anciens textes français* (SATF). Meanwhile, at Harvard University in the United States, medieval studies had become central to the literary curriculum by the 1890s, and soon afterwards was found in many of the major universities.

---

[7]   Gossman, *Medievalism and the Ideologies of the Enlightenment*, 45–46.
[8]   On Hickes see Richard L. Harris's entry in Damico, with Fennema and Lenz, eds., *Medieval Scholarship: Biographical Studies in the Formation of a Discipline*, vol. 2, 19–32.
[9]   Theodor Harmsen, "Hearne, Thomas (bap. 1678, d. 1735)," *ODNB*, http://www.oxforddnb.com/view/article/12827, accessed 19 September 2012.

It was hardly the case that the grip of classical education had been broken. Greek and Latin literature would continue to be taught in elite schools well into the twentieth century. But there was certainly a fresh assumption among the dominant European nation-states that their own national, vernacular literary traditions were worthy of attention. It is not coincidental that Germany and France had fought a war just five years before the establishment of the SATF and refounding of the MGH. Such scholarly developments represented organised and to a degree state-sponsored attempts to investigate the medieval past in a context of rising national self-definition. When education spread and universities expanded in the last third of the century, academic medieval studies took an important place in the larger movement. Medieval studies was central to university departments of history and literature as these disciplines entered the twentieth century.

In summary, then, medieval studies began with quasi-official sanction in the Reformation period, before its symbolic capital sank in the seventeenth century. It consequently became the pursuit of largely amateur antiquarians during the eighteenth century and much of the nineteenth, before its symbolic capital was raised once more with nation-building initiatives at the end of the nineteenth century. This was followed by academic acceptance in the early twentieth century which conferred educational capital on medieval texts and cultural objects. The study of the classical past, meanwhile, dominant for so long, has itself declined as classical languages are no longer learnt.

Many medievalists today feel that the educational and symbolic capital of medieval studies and its practitioners had sunk again by the end of the twentieth century. The entry of medieval studies into the academy in the 1890s reduced its dependence on nineteenth-century patriotism but the institutional safety thereby achieved did not equip it for competition with later developments. Medieval history is not necessarily central in a world which features postcolonial history. Medieval literary studies, based on philology, only belatedly adjusted to methods based on close reading (such as New Criticism). Medieval studies in the anglophone world was also belated and partial in its acceptance of structuralism, and came late, if ultimately more convincingly, to cultural studies and historicism. Departments of History and English once regarded medieval studies as central; now, many such departments do not teach medieval studies at all. The days of widespread compulsory teaching of medieval languages in English departments are long gone (and little lamented).

In general the discipline's image is not strong. In Britain in 2003 the then Education Secretary in the Blair Labour Government, Charles Clarke, seemed to capture a popular attitude to medieval studies when he reportedly said in a speech at University College Worcester that he "did not mind there being some medievalists around for ornamental purposes, but there is no reason for the state to pay for them."[10] Clarke here represented the stereotypical view of medieval studies as an obscure and conservative discipline, devoted to such highly specialised techniques

---

[10] Woodward and Smithers, "Clarke dismisses medieval historians," *The Guardian*, 9 May 2003.

as palaeography and genealogical editing. Yet in contexts other than medieval studies, obscurity is highly valued. Classical studies also employs such specialisms as palaeography and philology, yet without quite attracting the same opprobrium. A grasp of Latin simply commands more general respect than a knowledge of Old English or Middle High German; the word "classical" cannot be used as a put-down in the way that "medieval" so frequently is.

The signs for the discipline are not all negative, however. Many departments of History, Art History, and English still regard a medievalist presence as important to their curricula. Several thousand medievalists from all parts of the discipline converge each year on the two major international congresses in the field at Leeds in the UK and Kalamazoo in the US. Given the postwar expansion of higher education in the UK and America, there are probably more jobs in academic medieval studies than ever before. It is also the case – despite such lazy stereotypes of out-of-touch academic medievalists as Charles Clarke's – that a broad public interest in the Middle Ages remains very strong. This is suggested by an abundance of television programmes in recent years on the period, both in documentary and drama, and the success of the Medieval and Renaissance galleries at the Victoria and Albert Museum and the Medieval Europe Gallery at the British Museum, both opened in 2009. The discovery of a Roman bronze ceremonial helmet in a field in Cumbria in 2010 excited much attention, but so too did the Staffordshire Hoard of Anglo-Saxon gold found with a metal detector in 2009, and Viking coins found in Furness in 2011, while the discovery of the remains of Richard III made news around the world in the summer of 2012, and again a few months later when DNA tests verified that this was indeed the late king.

Stereotypes of the Middle Ages persist, but there is a sense that the period now holds its own alongside the classical past which for so long displaced it in importance. At the same time, medieval culture maintains a presence in the modern world in far more insidious ways. Supposed precedents from medieval history are used to justify oppressive modern nationalisms, as Patrick Geary has so ably documented; the modern rhetoric mobilised by western powers against the Islamic world similarly draws on medievalism, as Bruce Holsinger has persuasively argued.[11] These examples, too, are signs of the continuing influence of the Middle Ages in modernity, much as modern practitioners might and should want to resist them.

I have suggested above that medieval studies can in some form be traced back to the end of the Middle Ages and indeed that the process of studying the Middle Ages is bound up with the possibility of making the chronological distinction itself. After the Reformation and Wars of Religion in Europe, medieval studies persisted in one form or another into the seventeenth century, though often in increasingly attenuated forms. In the eighteenth-century Enlightenment, with its commitment to classical philosophy and reason, medieval culture was relatively

---

[11] Geary, *Myth of Nations*; Holsinger, *Neomedievalism, Neoconservatism, and the War on Terror*.

under-privileged (though as Lionel Gossman's magisterial study of Sainte-Palaye shows, medieval studies was by no means completely incompatible with Enlightenment thought). The second half of the eighteenth century then saw a Europe-wide turn to the primitive in all its forms. Whether in the Highlands of Scotland or the islands of the Pacific, the distant past or the present day, scholars and artists looked to what they believed was a simplicity lost to modern Europe. James MacPherson's translations of the bardic poet Ossian, supposedly culled in the Highlands of Scotland, were rapturously received in the 1750s. The Swiss Paul-Henri Mallet produced a paean to the Norsemen in his history of Denmark, translated into English by Thomas Percy as *Northern Antiquities* in 1770; Percy's own *Reliques of English Poetry* (1765) helped spark a general revival of interest in the ballad. In another sphere Louis-Antoine de Bougainville's voyage to Tahiti in 1768, recounted in his *Voyage autour du monde* (1771), appeared to confirm Jean-Jacques Rousseau's notions of noble savagery. The turn to folklore, too, best known through the Grimm brothers' collection of folktales, is part of this strand.

Within this larger movement, a turn to the Middle Ages is clearly visible, at least to hindsight. Percy's *Reliques*, along with the *History of English Poetry* produced by Thomas Warton in 1774–81, chiefly concerned itself with the Middle Ages. The Grimms were of course not only folklorists but are usually taken as foundational figures in German medieval studies.[12] German and British romanticism likewise seized on the primitive, with a particular interest in medieval culture evidenced in the poetry of John Keats, the architecture of Friedrich Schinkel, and the paintings of the Nazarenes, founded in Vienna in 1809 by Friedrich Overbeck and Franz Pforr. The medieval revival of the last third of the eighteenth century (with its long aftermath in the nineteenth) lies behind the second major strand I want to look at here, *medievalism studies*.

It was as the fortunes of academic medieval studies seemed to decline in the last third of the twentieth century that the study of *medievalism* arose. Sessions on the reception of the Middle Ages featured at Kalamazoo throughout the 1970s and led to the publication in 1979 of the first issue of the American journal *Studies in Medievalism* (*SiM*). In the same year a conference on the reception of medieval poetry was held in East Germany and the inaugural Salzburg conference resulted in publication of a volume on *Mittelalter-Rezeption*.[13] This German term, literally meaning "reception of the Middle Ages," is the rough equivalent of "medievalism" (a synonymous term, *Mediävalismus*, is more rarely used).[14] Just as "medievalism" was held to be different from medieval studies, and to an extent was set up in

[12] See Peck, "'In the Beginning was the Word': Germany and the Origins of German Studies," 129–32.

[13] The proceedings of the East German conference were published as Birnbaum, ed., *Rezeption deutscher Dichtung des Mittelalters*; the Salzburg volume is Kühnel, Mück, and Müller, eds., *Mittelalter-Rezeption: Gesammelte Vorträge des Salzburger Symposions*. For a description of the impulses behind the Salzburg conference, see Gentry and Müller, "The Reception of the Middle Ages in Germany."

[14] See the entry for *Mediävalismus* in Dinzelbacher, ed., *Sachwörterbuch der Mediävistik*; see also Gentry and Müller, "The Reception of the Middle Ages in Germany," 399; Utz, "Coming to Terms with Medievalism," 110 note 3.

opposition to it, *Mittelalter-Rezeption* is held to be distinct from the scholarly discipline practised in Germany as *Mediävistik*.

The most influential scholar of medievalism in its first decade was the British-born but American-based Leslie J. Workman, who was responsible for the early Kalamazoo sessions and founded *SiM*. As he described it, medievalism is the "*process* of creating the Middle Ages" and "the study not of the Middle Ages themselves but of the scholars, artists, and writers who ... constructed the idea of the Middle Ages that we inherited."[15] Workman was particularly concerned with those diverse figures mentioned above who began refashioning the image of medieval culture in the late eighteenth century. He distinguished medievalism from medieval studies in that it is about everything *after* the Middle Ages. Whatever knowledge it might require about medieval culture, it is not finally about the medieval period.

Initially, the American-based group and the German-speaking group were unaware of one another's activities. The coincidence in the rise of their shared interest is provocative, suggesting that on both sides of the Atlantic, the parent discipline, medieval studies, had arrived at a particular juncture, even a crisis. Of course what appears to be a new interest did not spring from nowhere. The Medieval Revival, with its origins in the late eighteenth century, had been much written about by 1979. It was scarcely possible to understand either romanticism or its sub-strand, the Gothic novel, without a knowledge of the rediscovery of the Middle Ages that began in the 1760s. Arthur Johnston's book *Enchanted Ground* was important in this regard; another early work was Janine Dakyns's *The Middle Ages in French Literature*.[16] But it was not only in literary studies that discussions were advanced. Significant work on the continuing use of the Middle Ages in nineteenth-century British political and historical thought was represented in Alice Chandler's *A Dream of Order: The Medieval Ideal in Nineteenth-Century English Literature*, a book frequently cited as foundational by Workman.[17] Given the importance of such medievalist phenomena as the Pre-Raphaelite Brotherhood and the nineteenth-century spread of neo-gothic architecture, medievalism was nothing new to most art historical and architecture studies; it was also quite prominent in historiography, even if the term "medievalism" was not explicitly used.[18]

---

[15] Workman, "Editorial"; qtd Utz and Shippey, "Medievalism in the Modern World: Introductory Perspectives," in Utz and Shippey, eds., *Medievalism in the Modern World*, 5; emphasis theirs; Utz, "Speaking of Medievalism: An Interview with Leslie J. Workman," ibid., 439.

[16] Johnston, *Enchanted Ground*; Dakyns, *The Middle Ages in French Literature*.

[17] Chandler, *A Dream of Order*.

[18] Among works belonging to what might be called the prehistory of medievalism studies, Gossman's *Medievalism and the Ideologies of the Enlightenment* has already been mentioned. See further, in historiography, Voss, *Das Mittelalter im Historischen Denken Frankreichs*; Dellheim, *The Face of the Past*, which will be further discussed in chapters 2 and 4; in art, Banham and Harris, eds., *William Morris and the Middle Ages*. Another field that witnesses a flourishing of "pre-medievalism" is that of Victorian literary studies: see for example Bump, "Hopkins, Pater, and Medievalism" and "Hopkins's Imagery and Medievalist Poetics." Another example

What *was* different in 1979 was the attempt to unify, under a single disciplinary heading, such work as that represented by Johnston, Chandler and Dakyns with work in art history, under the understanding that the re-use of the Middle Ages in all periods ought to constitute the material for a single, albeit broad, discipline. The two sets of scholars at work in 1979 began to define medievalism as the re-use of medieval motifs, themes, genres and topoi in post-medieval culture, in architecture, art, social and political theory, novels, plays, poetry, film. Later, computer games and tourist sites would be included. The word "medievalism" itself was a nineteenth-century coinage, then attributed by the *OED* to John Ruskin. Workman enthusiastically adopted this term and his journal, *Studies in Medievalism*, effectively dubbed the new discipline for English speakers, at exactly the same that *Mittelalter-Rezeption* was formalised in the German-speaking world.

Evidently, this new discipline was an offshoot of medieval studies, and it has been rare to see antagonism towards the parent discipline from within medievalism studies. In fact practitioners of medievalism studies generally began (and in many cases, continue) their careers as medievalists. They have often proposed that the newer kind of work could return the larger medieval studies to a sense of relevance in the modern world, just as its stock seemed to be falling. The parent discipline, however, was slow to accept the child as its own. As the volumes of *SiM* continued to appear in the 1980s, advancing the frontiers of the new discipline, medievalism met with the kind of scepticism that is often directed at what are perceived to be upstart fields. In Richard Utz's view, medieval studies had cordoned itself off from "any self-reflexive, subjective, empathic, or playfully non-scientific discussion of medieval culture."[19] For many traditional medievalists, in short, medievalism studies was a secondary or meta-discipline which came with too strong a whiff of postmodernism about it.

Nevertheless, a generation after its initial appearance, medievalism today seems to have achieved acceptance. It is firmly lodged in university study as a discipline, or perhaps sub-discipline. Courses in medievalism are widely available in universities in the US, UK, and Australia. Sessions on medievalism are now routinely accommodated not just at Kalamazoo and Leeds but at the meetings of the Medieval Academy of America and the New Chaucer Society. In her presidential address to the New Chaucer Society in July 2012, Carolyn Dinshaw noted that medievalism was now certainly a part of the business of late medieval studies, a judgement that seemed amply confirmed by the "Middle Ages in the Modern World" conference the following year in St Andrews, Scotland.[20] Indeed, the existence of this series at Boydell and Brewer, simply entitled "Medievalism," is itself a marker of the field's acceptance alongside the more traditional medieval studies in which Boydell has specialised. It is furthermore indicative of the security

appears in the first issue of *SiM*: Clark and Wasserman, "*Tess of the d'Urbervilles* as Arthurian Romance," discussed briefly in the conclusion. See also, for some of the foundational German work, Kühnel, Mück, and Müller, eds., *Mittelalter-Rezeption*, and Wapnewski, *Mittelalter-Rezeption: Ein Symposion*.

[19] Utz, "Coming to Terms with Medievalism," 107.

[20] Dinshaw, "All Kinds of Time," esp. 22–24.

of the new field (if a slightly ironic one) that it has generated a splinter movement: neomedievalism.[21]

If the signs are positive for medievalism studies, however, this does not mean that it is yet entirely clear what the discipline actually is, could be, or should be. It shares with cultural studies (significantly) the fact that it is relatively easy to give a broad sense of what it is but quite difficult to define with any precision. It is simple enough to say that medievalism is the study of the Middle Ages after the Middle Ages, but very difficult to discern a precise method. And like cultural studies, medievalism has proved difficult to house within traditional disciplines. Should it sit in departments of History, Art History, or English? Should it be part of medieval studies, or Victorian studies? In some ways medieval studies and cultural studies are *not* a natural fit, given the latter's tendency to a "focus on the contemporary" as Simon During observes.[22] Even more of a challenge to the disciplinary status of medievalism studies is the question of whether it should be regarded as a particularised phenomenon at all. Raphael Samuel has argued that there is in modernity an "expanding historical culture." Where history is concerned, Samuel suggests, "the work of inquiry and retrieval is being progressively extended into all kinds of spheres that would have been thought unworthy of notice in the past," and because of which "whole new orders of documentation are coming into play."[23] Is medievalism – which emerged from late eighteenth-century antiquarianism – simply rejoining a more broadly conceived attitude to the past?[24]

Even the term "medievalism" itself, despite the many definitions that have been offered, has a puzzling lack of clarity when probed more closely. An initial though minor problem is that "medievalism" is often used as if it were the discipline itself (see the Shippey definition cited above), while for others, *medievalism* properly refers only to the object of study (medievalist art, medievalist literature, and so on). There has been a tendency in recent years to solve this by separating "medievalism," which describes the object of study, from a more formally defined "medievalism studies." This seems an obvious solution (and is the one adopted in this book). There are wider problems, however. The definition on the *SiM* website already quoted – "the study of responses to the Middle Ages at all periods since a sense of the mediaeval began to develop" – is supposed to describe the study of medievalism but in fact could just as easily describe the traditional discipline of *medieval studies*. What is medieval studies itself, after all, but a set of responses to the Middle Ages? Compounding this, it is still quite common to see the term "medievalism" used as a synonym for "medieval studies" – presumably a back-formation resulting from the fact that practitioners of medieval studies are univer-

[21] More will be said about this in the conclusion. See volumes 19–20 of *SiM*, 2010–11.
[22] During, *Exit Capitalism*, viii.
[23] Samuel, *Theatres of Memory*, vol. 1, 25.
[24] On a specific case, see Higson, "'Medievalism', the Period Film and the British Past in Contemporary Cinema," in Bernau and Bildhauer, eds., *Medieval Film*. Higson argues that in the context of a general turn to the past in Western film in recent decades, films purporting to represent the Middle Ages *are* distinct from those dealing in later historical periods.

sally known as "medievalists."[25] Is the distinction between medievalism studies and medieval studies then as clear as a simple definition suggests?

As I will argue here, this question is not simply a dispute over terminology. The purpose of this book, in the context of this series, is to answer some of these questions, providing some disciplinary shape and purpose to medievalism, a brief historical account of it, and to suggest possible future directions. I aim to show how medievalism might be used, and how it speaks to medieval studies. As things stand – as I will argue here – the proliferation of *studies* in medievalism has far outstripped the development of a discipline of *medievalism studies*. The journal *SiM* and many essay collections over the past three decades have given us an expanded sense of the *impact* of the Middle Ages in post-medieval culture. But they have done little to establish a discipline.[26]

As things stand, good guides to British medievalism in its major phase between the medieval revival in the late eighteenth century and high modernism in the twentieth, do exist. Michael Alexander's *Medievalism: The Middle Ages in Modern England* (2007) is the most recent to offer this, while Chandler's seminal *A Dream of Order* is still the best starting place for medievalism in nineteenth-century thought. Mark Girouard's *The Return to Camelot: Chivalry and the English Gentleman* (1981) views medievalism from a slightly different angle, charting its influence in popular and elite culture up to World War I. Veronica Ortenberg has provided a more general, pan-European history in her *In Search of the Holy Grail* (though one which suffers from the necessary compression forced on it, and lacking any distinction between medieval studies and medievalism).[27]

In this book, I will not be trying to re-do the histories of medievalism presented by such writers – though I will at many points revisit their contentions and often contest them. My aim is neither comprehensiveness nor a fresh linear history, but rather an attempt to establish the basis for a discipline of medievalism studies and to articulate its relation to medieval studies.

---

[25] "Medievalism" for "medieval studies" is not offered in the *OED* and is perhaps more characteristic of American English. See for example Freedman and Spiegel, "Medievalisms Old and New: The Rediscovery of Alterity in North American Medieval Studies." As the title of the article suggests, there is some distinction between "medievalism" and "medieval studies," yet there are places in the essay where they seem synonymous.

[26] It must be said that four recent volumes of *SiM*, 17–20, have exhibited a marked turn to self-reflexiveness.

[27] Alexander, *Medievalism*; Girouard, *The Return to Camelot*; Ortenberg, *In Search of the Holy Grail*; Trigg and Prendergast, *Medievalism and its Discontents*.

I
TAXONOMIES

1

How Many Middle Ages?

I N A CASE that came before Southwark Crown Court in 2010, a woman found guilty of slashing her lover's face with a broken glass was let off with a conditional discharge and a suspended prison sentence because the judge believed she had been threatened with medieval behaviour. During a drug-fuelled sex session – Britain's *Daily Mail* reported – the defendant's lover had wanted to use nipple clamps and hot wax; she had resisted, which led to an assault. Judge Michael Gledhill sounded sympathetic as he said to her, "I've seen at least two implements which looked to the untrained eye as medieval torture instruments and not surprisingly you did not want to have pain inflicted upon you." The sex was consensual, and indeed the couple were lovers of long standing. But things got medieval, so the law stepped in.[1]

It is easy to hear the forlorn voice of the expert in medieval studies trying to object to the stereotypes here: "How did you know they were *medieval* torture instruments? Do you realise that torture was illegal for much of the Middle Ages? That in fact this kind of thing really belongs to the Tudor period?" Warming to a theme, that medievalist might also want to add that the burning of witches was more a feature of the sixteenth century than the Middle Ages, and that on the whole, many practices we regard as barbaric were more prevalent in the Renaissance than in the preceding era.

That medievalist, of course, would be missing the point. In the popular view, instruments of torture are *always* medieval. So, too, is the burning of witches, and many another grotesque practice. This conception of the Middle Ages is deeply entrenched. A Crown Court judge knows what he means by talking about medieval practices and a tabloid newspaper editor knows that readers will understand and even take perverse pleasure in this modern manifestation of the "medieval." Conversely, if the defence had been constructed on an objection to "Elizabethan" torture, or "Tudor" barbarism, there would have been no matrix of accepted

---

[1] Camber, "Top lawyer, his lover and a sex session that led to bloodshed at the Hilton," 21.

1. *The Knight Errant* (1870). Sir John Everett Millais, Bt (1829–1896).
© Tate, London 2014.

understandings to make it effective. The "medieval" character of the torture instruments helped the defendant in this case avoid a conviction for assault with a defence that effectively relied on her lover's ill-advised slip into the Middle Ages.

Although John Everett Millais's medievalist painting *The Knight Errant* (1870; Tate Gallery) (Figure 1) also hints at sexual violence, it tells a quite different medieval tale. A naked young woman, her face averted from the viewer, is tied to a huge birch tree, her long unbound hair rippling in the breeze but doing nothing to conceal her body. Before her on the ground lies her torn-off robe. Behind her, a young knight in elaborately detailed armour cuts through her bonds with a massive sword. Behind him lies a man presumably slain by the knight while, deep in the background, two other men flee. Clearly, a chivalrous deed is being performed here, and the implied narrative, in which a handsome knight errant delicately rescues the woman, is that of a medieval romance.

The two visions of the Middle Ages offered in these narratives are recreations, in modernity, of views of the Middle Ages. They are both medievalisms. They seem on the surface to be quite different tales, drawing on fundamentally different ideas of the Middle Ages. On the one hand, in the modern news story, there is what we can call a *gothic* or *grotesque* Middle Ages, entailing the assumption that anything medieval will involve threat, violence and warped sexuality (conversely, and somewhat self-fulfillingly, this view assumes that where the threat of sexual violence is made, something medieval is going on). On the other hand, there is what can be called a *romantic* Middle Ages. While Millais's painting concedes that violence against women exists, it also proposes that help is at hand in the form of knights, shining armour, and chivalry. There are, as we shall see, other ideas of the Middle Ages in existence, offering different inflections. But this distinction between a gothicised and a romanticised medieval is one I take to be fundamental, and I will draw on it throughout this book. It is the chief dualism in contemporary understandings of the Middle Ages, whether scholarly or popular.

It must immediately be clarified that these two modes are not necessarily mutually exclusive. Walter Scott's *Ivanhoe*, the 1819 novel that is foundational in any consideration of modern medievalism, employs the framework of medieval romance that Scott knew well, featuring love and chivalric deeds. But these sit alongside many darker and more gothic elements. Medievalist films often understand the Middle Ages in terms of a fundamental tension between the gothic-grotesque and the romantic, so that scenes of love and minstrelsy will alternate with gory battles or torture scenes. What *kind* of Middle Ages is presented by a narrative is often a matter of where it ends up in relation to these poles. Brian Helgeland's *A Knight's Tale* (2001) uses a romance framework to show that an individual can (in the film's verbal leitmotif) "change his stars." Whatever the limitations of the feudal Middle Ages – represented in the film by such gothic motifs as a gibbeted felon and the hero placed in the stocks – the romance framework recuperates the Middle Ages as a time when romance could overcome gothic. Mel Gibson's *Braveheart* (1995) also understands romantic love as a powerful force that alters the course of history, and is sufficiently invested in this notion as to introduce a historically impossible affair between William Wallace and Edward II's queen, Isabella. But by concluding with the judicial execution of the captured

Wallace, the film shows an understanding of medieval history as entirely framed by and ultimately unable to escape from its own gothic violence. The hero dies with the word "freedom" on his lips, but this can function only as a hopeful prophecy for modern Scotland. Medieval "freedom" is not finally possible in this film's vision.

This picture can be complicated still further. Although the gothic and romantic modes of apprehension of the medieval arose from different impulses at different times, they are not always straightforwardly distinguishable from one another. The two examples above, the *Daily Mail* story and Millais's painting, are quite different tales which nevertheless *both* assume a Middle Ages of sexual threat that requires violent action and sympathetic chivalry. In 2010, just as in 1870, a woman needs a chivalrous knight who recognises medieval oppression when he sees it. Judge Gledhill is the chivalrous knight of the *Mail* story, gently loosing the bonds of distressed maidens.

The gothic-grotesque and the romantic Middle Ages are then extreme perceptions, but the opposition between them is an unstable one with many intervening nuances. There is no fixed popular idea of the medieval at work today, and the first task is then to think about some ways of classifying the modern apprehension of the Middle Ages. Medievalism studies has laid claim to a very wide range of cultural artefacts as its objects of study: from neo-gothic cathedrals to medievalist computer games; from the activities of re-enactment societies to films and novels to medieval tourist sites, not to mention tabloid narratives, nineteenth-century painting, and many, many more. While it is relatively easy to carry out individual case studies within any one of these fields, it is enormously difficult to try to synthesise them.

Given the diversity of medievalism and the approaches to it, as Stephanie Trigg has written, "we might expect the methodological aspect of its inquiries to be foregrounded." Instead, as she notes, "it must be said that medievalism still struggles on this front." A decade on from Trigg's statement, change is slowly coming. Recent issues of *Studies in Medievalism*, for example, have devoted themselves to disciplinary self-reflection. Yet it is still the case that many scholars practising medievalism studies "restrict themselves to empiricist, broadly descriptive work," and that "the dominant scholarly genre in the field remains the essay, rather than the monograph."[2]

Responding to these problems, Trigg herself has proposed several different kinds of medievalism, worth examining here:[3]

> [1.] The first kind of medievalism relevant here, traditional medievalism, became available even before people started to talk about a thing or epoch called "the medieval." By traditional medievalism I mean any kind of reference to a medieval practice, discourse or icon that takes for granted its self-evident truth. This sensibility assumes that the meaning of this (medieval)

---

[2]   Trigg, review of Gallant; see her own response, the substantial longitudinal study *Shame and Honor*, or what she herself calls a *"symptomatic long history"* (14).

[3]   Trigg, "Once and Future Medievalism," numbering added.

object is palpably present to us, both then and now, through an unbroken lineage of embodied or ritualistic connection. This is the sensibility that allows for the endless "straight" re-tellings of Arthurian legend, for example, or that naturalises the use of medieval forms and practices in religious and parliamentary tradition.

[2.] By contrast, what we might call modernist medievalism might be characterised as a form of reconstruction. Even if they romanticise the content of a "medieval past," modernists, or neo-traditionalists, in comparison to traditionalists, tend to be already modern in form, appealing to historiography, empiricism (much of medieval studies), and antiquarianism (Spenser).

Trigg regards the "new medievalists" – such academic practitioners as Howard Bloch and Stephen Nichols associated with the "new philology" and "new medievalism" in the 1990s – as also belonging in this category, as they use "quasi-scientific ideological analysis or critique to uncover the underlying assumptions about the medieval period and academic institutions in the work of the most influential scholars."

[3.] The third form, postmodern medievalism, tends to occur as ironical reference or as romanticising pastiche, often condemned as ahistorical or simply "wrong" by old-fashioned historicists. While postmodern romanticism is prevalent in the fringe cultures of gothic groups and societies of medieval re-enactment, in the endless quotations from medieval tradition in popular culture (in film, television, fiction, advertising), postmodern reflexivity also characterises much of the most interesting writing in both medieval and medievalism studies, when that writing reflects not only on the medieval phenomena under discussion, but also the shaping cultural forces that mediate the medieval past for us in this way.

Some years earlier than Trigg, Umberto Eco outlined a rather different taxonomy, which has become perhaps the best known intervention in the field. In his essay, "Dreaming of the Middle Ages," Eco outlined no fewer than ten different kinds of Middle Ages:

1. "The Middle Ages as a *pretext.*" For Eco, the Middle Ages of opera, or what he calls cloak-and-dagger novels (as opposed to more serious historical novels); the historical background of the Middle Ages is used as a setting, but there is no real interest in the history.

2. "The Middle Ages as the site of an *ironical visitation.*" "Ariosto and Cervantes revisit the Middle Ages in the same way that Sergio Leone and the other masters of the 'spaghetti western' revisit nineteenth-century America, as heroic fantasy …"

3. "The Middle Ages as a *barbaric* age, a land of elementary and outlaw feelings." Eco has in mind the early films of Ingmar Bergman and suggests that "These ages are Dark par excellence, and Wagner's *Ring* itself belongs to this dramatic sunset of reason." He finds a celebration of Aryanism in this form,

memorably identifying "a shaggy medievalism." To his suggestions could be added John Milius's 1982 film, *Conan the Barbarian*, based on stories by Robert E. Howard.

4. "The Middle Ages of *Romanticism*, with their stormy castles and their ghosts."

5. "The Middle Ages of the *philosophia perennis* or of neo-Thomism." By this, Eco meant the presence of medieval philosophical thinking in modern theory – especially structuralism and semiotics: "In this sense, the perennial vigor of the Middle Ages is not derived necessarily from religious assumptions, and there is a lot of hidden medievalism in some speculative and systematic approaches of our time, such as structuralism." More recently, this idea has been greatly extended by research into the medievalism of *post*-structuralist theorists by Bruce Holsinger and Erin Labbie.[4]

6. "The Middle Ages of *national identities* ..." This theme has been greatly extended by Patrick Geary.[5]

7. "The Middle Ages of *Decadentism*." Eco has in mind Ruskin, the Pre-Raphaelites, Huysmans.

8. "The Middle Ages of *philological reconstruction*, which goes from Mabillon through Muratori to the *Annales* school..." "[T]hese Middle Ages help us ... to criticize all the other Middle Ages that at one time or another arouse our enthusiasm. These Middle Ages lack sublimity, thank God, and thus look more 'human.' "

9. "The Middle Ages of so-called *Tradition*." Eco refers to the Templars, Rosicrucians, alchemists and others "drunk on reactionary poisons sipped from the Grail, ready to hail every neo-fascist Will to Power ..." This version of the Middle Ages has been supremely realised since Eco's essay in Dan Brown's *The Da Vinci Code* (2003) (and heavily satirised in Eco's own novel *The Prague Cemetery* [2010]).

10. Eco writes at most length on 9, above, before turning to one more: "Last, very last, but not least, the *expectation of the Millennium* ... Source of many insanities ..."[6]

Eco's list – which was perhaps never meant to be taken too seriously – is a strange one combining several different principles of organisation and involving overlaps and questionable boundaries. Versions 1, 2, and 3 seem continuous with one another, variations on a theme rather than wholly discrete categories. Above,

---

4   Holsinger, *The Premodern Condition*; Labbie, *Lacan's Medievalism*. See also the essays in Cole and Smith, eds., *The Legitimacy of the Middle Ages*, and especially Cole and Smith's "Introduction: Outside Modernity."
5   See Geary, *Myth of Nations*.
6   Eco, *Faith in Fakes*, trans. Weaver, 68–72. See further the rewritten list of five (pertaining essentially to film) in Lindley, "The Ahistoricism of Medieval Film."

I placed *Conan the Barbarian* in Eco's third category as illustrative of barbaric medievalism. Eco himself actually has this film in category 9. His Middle Ages of Romanticism seems chiefly to refer to the gothic novel, but it is difficult to tell given that the only example he offers is William Beckford's *Vathek* (1787) – which is sometimes taken as a gothic novel but is really an eastern tale. His Middle Ages of Decadentism surely overlaps with that of Romanticism. Where does Tolkienian fantasy belong? Such fantasies are at times shaggy enough to belong in category 3, but are also romantic and sometimes philological.

It is notable, furthermore, that most, perhaps all of these different versions of the Middle Ages – as Eco's lashings of irony indicate – have something wrong with them. They are almost all the object of mockery. The principal possible exceptions to this are versions 5 and 8, the Middle Ages of neo-Thomism and "philological reconstruction." But what Eco apparently means by these is, quite simply, medieval *studies*. In all, this is very much an academic medievalist's list, with a medievalist's sense of irony. Whatever the advantages of both Eco's and Trigg's ways of breaking up medievalism, they both to some extent assume a knowledge of medieval studies and the Middle Ages.

In what follows I want to step back a little. Drawing on some of the myriad cultural productions that are relevant to considerations of medievalism, I will propose just two basic kinds of medievalism – two different kinds of Middle Ages, corresponding to the two different types with which this chapter opened. I will then distinguish subsets before attempting to sift through the different ways in which those Middle Ages are represented. It is important to say at the outset that no one version of the Middle Ages should be privileged – though it is true that different versions have held more or less sway at given historical periods. As Tison Pugh and Angela Weisl note, it is necessary to look "at the various intersections of medievalisms uniting in a given work."[7] To use Raymond Williams' terms, medievalism may be, within a given phase of a culture, dominant, emergent, or residual. I argue that culturally speaking, medievalism is rarely dominant, though it has sometimes been taken to be so. I use these terms in a somewhat weaker sense than Williams, but nevertheless, medievalism can be said to be what Williams calls "residual": a cultural formation "effectively formed in the past, but … still active in the cultural process, not only and often not at all as an element of the past, but as an effective element of the present." The question raised here – one I will return to at times in this book – is that of whether this residual cultural element has an "alternative or even oppositional relation to the dominant culture," or whether it "has been wholly or largely incorporated into the dominant culture."[8]

The Grotesque Middle Ages

I began, above, with an example of a shared understanding of the word "medieval" in the Southwark Crown Court. As far as the judge was concerned,

---

7 Pugh and Weisl, *Medievalisms*, 3.
8 Williams, *Marxism and Literature*, 122.

"medieval" meant pain, sexual deviance, coercion. This is the dominant sense of the word "medieval" in casual use. It represents what I have already called the gothic or grotesque Middle Ages. The word "grotesque" derives from "grotto," meaning a cave, which in turn derives from the Greek adjective *kryptos*, meaning "hidden" or "concealed." Hence "grotesque" connotes darkness, obscurity, the hidden and repressed. The prevalence of the grotesque Middle Ages today is in no way surprising, as it was to represent grotesquerie in all its forms that the Middle Ages was invented in the first place. That process needs brief examination here.

As Fred C. Robinson has noted, "renaissance" and "classical" do not get used pejoratively, while "medieval," by contrast, today means "barbaric," "primitive."[9] Hence to label something "medieval" is to place it in history to its disadvantage. It is true that a similar role is sometimes played by such terms as "prehistoric," "stone-age," or "neanderthal." A man accused of sexism might have any or all of these applied to him. But the force of these terms is rather different; to be *pre*historic is evidently to be in a non-time, outside history. Applying such terminology to sexism is to say that it is, or ought to be, extinct. To be accused of being "medieval" is subtly different: the person accused is very much *in* history, but lagging terribly behind.

Historically, this is in part because a middle, by definition, must come between two things. The "middleness" of the Middle Ages could therefore only become evident when the period itself could be thought of as completed. To describe a "middle" period is in the same moment to say that one is no longer in that middle. Hence, the longstanding tripartite division of history into Antiquity, Middle Ages, and Modernity – attributed in its first articulation to Petrarch – was formulated expressly to announce a *departure* from the Middle Ages, in favour of a new look back to Antiquity. For Petrarch, the immediate past was a dark age from which his culture was emerging.[10]

Where exactly the Middle Ages can be said to have ended, and a Renaissance to have begun, is always difficult to determine. But in Europe in the fifteenth, sixteenth and seventeenth centuries, references to a middle time or age, at first in Latin, later in vernacular languages, became increasingly common: the phrase *media tempestas* or "middle time" was recorded as early as 1469 in Rome, with variations on this expression occurring throughout the sixteenth century. What was to become the most common Latin term, *medium aevum*, was a relative latecomer, appearing in print early in the seventeenth century and making its first appearance in Britain by 1610. Before then, the term had already entered the English language, and is first recorded in 1570, when John Foxe referred to the "middle age" of the Church in the revised edition of his *Actes and Monuments*.[11] It is clear that by 1618 at the latest the term was well understood to refer to a past age of superstition, when the legal historian John Selden referred to "Those kind

---

[9]   Robinson, *"Medieval,* the *Middle Ages,"* 311.
[10]   See Mommsen, "Petrarch's Conception of the Dark Ages."
[11]   *OED,* "middle age" A.n.2. See further Robinson, *"Medieval,* the *Middle Ages,"* esp. 307.

of Acts and Legends of Popes and others ... usually stufft with ... falshoods, as being bred in the midle ages among idle Monks ...”[12]

Even before the terminology of a "middle" age became widespread, however, it was relatively common to see reference to the past as a "dark" time. In this respect, humanists took their lead from Petrarch. The construction of a dark age pre-dated the religious reformations of the sixteenth century, but reformers eagerly seized on that imagery. John Leland, in an often quoted phrase, wrote of bringing medieval culture "out of deadly darkenesse to lyvelye lyght ...”[13] But this is only one of the better known expressions of a thoroughly prevalent idea.

The humanist construction of a dark past then became conflated with the idea of a middle time or age. William Camden, anthologising examples of medieval poetry in 1605 in his *Remaines of a greater worke, concerning Britaine*, wrote, "I will onely giue you a taste of some of midle age, which was so ouercast with darke clouds, or rather thicke fogges of ignorance, that euery little sparke of liberall learning seemed wonderfull ...”[14] In 1632 William Struther, a Church of Scotland minister, contrasted "the middle Ages of darknesse" with "so great a light of the Gospel" as existed in his own time.[15] "Middleness," ostensibly a *chronological* characteristic, became in addition ineradicably *ideological* in the later sixteenth and the seventeenth centuries.

While attitudes to this Middle Age were particularly antagonistic in countries which, like Britain, espoused religious reform, they were not confined to such countries. Italy, after all, was a leader in the turn away from the dark past in order to embrace instead what was specifically claimed to be a renascent culture. (Even so, the term "Renaissance" itself did not come into use in its current broad sense, as "a concept of universal history, signifying a self-contained period inserted, as it were, between the Middle Ages and modernity ..." until Michelet and Burckhardt in the nineteenth century.[16])

In short, as Wallace Ferguson has outlined in a still classic book, the Middle Ages was quite simply invented to be the "other," the rejected past, the grotesque forebear of modernity.[17] From this historical process in the fifteenth and sixteenth centuries arose the abiding notion of the Middle Ages that we have clearly inherited today: that it was a time of uncultivated and often barbaric practices.[18] With this association made, it is clear that the *-eval* of the word, which refers to time, has been coloured by the word *evil*. There is no etymological link, but the homophone makes the pun in such titles as that of the video game series "MediEvil" irresistible.

---

[12] Selden, *The historie of tithes* ..., 44.

[13] Bale and Leland, *The laboryouse iourney*, Bviiir. See further Stanley, "The Early Middle Ages = The Dark Ages = The Heroic Age of England and in English."

[14] Camden, "Certaine Poemes, or Poesies, Epigrammes, Rythmes, and Epitaphs of the English Nation in former Times," 2.

[15] Struther, *A looking glasse for princes and people*, 93.

[16] Koselleck, "The Eighteenth Century as the Beginning of Modernity," in Koselleck, *The Practice of Conceptual History*, 154–69, 163.

[17] Ferguson, *The Renaissance in Historical Thought*.

[18] For a different interpretation placing emphasis on eighteenth- and nineteenth-century colonialism in periodization, see Davis, *Periodization and Sovereignty*, esp. 8–11.

It would be wrong to say that *nobody* in the sixteenth century could speak positively of the past. As Alex Davis's work makes clear, that was not the case.[19] My argument here is that whenever the *specific* terminology of the "Middle Ages" was used, it was uniformly to negative effect and it was only in the late eighteenth century that the idea of a middle age was turned to positive ends. Even so, something of the negative and gothic sense of the period always clings to it, especially in popular perception. Hence as we have seen torture is *always* medieval. The Middle Ages is a time of pain. The phrasal verb "to get medieval" apparently entered the language in Quentin Tarantino's *Pulp Fiction* (1994) when a gang boss turns the tables on the men who have just raped him and tells them, "I'm gonna git Medieval on your ass."[20] There is humour here, but of a particularly dark kind, as Carolyn Dinshaw has elucidated.[21]

The invocation of the Middle Ages in this guise can take a far more serious turn. Early in 2009, for example, a British citizen, Binyam Mohamed, claimed to have been tortured in Guantanamo Bay. His lawyer, Clive Stafford Smith, said that what his client had experienced in the penal facility "should have been left behind in the middle ages."[22] Mohamed himself, in a statement released by his lawyer, said, "It is still difficult for me to believe that I was abducted, hauled from one country to the next, and tortured in medieval ways – all orchestrated by the United States government."[23] At this level, the understanding of the medieval as grotesque has the capacity to provoke world events. It was enough, in 2006, for Pope Benedict XVI to quote an obscure medieval text in which a Byzantine emperor called Islam "evil and inhuman," for him to be accused of making what were called his "medieval" remarks. Responses turned the Middle Ages back on the pope himself: Salih Kapusuz, then deputy leader of the ruling AK Party in Turkey, was quoted as saying that the pope had "a dark mentality that comes from the darkness of the middle ages," and added: "He is going down in history in the same category as leaders such as Hitler and Mussolini."[24] Effortlessly, the "Dark Ages," the Middle Ages and barbarism are rolled up into one – and confounded with fascism in case the point is missed.

Extreme though it was, Kapusuz's view of the Middle Ages was just one example among many of a faultline between the Islamic and Judaeo-Christian worlds in understandings of the Middle Ages. Perhaps the most notorious statement of this kind was made on 16 September 2001 by the President of the United States, George W. Bush. The World Trade Center a smoking ruin, Bush stated, "This crusade, this war on terrorism, is going to take a while."[25] In response, al-Qaida adopted

[19] See Davis, *Renaissance Historical Fiction: Sidney, Deloney, Nashe.*

[20] The expression is recognised by the *OED*; see "medieval" 3.b.

[21] See Dinshaw, *Getting Medieval*, 183–91.

[22] Townsend, "Revealed: full horror of Gitmo inmate's beatings," 6.

[23] Mohamed, speaking through his solicitor on 24 February 2009: see http://www.independent.co.uk/news/uk/home-news/binyam-mohamed-8216i-wish-i-could-say-that--it-is-all-over-but-it-is-not8217-1630316.html. Accessed 22 February 2011.

[24] Hooper and Harding, "Muslim leaders demand apology for Pope's 'medieval' remarks."

[25] http://news.bbc.co.uk/1/hi/world/americas/1563722.stm Accessed 23 February 2011.

the same rhetoric of crusade. While Bush's remark could have been explained as an unfortunate slip, in the conflict that followed, as Bruce Holsinger notes, the crusade metaphor, tense with a thousand years of history, was perpetuated by US Defense Secretary Donald Rumsfeld and his underling Paul Wolfowitz, both of whom routinely branded Islamic regimes as medieval. As these usages frequently occurred "as part of comments scripted in advance by Wolfowitz himself and by the office of communications at the Department of Defense," Holsinger explains, "the medievalism of al Qaeda and the Taliban became a calculated and consistent part of Pentagon agitprop during the first year of the War on Terror."[26] In turn, during the 2011 "Arab Spring" rebellion in Libya, Muammar Al Gadaffi rhetorically resisted NATO intervention by repeated reference to a "crusader campaign."[27]

Such understandings of a grotesque medieval period, of course, need not be as serious as this, nor threaten retaliation on a global scale. Hardly a day goes by without a reference in the news to this or that "medieval" or "dark-age" practice in contexts where there is considerably less at stake. When the late Robin Cook, then Speaker in the British Parliament, referred to the House of Lords as a remnant of "the mediaeval age," or when Arsène Wenger of the Arsenal Football Club lamented what he called "Middle Age justice" applied by the media to footballers ("You burn someone quickly to satisfy people"), these represented the more light-hearted end of the spectrum of the grotesque Middle Ages.[28]

It is also evident that the grotesque Middle Ages is not necessarily always offered in a negative sense. The popularity of the Gothic novel of the late eighteenth century and its many derivatives, down to the vampire narratives currently in vogue, has to do with the *thrill* of the grotesque, the lure of the illicit. A grotesque medieval patina is intrinsic to such canonical Romantic poetry as Coleridge's *Christabel* (1797–1800). The antagonist Geraldine might be evil in this poem, but she is also attractive, mirroring her pure and innocent victim Christabel herself. Contemporary vampire narratives have entirely reversed the original convention in order to make the gothic central: gothic is no longer that which must be defeated in fiction.[29] Similarly, the dress and behaviour codes of today's Goths are a celebration of difference and acknowledge the grotesque-medieval origins of gothic.[30]

Whether celebratory or, as they more often are, condemnatory, these various versions of the grotesque Middle Ages must be recognised as reflecting the *original* sense of the term "Middle Ages." Historically, the grotesque medieval has

---

[26] See Holsinger, *Neomedievalism, Neoconservatism, and the War on Terror*, 43–54; quotation 48.

[27] For a discussion and spirited repudiation of the idea that cultural barbarism is "medieval," see further Simpson, *Under the Hammer*, 1–5.

[28] Cook: House of Commons debate, Hansard 13 May 2002, vol. 385, c529. http:// hansard.millbanksystems.com Wenger's comments were made in response to an edition of the BBC programme, *Panorama*, on "bungs" in football, aired in 2006: http://football. guardian.co.uk/comment/story/0,,1879373,00.html?gusrc=rss&feed=5

[29] On the vexed relations between gothic as a low form in the late eighteenth century and early nineteenth with the self-consciously high-art romanticism, see Gamer, *Romanticism and the Gothic*.

[30] See www.goth.net.

been *dominant* because a medieval period was brought into being in the sixteenth century precisely in order to promote the idea of a time or age which would be proverbial for its darkness. In his examination of pejorative uses of "medieval," Robinson laments "that we medievalists have an image problem on our hands."[31] But this misses the point: the reason "medieval" can be used pejoratively while "renaissance" and "classical" cannot is because the *medium aevum* was originally developed for precisely this purpose. And as Nancy F. Partner suggests, "perhaps it is time to admit that we get a lot of intellectual traction out of the bad old misrepresentations of medievalness, so reliably there to debunk again and again in ever newer and more surprising ways."[32]

Hence, when people invoke the grotesque Middle Ages they draw, whether knowingly or otherwise, on the dominant primary and original sense of the term "Middle Ages" established in the sixteenth century. They assume that their references will be understood to refer to a primitive past of barbaric practices, expecting this sense of the term to be immediately clear to their quite disparate communities of understanding, ranging from the handful of people in a courtroom to an implied worldwide community of Christians or Muslims. The disparate character of the possible communities of understanding testifies to the broad applications of the Middle Ages. From crusade to kinky sex, the grotesque is still the most common popular understanding of the term and the period.

The Romantic Middle Ages

Millais's painting shows a chivalric act but one which, at the moment of the painting, only the viewers can appreciate. The naked maiden herself is turning her face away in shame from her rescuer, and from the viewer. The story contains a threat: a more gothic and grotesque form of the Middle Ages has only narrowly been averted, it seems, in the minutes leading up to the moment captured by the image. What is promised in its future is romance: all will now be well, as the knight-rescuer is at hand. Chivalry has won out, as the figure of the dead assailant shows. But not everyone can appreciate this yet.

This instance of one of the enduring images of the Middle Ages – that of a beautiful woman rescued by a knight – suggests that despite the dominance of the concept of the grotesque Middle Ages, modern invocations of the Middle Ages are not entirely explained by an understanding of the period from Foxe to Wolfowitz. The image of chivalry was portrayed again and again through Victorian culture and if it is now a cliche, it remains a powerful one.

In short, the grotesque Middle Ages, while constantly invoked today, obviously does not tell the whole story. From the late eighteenth century onwards, a revival of interest in medieval culture was responsible for an idea counterposed to the sixteenth- and seventeenth-century understandings, which proposed that something valuable had been lost with the Middle Ages. Initially, the impact of

---

[31] Robinson, "*Medieval*, the *Middle Ages*," 311.
[32] Partner, "Foreword: Medieval Presentism before the Present," xi.

this revival was felt chiefly in poetry and literary studies, where the influence of
the French scholar Jean-Baptiste de La Curne de Sainte-Palaye and the German
Friedrich von Schlegel was registered in Britain in the work of such ballad collec-
tors as Thomas Percy, whose *Reliques of Ancient English Poetry* was first published
in 1765, and the literary historian Thomas Warton, whose *History of English Poetry*
appeared in three volumes between 1774 and 1781. Later, in the nineteenth century,
the influence of this romantic revival broadened: in particular, it is registered in
the novel and the visual arts. This is the Middle Ages of romance, of chivalric
deeds, but also of simple communitarian living and humanely organised labour, a
pastoral time when the cash nexus was unknown, a time of intense romantic love.
In Britain it was first seen in the work of a few scholars of the second half of the
eighteenth century who became interested in retrieving and imitating medieval
romances. These in turn had their influence on the poetry of the Romantics –
particularly on the early work of Coleridge, and Keats. In the nineteenth century
there was an explosion of medievalist poetry, novels, art, even social theory, a
great deal of it expressing a longing for aspects of medieval life. The early beginnings of organised medieval studies can also be seen in this period. This was the
inception of what we can call the *romantic* Middle Ages – a Middle Ages revalued
in largely positive ways.

Tame as much of this activity must appear today, conservative and nostalgic as
much of the art now seems, we need to recall that some of this medievalist activity
arose from rebellious impulses in the time of upheaval following the French Revolution. In 1790 Edmund Burke famously attributed the downfall of Marie-Antoi-
nette to a failure of chivalry, setting out a conservative appropriation of romance,
as David Duff argues, which was an obvious consequence of the literary histories
of Percy and Warton, and which would be enthusiastically espoused by Walter
Scott in the first decade of the nineteenth century. In this view romance was the
literature of chivalry, and chivalry itself was regarded less as a literary convention
than as an actual principle of order which had maintained civilisation in feudal
society. Such figures were not suggesting that the Middle Ages was *not* a time of
Gothic rudeness (which would have been a new argument) but rather that such
rudeness was kept in check by chivalry. In short the envisioned romantic Middle
Ages did not replace the Gothic vision but existed in tension with it.

There were alternatives to what Duff calls Burke's myth of "counter-revolutionary romance." It met its opposite in a myth of "revolutionary romance" among
his 1790s opponents. While from one perspective romance, with its manifest character, provided "a language of the absurd," it could nevertheless be adopted by the
revolutionary side; in the period of Revolution romance narratives "offered an apt
and accurate metaphorical language to write about the extraordinary phenomenon
that confronted them."[33] Hence the ordered feudal world which is the subject of
nostalgia in Scott's poems and novels was a powerful vision of the Middle Ages
but not the only one. In the 1790s Joseph Ritson, "the first [ballad] collector to be
a convinced radical, an enthusiast for the French Revolution and for Tom Paine's

---

[33] Duff, *Romance and Revolution*, 10, 13.

insistence on the Rights of Man," revived interest in the medieval outlaw, Robin Hood.[34] Later the Pre-Raphaelites of the 1840s boldly depicted scenes of sensual love, aiming to break with the authorised forms of painting sanctioned by the Royal Academy. In another tradition, entirely forgotten today, one of the most popular medieval figures of the nineteenth century along with Robin Hood and King Arthur was Wat Tyler, the leader of the 1381 rebels.[35] Later in the nineteenth century, such figures as the scholar Frederick Furnivall and the designer and writer William Morris found, in a communitarian Middle Ages, a model for the socialism they espoused.

Furthermore, there was one sphere in which this new romantic medievalism quickly grew dominant and became official. Neo-gothic architecture arose from impulses which were originally polemical, forming part of a reaction against the dominant neoclassicism of the eighteenth century in favour of a vernacular style. The Cambridge Camden Society (which moved to London and became the Ecclesiological Society in 1845) was at first a powerful force in this shift. The Society had decided by 1843 that it was the early Decorated style that was the most appropriate for modern imitations: "No one can, sensibly, employ Norman, and perhaps not judiciously even Perpendicular, when free to choose another style," the Society's pamphlet, *A Few Words to Church Builders*, stated in 1844. "Early English, though it must perhaps be allowed occasionally, should be used very sparingly. The Decorated or Edwardian style, that employed, we mean, between the years 1260 and 1360, is that to which only, except from some very peculiar circumstances, we ought to return."[36] The best known individual voice was that of John Ruskin, who similarly espoused Decorated: "I have now no doubt that the only style proper for modern northern work," Ruskin wrote in 1855, "is the Northern Gothic of the thirteenth century."[37]

By the middle of the nineteenth century, as the walls of the new Houses of Parliament rose in Westminster, neo-gothic had become the dominant architectural style in Britain. One of the architects of the Houses of Parliament, Augustus Pugin, had enormous influence, not least in the city in which I write these words, Manchester, where the university's earliest buildings, the assize court, the prison and the impressive town hall were all built in the neo-gothic style of Alfred Waterhouse, a follower of Pugin, while dozens of the churches are also medievalist recreations. As the Houses of Parliament and numerous buildings in Manchester and elsewhere show, the architecture of the Middle Ages was deemed suitable, in

---

[34] Knight, *Robin Hood: A Complete Study*, 154.

[35] The best known text of this tradition was Robert Southey's early dramatic poem, *Wat Tyler* (1794), published in illicit editions by his adversaries from 1817. But as Hannah Priest has shown, the Tyler tradition was a strong one outside of Southey's work. Priest's discoveries form part of a research project run by myself and Michael Sanders, "Rethinking Nineteenth-Century Medievalism."

[36] *A Few Words to Church Builders*, 3rd edn, 5–6; qtd in Andrews, *Australian Gothic*, 10. These words were not in the first edition of 1841, which was rather more tolerant of variation.

[37] Ruskin, *The Seven Lamps of Architecture*, 2nd edn, xiv.

the second half of the nineteenth century, for all kinds of civic building, from the church to the prison.

The medieval revival in architecture did not remain a British phenomenon. A New York Ecclesiological Society was established in 1848, and Pugin's influence was behind Richard Upjohn's Trinity Church in New York, completed in 1846. Another figure influenced by Pugin, George Gilbert Scott, won the competition to build the Nikolaikirche in Hamburg in 1845; in France around the same time there was fresh interest in gothic architecture, in part impelled by the pressing need to restore the cathedral of Notre Dame de Paris.[38] Even more markedly, neo-gothic is a feature of cities formerly belonging to the British empire, from Mumbai to Hobart.[39] Worship continues in such places, where the buildings also remain central to the civic spaces in which they appear.

This recapturing and reinvention of the medieval built environment was clearly a facet of what I am calling here the romantic Middle Ages, in that it power-fully and positively revalued an aspect of the medieval past. Neo-gothic was one of medievalism's spectacular successes, offering an official form of medievalism espoused by elite institutions of governance. Hence it is worth distinguishing this part of the revival as a subset, which I will call the *civic* Middle Ages.

Despite its revolutionary associations much of romantic medievalism is easy to write off as having been diverted into the dreamy fantasies of young men. British art galleries are full of Victorian depictions of armed knights variously rescuing or being tempted by mournful doe-eyed maidens with lustrous hair. Even more than Millais, Edward Burne Jones offers perhaps the best examples of this sublimation of masculine erotic fantasy in historical and legendary imaginings. In this vision, the same scenario is endlessly refigured: that in which the medieval feminine is hurt and vulnerable (abducted, stripped of rank, sometimes of clothes, threatened with loss of status, shame, and rape); the male figure, while outwardly protected by a carapace of armour, is himself inwardly soft and gentle as a woman; even as he unties the woman from a tree or otherwise restores her honour, his face is transformed with pity and empathy at her plight. In Burne Jones's paintings male and female faces are often very similar, suggesting a convergence of genders, which are therefore more strongly differentiated by outward markers (armour, female clothing). In Millais's *Knight Errant* all of these aspects are encapsulated; the woman's naked flesh is pale and vulnerable, shockingly incongruous against the setting of dark, ancient woodland. The knight's highly polished armour is fantastically detailed, a triumph of artifice next to the natural body of the woman. Yet we can tell from his youthfulness, the near bashfulness of his facial expression, that beneath the armour is another vulnerable, pale human body. In the present of the picture, only the massive sword poised between the pair – at the moment pointed safely down to earth and engaged in cutting the woman's bonds – phal-lically gestures to the necessary sexuality to which this painted incident is going to lead.

[38] Camille, *The Gargoyles of Notre-Dame.*
[39] See Andrews, *Australian Gothic* and Andrews, *Creating a Gothic Paradise.*

It is true that by the time such versions of romantic medievalism proliferated in the second half of the nineteenth century, much of the rebellious force had been lost. Romantic medievalism is easy to mock, then and now, because its essential character appears to be escapist, a turning away from the exigencies of real life. The committed socialist and reformer William Morris exemplifies some of the paradoxes. In early work in the 1860s, Morris wrote in *The Earthly Paradise*:

> Forget six counties overhung with smoke,
> Forget the snorting steam and piston stroke,
> Forget the spreading of the hideous town;
> Think rather of the pack-horse on the down,
> And dream of London, small, and white, and clean,
> The clear Thames bordered by its gardens green ...[40]

These lines enjoin the reader to *repress* the present in order to make the past alive. But the past of Chaucer that Morris represents here shows no sign of the Black Death (1348, 1361), the Peasants' Revolt (1381), the schism of the Church (1378), the strife between Richard II and the nobles (1388), or Richard's deposition and death (1399). The vision here is reminiscent of Ford Madox Brown's painting, *Chaucer Reading at the Court of Edward III*, in which gorgeously attired nobles, surrounding the aged but serene king, watch the poet recite, while distant in the background a lone ploughman drives his team, presumably knowing his place, far from court.

Morris's view of a romantic late fourteenth century was tempered in his later writing by a sense that the period's turmoil cannot be ignored. In a talk in 1889 on gothic architecture, Morris falls in with Ruskin's opinion that it was the architecture of the late thirteenth and early fourteenth centuries above all which ought to be upheld. But "the turning point of the Middle Ages" was shortly afterwards reached, with the advent of the Black Death and "the no less mysterious pests of Commercialism and Bureaucracy."[41] Morris, at this date a more committed and aware Marxist socialist than he was when writing *The Earthly Paradise*, now concedes the entry of the cash nexus into human relations in the fourteenth century. Chaucer goes unmentioned here, but it must have been difficult to reconcile this later view with the earlier vision of "London, small, and white, and clean." After all Chaucer, who was a bureaucrat and customs controller central to the operations of commerce, should be seen as an agent of the corruption Morris describes.

In his final years, Morris turned to writing a series of medievalist prose romances which have often baffled his adherents in their apparent turn away from a world of social injustice which Morris was otherwise devoted to changing. Morris did reinvent romance to some degree in such works as *The Water of the Wondrous Isles* (1895), giving a proto-feminist spin to the genre by putting his women in charge

[40] Morris, *The Earthly Paradise: A Poem*, Prol. 1–6.
[41] "Gothic Architecture," in Morris, *News from Nowhere and Other Writings*, ed. Wilmer, 343. The lecture was originally given to the Arts and Crafts Exhibition Society London in 1889 and published by the Kelmscott Press in 1893.

and blending a vision of socialist communitarianism into his feudal settings. In Morris's fantasy Middle Ages, there is an odd power vacuum at the very top; kings and queens are never among the major characters. The point Morris was trying to make by bringing a socialist vision to romance was largely missed by two twentieth-century writers who were deeply influenced by him. In the work of J. R. R. Tolkien, as was frequently objected in early criticism of *The Lord of the Rings*, the female characters are pushed once more to the background. In the Narnia books by his friend and colleague, C. S. Lewis, there is slightly more evenhanded treatment. But in the work of both, the Middle Ages of romance seems to have retreated to a world of stereotyped gender roles, fear of technology, and dreams of powerful monarchies. In their novels it is above all the return of kings that guarantees order.

Once again, this legacy should not obscure the fact that there was both an official and a practical side to Victorian romantic medievalism – and not simply in the architecture. As Mark Girouard reminds us, the nineteen-year-old Queen Victoria mocked the Eglinton Tournament (the Scott-influenced medieval recreation of 1839), but two years later medievalism was espoused at the highest level when she and her German-Romantic inspired husband Albert held an expensive themed ball in which they appeared in the guise of Queen Philippa and Edward III.[42] At the same time, serious thinkers proposed solutions based on medieval models to England's increasing working-class unrest in the 1840s. Such diverse figures as Benjamin Disraeli and Thomas Carlyle were far from being dreamy adherents of medieval romance, yet nevertheless each thought there was a calm order in medieval feudalism which, restored, would benefit nineteenth-century society.[43]

It is easy to look back and see such ideas as absurd – as empty as the appeals sometimes made today to a lost English prewar innocence. Disraeli's proposals for a return to medieval aristocracy translate to racialised fantasies: in his novel, *Sybil*, the romance plot brings together two figures depicted as truly aristocratic, and Disraeli sees "the noble English blood, of which in these days few types remain," as consisting of "the Norman tempered by the Saxon; the fire of conquest softened by integrity."[44] Logically, this would lead to the expulsion of all aliens, or a programme of eugenics (neither of which would have benefited the Jewish Disraeli). Yet those who made such calls were genuinely concerned about what the industrial revolution had produced, and wanted to achieve a programme of social renewal. As Michael Alexander argues, the "social medievalism" of the 1840s cannot be simply written off as "nostalgic or escapist" and he holds up the example of teachers at the Working Men's College, whose "paternalism and quixotisms did some good, and exemplified the medieval ideals of chivalry, generosity and charity."[45]

To find something worth retrieving from the Middle Ages did not necessarily mean that the enthusiast thought that *everything* medieval was equally good. A

[42] Girouard, *The Return to Camelot: Chivalry and the English Gentleman*, 112.
[43] See especially Disraeli's *Sybil, or the Two Nations* (1845), Carlyle's "Chartism" (1839) and *Past and Present* (1843). Fuller reference to these works appears in the next chapter.
[44] Disraeli, *Sybil*, 64.
[45] Alexander, *Medievalism*, 97, 172.

central tension in Karl Marx's thinking, as Bruce Holsinger and Ethan Knapp outline, arises from "the timeless stability of feudal mutuality" on the one hand, "and the sinister adumbration of capitalist expropriation" on the other.[46] As this suggests, in Marxist thought the grotesque Middle Ages co-exists with the romantic. The Victorians were – mostly – well aware of this coexistence. As we have already seen, in the background of Millais's *Knight Errant* the two men fleeing in terror and the dead man are presumably the would-be abductors or rapists. They leave a question behind them: has the knight arrived in time? He has evidently saved the woman's life, but what of her honour? The Middle Ages of this image is a time in which resplendently armed knights rescue damsels – but only because someone else was stripping damsels of their clothes and tying them to trees. The *emergent* romantic Middle Ages to some extent presupposed a *dominant* grotesque Middle Ages, with the assumption that romanticism would effect the rescue from the grotesque, without always effacing that grotesque.

Both what I am calling the romantic Middle Ages and the civic Middle Ages flourished alongside one another through Victoria's reign. Both then received a severe check in Britain in the early years of the twentieth century. To some advocates, civic neo-gothic still appeared dominant towards the end of the nineteenth century. In his 1889 lecture, Morris wrote, "Gothic Architecture is the most completely organic form of the art which the world has seen," and he proposed that Gothic architecture was the only style "on which it is possible to found a true living art, which is free to adapt itself to the varying conditions of social life, climate, and so forth."[47] In fact even as he uttered these words, the boom in neo-gothic was faltering, and a few years after his death in 1896, it was over. Neo-gothic was entering its long residual phase. Manchester's John Rylands Library, designed by Basil Champneys and opened in 1900, was among the last public gothic buildings in Britain. Although Liverpool's Anglican Cathedral took most of the twentieth century to build, its design by Giles Gilbert Scott (grandson of George Gilbert Scott) dates from 1903.

Other aspects of Victorian medievalism did not survive World War I, as Mark Girouard argues. By the end of the nineteenth century British men conducted themselves in battle and colonial expeditions alike according to what they thought were chivalric ideals based on medieval models. By 1914, "the ideals of chivalry worked with one accord in favour of war," but in the war itself chivalry died, "[o]r at least it received its death-wound."[48]

The civic Middle Ages is still with us in some quite obvious ways. Alfred Waterhouse's neo-gothic Manchester town hall is still the centre of Manchester's government, his prison is still a prison and his many university buildings in northern cities fulfil more or less their original purposes (while lecturers themselves have spread into the post-war outlands of the campus, the castellated citadels have been taken over by the feudal lords and their phalanxes of clerks). Charles Barry's

---

[46] Holsinger and Knapp, "The Marxist Premodern," 465.

[47] Morris, "Gothic Architecture," 332, 346.

[48] Girouard, *Return to Camelot*, 276, 290; for more detail see also Frantzen, *Bloody Good*.

Unitarian Chapel on Upper Brook Street in Manchester is now part-ruin, part Islamic Academy; St George's church in Manchester's Castlefield is an apartment block, but most neo-gothic churches are still simply churches.

The romantic Middle Ages mutated and was soon reused in the time of modernism. Jackson Lears argues for a profound antimodernist impulse in American culture at the end of the nineteenth and the beginning of the twentieth century, which in its turn gave rise to neo-medievalism in America – such a text as Ralph Adams Cram's medievalist utopian work of political theory, *Walled Towns* (1919), is one result.[49] The end of Victorian medievalism in Britain was followed, as Alexander describes it, by a phase of Edwardian medievalism, in which the Middle Ages emerged in new if somewhat more occulted forms.

Chivalry might have died in the trenches of the Somme, as Girouard has it, but some artists, nevertheless, reacted to World War I with renewed medievalism. It was while recovering from trench fever in 1917 that Tolkien began his medievalist epic, and around the same time that the Welsh poet David Jones wrote a short narrative entitled "The Quest," in which "A Victorian ethos of self-sacrifice is expressed in familiar, archaizing language."[50] Thereafter, these two writers would go in very different directions, one writing epic romance, the other, within ten years, embarking on modernist poetry in which "the Middle Ages would become invested with ever-greater symbolic power, offering a key to the meaning of Western history in *The Anathémata* and rising to visionary intensity in *The Sleeping Lord*."[51]

Hence while conventionally modernism is seen as a reaction against Victorianism of all kinds, including medievalism, David Jones's work shows how medievalism might remain nested within modernism. In fact high modernism everywhere shows itself to be attentive to medievalism. Such a central modernist work as T. S. Eliot's *The Waste Land* (1922) gestures in its title alone to the medieval Grail myth. Eliot was candid about this, attributing his interest in the Grail to a reading of Jessie L. Weston's influential *From Ritual to Romance* (1920), a work which is in part an attempt to understand the Arthurian story.[52] Even more ubiquitous than Arthurian legend is Dante, a medieval poet whose work subtends a great deal of modernist literature, as Daniela Caselli demonstrates.[53] In modernism, nostalgic and romantic medievalism was not only renewed, but pushed in the direction of self-consciously fashioned high-art forms in a manner arguably not seen in the English language since the death of Tennyson in 1892. A more general

---

[49] Lears, *No Place of Grace*; I discuss Cram's work in chapter 4.

[50] Robichaud, *Making the Past Present*, 1. Tolkien's work of this time was published in two parts as *The Book of Lost Tales*.

[51] Robichaud, *Making the Past Present*, 2.

[52] John Ganim brilliantly if briefly discusses the medievalism of the poem in his "Medieval Film *Noir*: Anatomy of a Metaphor," in Bernau and Bildhauer, eds., *Medieval Film*, 182–202.

[53] See Caselli, *Beckett's Dantes*; Caselli's current work extends her insights to other major modernist figures. See also Havely, ed., *Dante's Modern Afterlife*, and, especially on the American afterlife of Dante, see Verduin, "Dante's Inferno", Verduin, "Grace of Action," and also Verduin, "Sayers, Sex, and Dante."

sense of the medieval is pervasive in modern poetry: Chris Jones has extensively documented the role played by Old English verse in twentieth-century poetry, from Pound and Auden to Heaney.[54] Clearly, then, it would be mistaken to see modernism as having ended the medievalist impulse. Modernism turned medievalism to different purposes, and perhaps hid it better than the Victorians had done, but it remains in places a powerful presence behind modernist symbolism.

Romantic medievalism did continue in its more overt guises, down to the present day. But in the twentieth century, it became a residual form, less likely to be found in elite than in popular culture. Tolkien's children's story of 1937, *The Hobbit*, was a medievalist work which drew on the author's deep knowledge of philology and Old English and Old Norse texts. In 1954–56 Tolkien published a sequel, *The Lord of the Rings*, a much more expansive work about Middle Earth, his imagined past version of our own world. A neo-medievalist industry was born. Tolkien, a man of conservative political opinions, presented a starkly binary struggle in Middle Earth between virtuous craft and threatening industry. The Shire, the hobbits' homeland, is part ideal and part satire of a very Little England of agrarian community and small government. In the 1960s, to his puzzlement, Tolkien found his work central to libertarianism and the environmental movement. *The Lord of the Rings* and hippies met where they shared antimodernist distrust of technology and love of nature. They shared little else. But this antitechnological Middle Ages of the little person has become one of the defining images of the Middle Ages around the world.

One manifestation of the medieval in this form is found in the enormously popular medieval markets and fayres (the archaic spelling is mandatory) by which small towns celebrate their own local cultures and promote an anti-capitalist, nonglobalist way of life: agrarian, community-based, poetic. A medieval market will feature local produce, organically grown products, home-brewed, non-mainstream drinks such as mead, and wooden toys, with perhaps a musician or jugglers. Such things are synecdochically understood to be medieval. A *mercado medieval* in the Cantabrian town of Cabezón de la Sal which I visited in August 2011 took place adjacent to the regular Saturday market. It featured local produce – for example, local honey, the cheeses for which the area is known, and cured hams. A few of the stall holders had made an effort with medievalist dress. Several stalls sold distinctly non-medieval tourist souvenirs (one, mysteriously, offering cacti) while children were catered for with pony-rides. The market's medievalness was signalled chiefly in banners with heraldic devices at either end of the market and the fact that the stall awnings had decorative scalloped fringes.

Given its position next to the regular market, where exactly the same kinds of things are on sale every week, the medieval character of this market consisted chiefly in these little touches of colour and quaintness. The sheer excess of the huge pile of hams was perhaps also a marker of medievalness. But in most ways the medieval market struggled to differentiate itself from the main market. What is

---

[54] Jones, *Strange Likeness.*

suggested here is that all that "medieval" means in this context is "pre-industrial." The street market is therefore a "medieval" technology, wherever it is found.

Medievally themed festivals have also been common in recent years in Europe, in which jousting knights are particularly popular. Their lineage goes all the way back to the Eglinton Tournament and *Ivanhoe*. A *Gigantisches Mittelalter Spektakel* in Biebesheim, Germany, in September 2011 promised a historically improbable tournament of "knights versus Vikings" (Figure 2). Here, the medieval spectacle meets the computer game. Offering even more participation, a *fête médiévale* could be enjoyed in Saint-Benoît-du-Sault on 14 July 2012 for a price of 10 euros, with a *buffet spectacle* enlivened by twenty comedians and three musicians.

It is to these destinations that the paths of nineteenth-century romantic medievalism have led. Romantic medievalism is no longer a matter of the kind of state policy that sanctions a neo-gothic building programme, nor of the canonicity that sees its widespread adoption in art. Instead, contemporary romantic medievalism is chiefly a carnivalesque Middle Ages. The fairs and spectacles signal their medieval character by adding jugglers, colourful, decorative awnings, perhaps a fire-eater; they are often *excessive*, piling high their cured hams and cheeses in a manner to please a Friar Tuck. They are overtly pre-industrial. This is a Middle Ages understood as perpetual carnival.

This is not, however, the only destination of the romantic Middle Ages. In one minor strand, a romanticised medievalism is turned back into a gothicism: this is Eco's Middle Ages no. 6, the medievalism of national identities. In medieval romances themselves, ideologies of race, blood, and faith are prominent. The true knight is the knight of the right blood; the monstrous other (a giant, Saracen, or simply a felon knight) must be expelled or converted. This discourse of racial and religious purity has lurked in modern romances like a virus since Scott's blond, Saxon Wilfrid Ivanhoe took on his swarthy adversary. In Tolkien's *The Lord of the Rings*, tall men of ancient noble races from the west turn back dark-skinned invading easterners and southerners. Like the Nazis before them, contemporary fascists often seek authorisation in the medieval past.[55] On St George's Day – 24 April – in 2010, the polemical songwriter Billy Bragg confronted a member of the right-wing British National Party in east London who was on horseback and dressed as St George. Bragg asked the BNP member whether he knew that St George had come from Lebanon.[56] In 2011, the Norwegian mass murderer Anders

[55] Medievalism has been said to be "essential to Nazi ideology" (Morgan, "Medievalism, Authority, and the Academy," 65). While a medievalist element in Nazi mythology can certainly be detected, this is somewhat overstated, particularly in light of the neoclassicism of Nazi building programmes. See Koerner, "Nazi Medievalist Art and the Politics of Memory," who argues that it was the far right of the Weimar Republic that more systematically espoused medievalism, and that "the Nazi elite did not consider medievalism a political program ... [but] rather, a general idiom of reverence, a diffused nostalgia" (48); on Hitler's own anti-medievalism see 53. Lears discusses the link between antimodernism and fascism in *No Place of Grace*; see e.g. 6, 32, 160. On medievalism and the modern extreme right, see Geary, *The Myth of Nations*; see also, note 65 below, on Bildhauer's discussion of the 1937 film *Condottieri*.
[56] "Billy Bragg and BNP clash over St George's Day," *The Guardian*, 24 April 2010.

2. Poster: "Gigantisches Mittelalter Spektakel, Biebesheim".
Photograph: A. Bernau.

Behring Breivik claimed to be a member of a latter-day Knights Templar organisation, an anti-Islamic secret society. In such fantasies, the nineteenth-century Middle Ages of romance comes full circle and, fully realised in grotesque guise, finds itself in the crypt once more.

Representing the Middle Ages

I have to this point described the two major forms which understandings of the Middle Ages take today, with some of their variations. It would be wrong to suggest that these are absolute and always separable categories: as I have made clear, what I have called the civic and the romantic Middle Ages go side by side and are often closely related to one another; such figures as Ruskin, Pugin, and Morris are crucial to both. And in the midst of the romantic Middle Ages the grotesque Middle Ages might intrude, as Millais's painting suggests. One of the seminal medievalist texts, Scott's *Ivanhoe*, presents much that is romantically nostalgic. But never far away are dark villains, hints of torture, and sexual deviance. The final tournament is won by Ivanhoe not through his own skill but because his adversary Bois-Guilbert simply drops dead, "a victim to the violence of his own contending passions."[57] After this peculiar anticlimax, Ivanhoe wins his fair maiden, Rowena, yet there is more than a hint of a residual attachment to the female character most readers have found more interesting, the Jewish Rebecca. Hence, the hero is denied his ultimate triumph in battle, while the presence of Rebecca disrupts the traditional romantic ending. The novel is conflicted: the good, romantic medieval represented by Ivanhoe cannot claim a total victory and the grotesque medieval other is not entirely defeated. Nor is the grotesque without some attraction. Scott, who could not resist closing *Ivanhoe* by expressing his doubts about another of its romantic heroes, King Richard the Lionheart, was not the uncomplicated champion of the Middle Ages he is often thought to be.

In short, the grotesque and the romantic Middle Ages may be found occupying the same places (as the fascist adoption of medievalism shows). And they do not exhaust the possibilities. When at the beginning of *Ivanhoe* the characters Gyrth and Wamba debate the Norman Conquest and its impact, we glimpse what might be called the *constitutional* Middle Ages. This is most obviously seen in the idea, predating Scott but popularised by him, of the "Norman Yoke": the belief that the democracy of which nineteenth-century England was a shining example had been anticipated by the Anglo-Saxon state, before being curtailed by the Conquest.[58] Entirely at odds with the grotesque Middle Ages, this version has more in common with Eco's Middle Ages of national identities.

As is becoming evident, one major problem that confronts medievalism studies is the sheer diversity of material. Already, to this point, I have drawn on poetry, novel, painting, architecture, and political theory. Within those broad genres, I

---

[57] Scott, *Ivanhoe*, 506.

[58] The classic statement is Hill, "The Norman Yoke," published in 1954 and reprinted in his *Puritanism and Revolution*, 1958. For a more recent summary see Chibnall, *The Debate on the Norman Conquest*.

have also indiscriminately mixed quite different examples. The novel alone, for example, offers quite varied kinds of medievalism. On the one hand, *Ivanhoe* gave rise to a novelistic tradition in which there was an attempt to represent a historical Middle Ages with a degree of realism. In 1843, Edward Bulwer Lytton showed himself to be the heir to this tradition with his *Last of the Barons*, a novel which opens in 1467 and depicts events of the Wars of the Roses in the mode established by Scott, mixing fictional and historical characters, with a narrative point of view fully imbued with hindsight and aware of later history. (Victor Hugo's 1831 novel *Notre Dame de Paris* is also in this tradition.) Two years later, Benjamin Disraeli published a very different kind of novel, *Sybil, or the Two Nations*. As we have seen, this novel was set in the recent past, in the mode characteristic of realism as practised by Balzac and Stendhal. Yet it falls under the view of the medievalist because the novel's narrator frequently identifies his hero and heroine as being of Saxon and Norman stock, and discusses contemporary social problems in terms of solutions that can be drawn from the Middle Ages. Formally, of course, these two novels are quite different works. Medievalism studies wants to claim both of them. If it does not claim them, then it limits what medievalism studies can be. But how can the different apprehensions of the Middle Ages in these two novels be distinguished? Conversely, what is gained by thinking of them as belonging in the same category? How can different medievalisms be compared?

One basic taxonomy has been proposed by Francis Gentry and Ulrich Müller – the latter one of the original founders of the field of *Mittelalter-Rezeption*. They propose that "Four distinct models of medieval reception can be determined":

> (1) The productive, i.e., creative reception of the Middle Ages: subject matter, works, themes, and even medieval authors are creatively re-formed into a new work;

> (2) The reproductive reception of the Middle Ages: the original form of medieval works is reconstructed in a manner viewed as "authentic," as in musical productions or renovations (for example, paintings or monuments);

> (3) The academic reception of the Middle Ages: medieval authors, works, events, etc., are investigated and interpreted according to the critical methods that are unique to each respective academic discipline;

> (4) The political-ideological reception of the Middle Ages: medieval works, themes, "ideas" or persons are used and "reworked" for political purposes in the broadest possible sense. e.g. for legitimization or for debunking (in this regard, one need only recall the concept "crusade" and the ideology associated with it).

Gentry and Müller concede that "In many, indeed possibly in all instances, the above forms of reception merge," and suggest that only in the case of models (2) and (3) is it possible to analyse "right" and "wrong" (the suspensive quotation marks are theirs).[59]

---

[59] Gentry and Müller, "The Reception of the Middle Ages in Germany," 401.

The main problem with this taxonomy is that (4) is of a different order from the first three; to make it separate unfortunately implies that the first three models of medieval recovery are somehow free from the "political-ideological." In fact, a great amount of the effort in medievalism studies and histories of the discipline of medieval studies is aimed precisely at exposing their political-ideological investments. In any case, as Gentry and Müller themselves concede, the borders are porous. Even such an apparently uncontroversial category as "The academic reception of the Middle Ages" is very fluid. Thomas Warton's *History of English Poetry* (1774–81) was once an academic work, as was, even more obviously, Stubbs's *The Constitutional History of England* (1873–78). The former, at least, is now considered only as medievalism, not medieval studies.

The problems inherent in creating a workable taxonomy for medievalism are intractable. Here, I will propose a working model. In my study, I regard medievalism as a *discourse*, which can appear to greater or lesser degrees in cultural works. It can suffuse them almost entirely; it can be a barely detectable substrate. I arrange various possibilities here on a spectrum.

1. The Middle Ages "as it was." The Middle Ages is depicted as if realistically: medieval motifs are used to create a medieval setting; there is an apparent attempt to represent or invoke the period "as it really was." *Ivanhoe* and the historical novel to which it gave rise, down to Ken Follett's *Pillars of the Earth* (1989) and Ariana Franklin's Mistress of the Art of Death series, are all examples. So too are the films and television series that treat the Middle Ages in something like a realist fashion (most recently, *The White Queen*, a BBC adaptation [2013] of Philippa Gregory's novels focused on Edward IV's queen Elizabeth Woodville). Neo-gothic churches are another way of representing the Middle Ages "as they were"; so too are performances of medieval music on reconstructed instruments. Many medieval tourist sites similarly aim to create this level of realism, either by building on an actual medieval original, or through sheer invention.

But also pertinent here is the labelling of the war on terror as a crusade, and al-Qaida's retributive labelling of Westerners as crusaders. Both are attempts to use a "real" Middle Ages, to say in effect: Westerners were crusaders then, and they are crusaders now. The many differences between the crusades and the war on terror serve to remind us that we are dealing here with an *effect* of the real, not with any historical reality itself.

2. The Middle Ages "as it might have been." The Middle Ages is depicted, through or as legend; this might be done realistically or through a fantasy realisation, but either way, there is an implicit concession that it is not history but a fantasy that is on display. Much Pre-Raphaelite art self-consciously depicts matter from *legend* rather than history; so too does Wagner's Ring Cycle. The story of King Arthur, with its many offshoots, usually fits into this category; it can be represented as fantasy, or as realism; with greater or lesser magic. Marion Zimmer Bradley's *Mists of Avalon* (1982) is at the legend end of the possibilities; Mary Stewart's Arthurian novels (commencing with *The*

Crystal Cave [1970]) are more grounded in historical realism; Bernard Corn-well's Arthur trilogy (1995–97) sits somewhere in between, and Channel 4's *Camelot* keeps its fantasy in the background, implicitly claiming to represent a realistic Christian, dark-age Britain, emerging from the collapse of the Roman empire. Antoine Fuqua's film *King Arthur* (2004) eschewed magic and laid a heavy emphasis on a historical Arthur, and so perhaps belongs in the first category rather than here. Sometimes, legend is in the eye of the beholder: there is a small industry in books about the "real King Arthur" which for some are history, for others, the purest legendary medievalism.

3. The Middle Ages "as it never was." A quasi-, pre-, parallel or non-Middle Ages is depicted, using medieval motifs which create a medieval appearance. Tolkien's *The Lord of the Rings* is routinely thought of as medievalist, but the setting is explicitly in a time long *before* the Middle Ages; George Lucas's *Star Wars* films (1977–2008) have some medievalist elements but are set "a long time ago, in a galaxy far, far away." Tolkien himself invented ingenious explanations for the anomalies he created: the men of Rohan may *appear* to be speaking Anglo-Saxon but, he explains, this was just his way of repre-senting what they actually did speak, which was something quite different. More frequently, there is simply no need for explanation of these "off-world" medievalisms. Lucas's Jedi knights are a mix of Templars, Shaolin monks, and Knights of the Garter, but this magpie approach to culture receives no explanation nor, strictly, does it require one. Abundant science-fiction narra-tives depict what look like feudal or otherwise medievalised states, but take place where there cannot be a Middle Ages. Iain M. Banks's *Matter* (2008) features a civilisation in what looks like a feudal stage of development, but which also has steam engines.

To these three basic modes of medievalism we can add two counterposed ways in which the Middle Ages are apprehended:

4. A cultural production based largely on medieval elements incorporates modern references or motifs. The 1994 recording *Officium*, by Jan Garbarek and the Hilliard Ensemble, is to a great extent scholarly, in that it features the Ensemble's singing of various Gregorian and other chants from the thirteenth to sixteenth centuries. But these are anachronistically threaded through with Garbarek's modern jazz saxophone. Many further examples are found in the neo-medieval music movement: much of the work of the pioneering Hamburg band Ougenweide, founded in 1970, with its Middle High German lyrics, belongs here.[60]

5. A cultural production, essentially of its own time, looks back to the Middle Ages with greater or lesser explicitness. Michael Powell and Emeric Press-burger's *A Canterbury Tale* (1944) stands as a neat exemplar. Set at the time it

---

[60] See www.ougenweide.eu. See also Kreutziger-Herr, "Imagining Medieval Music: A Short History."

was made, it has a title which makes it impossible not to think of Chaucer's great medieval work. Yet after an opening which depicts a moment from the Canterbury pilgrimage, there is a famous jump-cut to the present day; subsequently there are only fleeting and indirect references to the medieval narrative. T. S. Eliot's *The Waste Land*, with its cryptic gestures to Arthurian legend via Jessie Weston, falls into this category, along with a great deal of modernist poetry. Modernist architecture, too, often gestures in a minimal way to medievalist motifs, using castellation or machicolation. Disraeli's *Sybil* is another example. In other kinds of novels, medievalism might appear as dreamlike fragments within a larger realist context, as in Randolph Stow's *Girl Green as Elderflower* (1980).[61] More recently still, the Welsh press Seren has commissioned and published ten novellas by Welsh writers, all of which are reworkings in various ways of tales from the *Mabinogion*. Heavy metal bands which sprinkle their music with medieval (chiefly gothic) motifs belong here, but so too does such neo-medieval music as that of the German band Corvus Corax, with its eclectic mix of gothic, folk, rock, reconstructed instruments, and Latin lyrics, and The Soil Bleeds Black, whose compositions are mostly original, but in a recognisably medievalist style. Some of this is what Louise D'Arcens has characterised as "'throwaway' medievalism … in which the presence of medievalist tropes is incidental, fleeting, and historically undiscriminating" (though poets, novelists and bands alike can take their medievalist references very seriously).[62]

Much in the second category, and everything in the third, would also correspond with what some scholars are now calling "neomedievalism." This term, first attested in the late nineteenth century and given some currency by Umberto Eco's use of it (see above), has recently been seized upon by scholars associated with the Medieval Electronic Multimedia Organization (MEMO). According to the MEMO website, neomedievalism:

> Involves contemporary "medieval" narratives that purport to merge (or even replace) reality as much as possible … Neomedievalism engages alternative realities of the Middle Ages, generating the illusion into which one may escape or even interact with and control – be it through a movie or a video game. Already fragmented histories are purposed as further fragmented, destroyed and rebuilt to suit whimsical fancy, particularly in video games, where the illusion of control is most complete … It is a seriously gleeful embrace of the absurd.[63]

---

[61] On Stow's medievalism in general, I am indebted to Melanie Duckworth's unpublished doctoral thesis, "Medievalism and the Language of Belonging in Selected Works of Les Murray, Randolph Stow, Francis Webb, Kevin Hart."

[62] See www.soilbleedsblack.com; D'Arcens, *Old Songs in the Timeless Land*, 6.

[63] http://medievalelectronicmultimedia.org/definitions.html. Accessed 9 November 2012. See further Robinson and Clements, "Living with Neomedievalism." Among several thoughtful responses in the succeeding issue, see in particular Grewell, "Neomedievalism: An Eleventh Little Middle Ages?"

There has been much discussion of neomedievalism in a short space of time, with some scholars reacting cautiously to the potential fragmentation of medievalism studies in the very moment in which it seemed to be establishing itself. Neomedievalism represents the decisive point at which medievalism studies floats free of any necessary connection to the Middle Ages and medievalist scholars. It is in one sense the logical destination of modern medievalism, which began in the eclecticism of something like Walpole's Strawberry Hill, passed through the increasingly rigorous demand for authenticity of the Ecclesiological Society's neo-gothic and Pugin's designs, before moving away from rigorism and towards a freer (if better informed) play with medieval motifs by the end of the nineteenth century. Neomedievalism relocates medievalism as a cultural-studies pursuit, not necessarily a medievalist one.

Without creating further categories, it is worth noting that any and all of these modes can be represented through such a heavily ironic, or clearly humorous and satirical manner, as to make it obvious that any surface realism is entirely vitiated. The hit French comedy, *Les Visiteurs* (1993), in which a medieval French nobleman and his servant are transported to the present day, provides an example. Indeed this film stands as a metaphor for our relation to the Middle Ages: it is a time in the distant past, yet it can irrupt into the present; when it does so, it confirms our stereotype of a grotesque time of dirt, smell, bad manners and violence. And yet – as the knight finally returns to his own time, farewelling the modern woman who has begun to fall for him – there is a moment of romantic tenderness. He melts from her view, representing that moment in which we perceive that a romantic Middle Ages is both desirable and, after all, beyond our grasp.

The "Real" Middle Ages?

As the nineteenth century furthered the idea of the grotesque Middle Ages, simultaneously developed a romantic Middle Ages, and ultimately produced professional medieval studies, where did the *true* Middle Ages lie? Should we, with Ruskin, Morris and many followers, consider the Middle Ages as principally a time of relative harmony and the pinnacle of architectural achievement, brought about by the church and by feudalism? Should we regard it as an attractively simpler time than our own post-industrial era? A time when contemplative monks and nuns offered much of the protective social structure today provided by the state? Should we see peasants the way medieval books of hours see them, as contentedly performing honest manual labour according to ageless seasonal rhythms? Or, instead, should those peasants be regarded as the victims of oppressive laws, unjust taxation, and virulent plagues? The Church, as corrupt and bloated on its revenues? The feudal system, as violent and exploitative?

Naturally – as the Middle Ages of the scholars tells us – the opposition that is set up between grotesque and romantic is simply not valid. Medieval Europe would have been a more dangerous place, it seems safe to say, were it not for the Church; but the Church became corrupt. Many lives on the land were conducted harmoniously enough, we may speculate – but there was little relief at hand during the famines of the early fourteenth century and the oppressive taxation that funded Edward III's wars in the 1330s. It can be argued that conditions were better for English peasants in the 1360s and 1370s as a result of the labour shortage after the Black Death. But the delightful images of peasant labour in the margins of manuscripts seem highly unlikely to tell the whole truth.

Such topics are not part of this book. The finer-grained, more detailed truth behind these oppositions can only be approached through the painstaking work of archaeologists, historians, and their fellow scholars in related disciplines of medieval studies. That is not what this book is about. Whether talking about the grotesque, the romantic, or the civic Middle Ages, this book is not about their relative truth value but about the ways in which these totally contradictory ideas of the Middle Ages came to coexist; what the significations of the medieval are today, and what we might do when we study those.

This is not always a dispassionate pursuit. In the essay referred to above, Umberto Eco famously issued a call to responsibility:

> [W]e have the moral and cultural duty of spelling out what kind of Middle Ages we are talking about. To say openly which of the above ten types we are referring to means to say who we are and what we dream of, if we are simply practicing a more or less honest form of divertissement, if we are wondering about our basic problems or if we are supporting, perhaps without realizing it, some new reactionary plot.[64]

Some medievalists have taken this seriously indeed. Discussing the 1937 film *Condottieri*, for example – an Italian-German co-production promoting fascist values – Bettina Bildhauer states that "Scholarship ... should aim to analyse and thereby shatter such illusions."[65] Debates about recreation and authenticity rapidly break down into tedium yet, conversely, it is clear that appeals to authenticity can have their uses. Reminding an extreme nationalist that his icon of Englishness, St George, was born in the Middle East can have a usefully deflating effect.

My working assumption in this book will be that the Middle Ages was a chronological period which took place in the past, and to which we can assign temporal boundaries (even if these are subject to challenge and modification). We have access to this period through the work of medieval studies, which sifts through the material traces of the period. The time of *medievalism* is rather different. Medievalism characteristically evokes a time in the past but does so in an often contradictory way, by positing that that past is in some sense still alive and still with us, or able to be with us. From that possibility arises the equally paradoxical possibility that there remain in this world medieval *places* that can be visited. Certain ideologies – that of al-Qaida, for instance – can be envisaged as bringing the Middle Ages alive, in a sense, in a contemporary time and place. The next two chapters, then, will explore these paradoxes of medievalism: those of medieval time and space in the modern era.

[64] Eco, *Faith in Fakes*, 72.
[65] Bildhauer, *Filming the Middle Ages*, 171.

II
TIME, SPACE,
SELF, SOCIETY

2

"Welcome to the Current Middle Ages": Asynchronous Medievalism

S HEKHAR KAPOOR'S 2007 film, *Elizabeth: The Golden Age*, sequel to 1998's *Elizabeth* with Cate Blanchett again in the title role, depicts the middle years of the Tudor queen's reign up until the defeat of the Spanish Armada in 1588. Continuing the central drama of the earlier film, it traces the virgin queen's establishment of her legitimacy as a woman on the throne. At the same time, in a scarcely less obvious way, the narrative is a triumphal drama of the forging of a Protestant nation, breaking free from and defining itself against a Catholic past of superstition and oppressive masculinity. As it builds towards the Spanish king's invasion of England the film shuttles between its English and Spanish settings, in scenes in which it becomes increasingly clear that Elizabeth inhabits a light-filled realm of incipiently renascent splendour. She receives emissaries in her luminous palace of Whitehall (in scenes shot in the cathedral of Ely with its massive lantern tower). In corresponding scenes set in Spain (shot in some of the darker corners of Westminster Abbey), her adversaries are depicted in shadows, attired in dark cloaks, showing us that the obscurity of their own inner ignorance moves with them. Ultimately, of course, the pernicious Armada, leading the forces of superstitious darkness, is defeated by a nation that is thereby left free to pursue its own destiny as an enlightened place which, among many other things, lets a woman remain on the throne.

The condition of the film's overt feminist promise, however, is the extirpation of the ignorant medieval past. The film thereby plays out a version of precisely the way in which sixteenth-century England itself portrayed the superstitious past. I have already, in the introduction, revisited the history through which the British Middle Ages was invented in the sixteenth century and conceived of, first as a dark time and then as a middle time (intervening between the classical and the "modern" sixteenth century). As I showed, these two ideas were effortlessly conflated: middleness became darkness, and vice versa. One of the reasons for the almost hysterical condemnation of the medieval period in the late sixteenth century was the quite genuine fear that, without ceaseless vigilance, that dark age could return. It was not a groundless fear: Elizabeth, after all, succeeded a Catholic monarch and, in France and Spain, faced invasion from two Catholic nations. Hence the state she ruled was consistently oppressive and intolerant in religious matters, fearful of a return of the Catholic past.[1]

What is at stake in the view of history in Kapoor's film is then no less than historical progress itself. The film neatly captures the fear – also apparent in the Elizabethan era – that the past can return. The past might be not too far away, indeed: just across a stretch of water in a neighbouring nation. In such depictions the Middle Ages is not entirely a period, a chronological era with fixed boundaries, but rather something that might come back, something that continues to exist in some places though it has been eradicated in others. William Camden's comment in 1605, already quoted in the introduction, refers to a "midle age" with its "darke clouds" and "thicke fogges of ignorance." This characteristic conflation of middle-ness and darkness makes the chronological middle more fluid. In theory, a middle age is fixed in the past, but in fact, just as dark clouds and thick fogs can quickly obscure a sunny day, so too can a middle age return.

In the sixteenth century and for a long time afterwards, in short, the Middle Ages was *never* simply a chronological concept, never simply a past time firmly fixed in the past. It was an ideological state of being, a state of historical development that might return and in fact could be re-entered much more easily than it could be left behind. Sermons of the period repeatedly warn against precisely this possibility: John Jewel, bishop of Salisbury under Elizabeth, was one who preached vigilance against Catholics who might bring back darkness, concerned that those who "rauine and spoyle the house of God" and by means of whom "forraine power, of which this realme by the mercie of God is happely delyuered, shall agayne be brought in vpon vs," and warning that "Suche thinges shalbe done vnto vs, as we before suffered: the truth of God shalbe taken away, the holy scriptures burnt and consumed in fire."[2] The overall mode here might be an admonitory subjunctive, but the simple future tenses rhetorically propose something that *will* happen.

Later, when interest in the medieval period was revived in the second half of the eighteenth century, the original threat of a Middle Ages that might return had greatly diminished. In the eighteenth century, as Linda Colley has argued, Great Britain was consolidating itself as a protestant nation and a British Empire was being founded in the 1760s on the gains made in the Seven Years War.[3] If Britain still demonised Catholicism, it nevertheless did so without quite the same sense, as in Elizabethan England, that Catholicism was always set to pounce on an unwary nation. It was then possible for such ministers of the Church of England as Thomas Percy to revive interest in the Middle Ages without provoking fears of an immediate lapse into Catholic superstition. It was possible for people to construct around themselves renewed medieval spaces – as Horace Walpole did with his house at Strawberry Hill – without threatening the immediate return

---

[1]   On the main issues here see further Parish, *Monks, Miracles and Magic*.

[2]   Jewel, Sermon on Psalm 69, in *Certaine sermons preached before the Queenes Maiestie*, 17v. The words were re-used by later preachers.

[3]   Colley, *Britons*.

of the medieval repressed. Hence the foundations were laid for a more scholarly approach to the Middle Ages in the 1760s, the period known as the Medieval or Romantic *revival*.

The initial impulses of the revival grew out of antiquarianism. In the eighteenth century all kinds of antiquities became the focus of interest – neolithic and Iron Age remains, coins, ballads and early poetry, folklore – as part of a general turn to the primitive. There was then a discovery of the past, in some cases quite literally a dis-covering as artefacts were unearthed, manuscripts retrieved, old tombs broken open. Out of disparate antiquarian impulses arose, in the medievalist sphere, such classic works as Richard Hurd's *Letters on Chivalry and Romance* (1762); Thomas Percy's ballad collection, *The Reliques of Ancient English Poetry* (1765); Horace Walpole's novel, *The Castle of Otranto* (1764), Thomas Tyrwhitt's edition of Chaucer's *Canterbury Tales* (1775), and the three-volume scholarly work by Thomas Warton, *History of English Poetry* (1774–81).

Pioneering though such works were in the British context, most work in Britain at the time was derivative, deeply indebted to such contintental scholars as Jean-Baptiste de La Curne de Sainte-Palaye, Claude Fauchet and the German romantics.[4] But the impact of Percy, Warton, and Hurd in Britain was extensive: it is hard to imagine Wordsworth and Coleridge's *Lyrical Ballads* (1798) without Percy's *Reliques*; Warton's *History* was the major account of early English poetry for at least a century; Walpole's novel spawned a series of imitations and redefined "Gothic." Walter Scott writes of the impact of the *Reliques* on him as a boy; his *Minstrelsy of the Scottish Border* (1802–3) can be regarded as the Scottish version of Percy's work, an early work in a career that also produced the hugely influential medievalist recreation, *Ivanhoe* (1819), and a series of works in the new genre, the historical novel.

Even as artefacts were dug out of the ground, oral ballads transcribed, and manuscripts retrieved from oblivion, the condition of this so-called revival was that nothing would actually come back to life. The Medieval Revival, by transforming the Middle Ages into a new object of study, in fact revived nothing, but rather secured the period as part of the dead past. This was History. At least implicit in this antiquarianism was the underlying eighteenth-century sense of historical progress; nothing had ever reached such a state of improvement as it now enjoyed. Correspondingly, there was little threat that the past might return. Medieval studies, which grew out of the amateur efforts of Percy, Scott, and others, would eventually deliver the Middle Ages as a historical period, fixed in the past.

And yet, acceptable as an interest in the Middle Ages became in the course of the nineteenth century, a strange temporality, as I want to show here, has persisted in all eras in ideas of the Middle Ages. "Historical linearity," Bettina Bildhauer and Anke Bernau write, "quickly proves an unsatisfactory model when seeking

---

4 See Johnston, *Enchanted Ground*, esp. 18–24; on Sainte-Palaye see further Gossman, *Medievalism and the Ideologies of the Enlightenment*; Busby, "An Eighteenth-Century Plea on Behalf of the Medieval Romances."

to understand contemporary investments in the medieval past."[5] And while they refer specifically to films about the Middle Ages, the remark is more generally true. We might think of the vision of a discontinuous history that results as a *queer* one. Carolyn Dinshaw, thinking in particular of mystical experience and Margery Kempe, writes: "in my view a history that reckons in the most expansive way possible with how people exist in time, with what it feels like to be a body in time, or in multiple times, or out of time, is a *queer* history – whatever else it might be."[6] As Dinshaw makes clear elsewhere, this is not necessarily a question of sexual orientation:

> By "queer" I thus don't only mean "gay" or "homosexual" ... And I don't just mean "odd" or "different," though there's inevitably some of that here, too. In my theorizing of temporality I explore forms of desirous, embodied being that are out of sync with the ordinary linear measurements of everyday life, that engage heterogeneous temporalities or that precipitate out of time altogether – forms of being that I shall argue are queer by virtue of their particular engagements with time.

Dinshaw's concern in her book *How Soon is Now?* is with "asynchrony as a motif that demonstrates the constant presence of other kinds of time in the *now*."[7] My concern in this chapter, with a couple of exceptions, is not with explicit stories of asynchrony. Rather, I trace a history of medievalism in which the potential for asynchrony is always just beneath the surface or, perhaps more appropriately, a moment or two away. I contend that the antiquarians and writers who aimed to revive study of the Middle Ages did so with a newly historical sense that they could construct an era in the past and know it as a past era. Out of that impulse, medieval studies arises. At the same time, however, many of the same people could not resist trying to bring that past alive in some sense, arguing that there was a role for the medieval in the present day. Out of this impulse, what we call medievalism arises.

It is easy to see the latter impulse at work. It often looks like nostalgia. One very intense period of such nostalgia, as we shall see, was the 1840s. But nostalgia is by no means its only form. Medievalist texts often portray something which is almost the reverse, paradoxically embedding the present in the medieval past. So in Rudyard Kipling's 1920 short story, "The Eye of Allah," a group of western Christians, among them Roger Bacon, discovers the existence of microbes with the help of a magnifying crystal retrieved from the Islamic world. This device is deliberately destroyed at the end of the story by the medieval clerics, who are fearful of the impact the discovery would have on faith.

Similarly, in Edward Bulwer Lytton's novel *The Last of the Barons* (1843) a

[5]   Bildhauer and Bernau, "Introduction: The A-chronology of Medieval Film," in *Medieval Film*, 1–19 (5); see their introduction more generally for reflections on representations of medieval time.
[6]   Dinshaw, "Temporalities," 109; see further Dinshaw, *How Soon is Now?*, ch. 3.
[7]   Dinshaw, *How Soon is Now?*, 4, 43.

character named Adam Warner has invented a machine in 1467 which, it becomes clear, is a steam engine. Adam is for a time protected and promoted by the villainous Friar Bungey, who sees the machine's potential; failing to understand it, however, Bungey is reduced to using it to produce boiled eggs. The engine is eventually smashed by a mob and Warner murdered as a wizard because people believe that the machine will deprive them of their livelihoods: "Did he not devise a horrible engine for the destruction of the poor – an engine that was to do all the work in England by the devil's help?"[8] Bulwer Lytton's avowed concern in this novel is with the course of political history, and the counterfactual possibilities arising if the earl of Warwick had not been killed at the battle of Barnet by the triumphant Edward IV. As Warwick had always been an enemy of despotism, the narrator argues, had he lived "the great baron would have secured and promoted liberty according to the notions of a seigneur and a Norman, by making the king but the first nobleman in the realm."[9] Furthermore, Warwick's tolerance towards the Lollards might have led to greater religious toleration, meaning that there might have been no need for the development of Puritanism.

These are things which, in the narrator's (or Bulwer Lytton's) view might have happened, although they did not. Of a different order is the invention of the steam engine, which might have happened, but if it did, it certainly had to happen again. In such tales as *Last of the Barons* and "The Eye of Allah," technology is suppressed in order to keep the Middle Ages medieval. These narratives toy with the instability of temporal boundaries; time is confused. Bulwer Lytton's novel asks, Did the industrial revolution have a false start in the Wars of the Roses? Kipling wonders, Could the scientific revolution have arisen in the late Middle Ages because of contact with other cultures? Just as the creation of a sense of the Middle Ages can be traced to sixteenth-century acts of destruction, in these narratives acts of iconoclastic destruction must take place in order to guarantee the integrity of the temporal boundaries that earlier iconoclasm created. If one of the enabling conditions of medievalism is unending play with the instability of temporal boundaries, medievalism also finally requires the iconoclasm which confirms a sense of the Middle Ages as a discrete time in the past.

The Middle Ages Revived

One day in July 1839, a well-to-do young woman went along to Hyde Park in London with a friend to watch knights tilting. It is likely that they were practising for the great tournament re-enactment at Eglinton in Ayrshire which took place the following month. Whatever they were doing, there is nothing in the onlooker's reaction to suggest that she regarded this form of entertainment at the dawn of the Victorian period as particularly unusual: twenty years after Scott's *Ivanhoe*, the imagery of knightly endeavour had clearly become quite commonplace. The novel had provoked dramatic imitations soon after its initial publication; in London in

---

8   Bulwer Lytton, *The Last of the Barons*, 2:189.
9   Bulwer Lytton, *The Last of the Barons*, 2:426.

1820, Mark Girouard notes, *five* such dramatised versions were running, including one at Astley's amphitheatre which culminated with twenty mounted knights taking part in a joust. A new subgenre of entertainment had been born. In the summer of 1838, an opera, *The Tournament*, was running at St James's Theatre while in April of the same year Samuel Pratt's armour showrooms opened in Lower Grosvenor Street. "It was inevitable," writes Girouard of the event at Eglinton, "that someone would give a tournament in the end."[10]

In Hyde Park, however, the onlooker was not seduced by the spectacle, thinking the whole thing "a ridiculous failure." The jousters kept missing one another, she wrote, "and looked extremely clumsy in their heavy armour." She noted that "For fear of accidents, which were not very likely to happen, they had their lances sawn across that they might break at a slight shock, and so absurdly particular had they been in this respect that some of the lances broke with their own weight and fell to pieces to the no small amusement of the bystanders."[11] The Middle Ages were back in Hyde Park in 1839. Yet not really back, as anyone with eyes to see the sawn-through lances knew. It was unlikely that any distressed damsel would want to look to this kind of phallically compromised masculinity for rescue.

Nevertheless, foolish though she found this spectacle, this particular young woman was herself deeply immersed in medieval culture. Lady Charlotte Guest had recently commenced her translation of the Welsh *Mabinogion,* which she would complete ten years later. Hers was just one of the many initiatives going on in the 1840s aimed at bringing the Middle Ages to a wider public. Alfred Tennyson commenced his major work the *Idylls of the King* with the publication of his poem "Morte D'arthur," which first appeared in his two-volume *Poems* of 1842. Here, Tennyson gave the tale of Arthur's death a framing tale (later omitted) in which a narrator, having heard a modern poem about Arthur, falls asleep on Christmas eve. Near dawn, he dreams he sees Arthur aboard a ship, and hears people calling on Arthur to return. The hint that Arthur might come back is of course provided by medieval romance itself. Thomas Malory, Tennyson's chief source, was circumspect about Arthur's survival and refused to commit himself to it. Nineteenth-century poets, like twentieth-century novelists and filmmakers, take it as a given that they can bring Arthur back.

Twenty years on from *Ivanhoe* and more than half a century on from Percy and Warton, there was extraordinary interest in the Middle Ages, at least in elite culture. The first Victorian decade is known as the "Hungry '40s" – a time of deprivation and poverty, culminating in mass movements and revolution. This was also the period that was decisive in setting ideas of what the medieval was, what it could do, and what it was for. By 1840 it was possible to think about the "medieval" in a new way. As we saw in the previous chapter, the idea of a "Middle Age" existed in Britain by the 1570s at the latest. Yet through all of the centuries from the English Reformation onwards there was no simple adjective that could be used to denote the period: the word *medieval* did not exist before the nineteenth

[10]   Girouard, *The Return to Camelot,* 90.
[11]   Bessborough, ed., *Lady Charlotte Guest,* 93.

century. The result was, in the context of the eighteenth-century revival of interest in the Middle Ages, a confusion of terms. Some would use the adjective *ancient* to refer to the Middle Ages. David Hume, in his *History of England*, referred to the "feudal" period when he wanted to indicate the Middle Ages, using the phrase "of the middle age," according to Clare Simmons, just once.[12]

At the same time, the highly complex term "gothic" was current. It could be used in a relatively simple sense to refer generally to the Middle Ages: in the second edition of his *Castle of Otranto* (1765), Walpole added the subtitle "A Gothic Story" and by it he meant simply that it was set in the Middle Ages. It was only later that the "gothic novel" was taken as requiring the trappings of *Castle of Otranto*: the repressed past, ghosts in the present, chivalry and villains, oppressed maidens, crumbling castles and cryptic subterranean spaces. Gothic "could be appropriated as representing a specifically British cultural tradition," as Catherine Spooner writes, "of political freedom and progressivism embodied in the achievements of the Middle Ages."[13] But as she notes, the term became distinctly divided by the end of the eighteenth century. By then some scholars were clearly uneasy with a term which was "vexed," as John Ganim states, "[f]rom its earliest formulation in English."[14]

In the field of architecture, "gothic" had become problematic and inadequate, even by the middle of the eighteenth century. "We have long wanted more distinct terms to express the several kinds and modes of ancient buildings that are found among us," wrote the historian of Ely cathedral, James Bentham, in 1758. "Modern writers have used the term *Gothick*," he noted, "to signify all kinds that deviate from the ancient proportions of the Grecian or Roman Architecture; but *Gothick* is in that sense a term too vague and general, for it will comprehend all our ancient Architecture."[15] Bentham also showed himself aware of a fact that made critics uncomfortable: the Goths were destroyers. Later in the century, after Edmund Gibbon's *Decline and Fall of the Roman Empire* (1766–88), it would have been difficult to think of the Goths as anything other than barbarians, which further compromised the term.

The consequent unease provoked by the term is clearly visible in John Milner's 1798 *Dissertation on the Modern Style of Altering Antient Cathedrals*, which uses *gothic* in an architectural sense throughout, but notes that it is "ludicrous and improper" to employ a term which properly applies to "real Goths, the destroyers of the arts and literature of preceding ages." In a later work, Milner settled the question of terminology by referring to "that beautiful style of architecture properly called the pointed, and abusively the Gothic, order."[16] The celebrated 1817

[12] Simmons, "Medievalism: Its Linguistic History in Nineteenth-Century Britain," 30.
[13] Spooner, *Contemporary Gothic*, 13.
[14] Ganim, *Medievalism and Orientalism*, 24.
[15] Bentham, Letter to Rev. Dr. Lyttelton, Dean of Exeter, in Stevenson, *A Supplement to the First Edition of Mr Bentham's History*, 7.
[16] Milner, *A Dissertation on the Modern Style of Altering Antient Cathedrals*, 44 note 1; Milner, "On the Rise and Progress of the Pointed Arch," in *Essays on Gothic Architecture*, 126–27. At about the same time (in words not translated into English until 1849), Friedrich von Schlegel insisted that "The objections urged by some few critics to the use of the term

work by Thomas Rickman, *An Attempt to Discriminate the Styles of Architecture, from the Conquest to the Reformation*, then established what remain the standard descriptive terms for ecclesiastical architecture, with the quadripartite division: Norman, Early English, Decorated, and Perpendicular.[17]

While Rickman's specialised terminology settled the question in relation to architecture, it did not offer an alternative to *gothic* in its other applications, which were of course extremely varied. By the end of the eighteenth century "gothic" was at least as readily associated with the fictions of Matthew Lewis and Ann Radcliffe as it was with the Middle Ages, and it had become a word of rich and unstable significations. As Ian Duncan summarises it:

> "Gothic" represents, in short, the crux or aporia of a myth of national culture, of "British" historical identity – one that retains its currency to this day. In it the alien and the familiar, the natural and the unnatural or supernatural, are richly confused: neither one category nor the other is clearly stable.[18]

Nevertheless, the fact that there was still no easy way of referring to the Middle Ages meant that the term "gothic" retained its association with it. Unsurprisingly, as antiquarian research into the Middle Ages deepened, a new and neutral adjective was coined. The word *medieval*, formed from the late Latin *medium aevum* (meaning "middle age"), was first used around 1817, by an antiquarian named Thomas Dudley Fosbroke. Using the spelling *mediæval* he introduced the word in the second edition of his book *British Monachism* in 1817. Whether or not Fosbroke invented this neologism himself (he shows no sign that he was aware of having done so), he was certainly responsible for popularising it, using it frequently in his contributions to the monthly scholarly journal, *The Gentleman's Magazine*, and then in 1825 publishing the first book to use the term in its title, his *Encyclopaedia of Antiquities, and Elements of Archaeology, Classical and Mediaeval*. By the late 1820s other scholars were using the new adjective; in the 1830s its use spread in scholarly circles and by the early 1840s *medieval* was clearly in popular use.[19]

The terms "gothic" and "romantic" are habitually seen as linked, but "medieval" has not been considered – as it ought to be – as the third term of the equation. "Medieval" took over some of the function of the other two words but did so, initially at least, in a way that emptied them of any revolutionary or subversive

Gothic, arise from an imperfect comprehension of its grand and universal signification." *The Aesthetic and Miscellaneous Works of Frederick von Schlegel*, trans. Millington, 157.

[17]　Rickman, *An Attempt to Discriminate the Styles of Architecture*; the second edition of 1819 was more widely known.

[18]　Duncan, *Modern Romance and Transformations of the Novel*, 22–23.

[19]　See Fosbrooke, *British Monachism*, 2nd edn, 1.vi. See further Matthews, "From Mediaeval to Mediaevalism." It seems clear that the English language was the leader here, just as it had been with the term "Middle Ages." Other continental languages introduced their equivalents to *medieval*, probably by analogy with the English term, in the second half of the nineteenth century. On the French case (where the early nineteenth-century usage, *moyenageux* and variations as adjective, was replaced by *médiévale* in the 1870s), see Hadjadj, "'Moyen Âge' à l'épreuve des dictionnaires." See also Voss, *Das Mittelalter im Historischen Denken Frankreichs*, esp. the helpful table at 391–419.

force. Fosbroke himself was not at all a devotee of the Middle Ages in the manner of a Percy or a Scott. Like many antiquarians, he was an ordained minister of the Church of England. He was anti-Catholic and remained overtly suspicious of the medieval past. The new adjective which he put into circulation was always used by him and others writing for scholarly journals in a scrupulously chronological sense. It was clearly the neutral word that fulfilled precisely what *gothic* could not, because it was free of any pejorative associations. Medievalist scholarship was beginning to flourish in the largely peaceful period after the end of the Napoleonic wars. If *gothic* thrived in the revolutionary period, a new and counter-revolutionary vision of the Middle Ages was taking shape after Waterloo. It was a version of the Middle Ages for which the strictly temporal *medieval* was the appropriate general term.

At the same time, *gothic* became a specialist term, referring in a technical sense to ecclesiastical architecture, and in another sense to a genre of the novel which was originally known for its medievalist trappings: castles, dungeons, the supernatural. Floating free of its medieval associations, it would come to refer to a certain mode of writing which need not be medievalist at all. Mary Shelley's *Frankenstein* (1816) is today perhaps the best known gothic novel, but it is about science and modernity rather than medieval superstition. In the literary sphere, gothic was becoming "a conspicuously 'low' form," as Michael Gamer puts it, "against which romantic writers could oppose themselves."[20]

Perceptions of the Middle Ages were changing, then, as more information was brought to light and medieval culture was more closely scrutinised. It was far from being the case, however, that as a result the old associations of the Middle Ages simply lost their hold on the imagination. It is an irony that while *gothic* was able to shed the original negative association with the Middle Ages to become a technical term, the new and neutral word *medieval* quickly attracted all of the old pejorative associations: by the early 1850s, this word which had begun its semantic career as a usefully unprejudicial way of referring to a period was quite clearly being used in derogatory senses.

This process can be observed with the formation, in the early 1840s, of a new noun. This was the word *medievalism* which, unlike the adjective from which it was formed, had a pejorative sense from the beginning. It was, at first, a very specific term, referring to the renewed Catholicism represented by High Church Anglicanism or the Oxford Movement (also known as Tractarianism and Puseyism). When first used, *mediaevalism* had this very specific meaning, and the only nuance concerned whether it was High Church Anglicanism that was referred to, or Catholicism itself. That depended on where the user stood. Some made no distinction between the two. But in 1850 the vicar of Leeds found it necessary to announce that while he was a committed High Churchman, he was, contrary to popular report, not among the "converts to mediaevalism; insinuating Romish sentiments; circulating and republishing Romish works; ... adopting

---

[20] Gamer, *Romanticism and the Gothic*, 7.

Romish prostrations; ... muttering the Romish Shibboleth, and rejoicing in the cant of Romish fanaticism."[21]

The Catholic Emancipation Act had been passed by Parliament in 1829; Catholics could now hold high office and sit in parliament. The first of the tracts announcing the Oxford Movement was published in 1833. To those who were troubled by such developments, the time was right for the dark Middle Ages to be invoked once again as a threat to all that was civilised in a modern, industrial, Protestant nation. Hence the neologism *medievalism,* introduced to the language around 1844 in reference to these retrograde tendencies in religion, was derogatory from the beginning.[22] Probably as a consequence, the once-neutral adjective *mediaeval* itself now began to take on pejorative colouring. It can be seen in that role in parliamentary debate by 1851, when a Lord Beaumont referred to "the obsolete doctrines and mediaeval prejudices of infallible Rome," whose adherents sought "to crush all freedom of conscience and spirit of independence."[23]

Medievalism, both the term and what it connoted, was taken very seriously in the decade of the 1840s. In her home in Wales, Charlotte Guest was so distressed by the high-church tendencies of her parish priest that, fearing the corruption of her children, she consulted the archbishop of Canterbury himself.[24] One marker of the anxiety surrounding the term is the rapidity with which it semantically mutated and took on several shades of meaning. While at first *medievalism* indicated either Catholicism or High Church Anglicanism, by 1848 the *Athenaeum* was using the term to refer to neo-gothic architecture (of which it generally disapproved), on one occasion disparaging what it calls "ultra-medievalism."[25] In 1851, Dante Gabriel Rossetti used the term to label the medievalist recreations of his own paintings.[26] It is also used to refer to the conservative Young England movement: Benjamin Disraeli, the movement's leading light, was said to have equipped the Tory party "with protectionism, mediaevalism, and territorial constitutionalism."[27]

---

[21] "False Reports about the Vicar of Leeds."

[22] The word was exactly parallel with the adjective "neo-Catholic," which also explicitly referred to the Oxford Movement and is first attested in 1842. *OED* s.v. neo-Catholic, A.*adj.* A long tradition has attributed the coinage of the noun "medievalism" to John Ruskin in 1853. See Gordon, "Medium Aevum and the Middle Age," 24. On the date of 1844, see my "From Mediaeval to Mediaevalism," where I show that the term had already been in written use for a decade when Ruskin employed it and argue that he was probably trying to re-establish it with a more neutral sense. Richard Utz notes that unlike other "-isms" coined around this time (such as *liberalism, republicanism, nationalism*), which migrated from continental languages to English, *medievalism* went in the other direction. "Coming to Terms with Medievalism," 105, 110 n 3.

[23] House of Lords Debate, Hansard 21 July 1851, vol. 118, col. 1110. Online at www.millbanksystems.org.

[24] See Bessborough, ed., *Lady Charlotte Guest,* 236–37, 238.

[25] "Architectural Drawings," 465.

[26] D. G. Rossetti to W. M. Rossetti (London, September 1851), in *Letters of Dante Gabriel Rossetti,* 104.

[27] "The New Protestant Leadership."

Very occasionally, the word could simply refer to the Middle Ages as a period.[28] Unlike the adjective *medieval*, a term which had remained semantically stable in scholarly use for thirty years, the new noun is quickly seen fitting a range of needs.

This was in part no doubt because of the sheer pervasiveness of the medieval in 1840s Britain when, as we have in part seen, interest in the Middle Ages was at a high. Scholarly and publishing societies were established in the period and numerous editions of both Old and Middle English texts appeared in Germany and Britain; France was becoming interested in both Old French and Anglo-Norman. The study of medieval Germanic languages was set on a new footing by Jacob Grimm's major work, *Deutsche Grammatik*, which originally appeared in 1819, with a second and greatly expanded edition in 1822–37. Public perception of the medieval period was also on the rise, in the wake of the publications of *Ivanhoe* and Victor Hugo's *Notre Dame de Paris* (1831, English translation *The Hunchback of Notre Dame* 1833), along with the spread of neo-gothic building.

The decade of the 1840s was bookended by two quite different medievalist events. In 1839, the Eglinton Tournament took place in Ayrshire, Scotland, at the arrangement of a group of young, Tory-inclined aristocrats. The event was widely lampooned, not least because on its first day pouring rain such as never fell in the pages of Walter Scott ruined the spectacle. Chris Waters has described it as "little more than a decorative aristocratic romp."[29] But even the satires extended Eglinton's impact as an idea, and it is thought that 100,000 people might have attended.[30] Then, in 1851, the Great Exhibition in the Crystal Palace featured the Mediaeval Court designed by Augustus Pugin, which was viewed by thousands.[31]

In the course of the decade, the walls of the Houses of Parliament (1836–67) designed by Charles Barry and Pugin continued to rise, marking the official espousal of neo-gothic architecture.[32] The period also saw the emergence of the Cambridge Camden Society, promoting Gothic architecture in church building and renovation; the establishment of the Pre-Raphaelite Brotherhood in 1848, in which the medievalist poets and painters Dante Gabriel Rossetti and William Morris launched their careers; and the publication of John Ruskin's *The Seven Lamps of Architecture* in 1849 (*The Stones of Venice* followed in 1851–53). In the literary sphere, Tennyson published his "Morte D'arthur" in 1842, while Charlotte Guest completed her translation of the *Mabinogion* in 1849.

The decade was also, of course, particularly notable for working-class insurrection and bourgeois revolution. In Britain, Chartism was constituted as the first working-class mass movement. In this context, the Middle Ages were genuinely put forward as offering practical solutions to contemporary problems. In 1843, even

---

[28] See e.g. Odard, "A Sentimental Journey through Normandy," 399. On all these shades of meaning, see further Matthews, "From Mediaeval to Mediaevalism."

[29] Waters, "Marxism, Medievalism and Popular Culture," 141.

[30] On the tournament see further Girouard, *Return to Camelot*, ch. 7; Anstruther, *The Knight and the Umbrella*.

[31] On the Mediaeval Court see Ganim, *Medievalism and Orientalism*, 99–100; on Pugin see Hill, *God's Architect*.

[32] For detailed description see Wedgwood, "The New Palace of Westminster."

as concerns rose over mediaevalism or a renewed English Catholicism, Thomas
Carlyle conjured up the image of the monastery of Bury St Edmunds in *Past and
Present*, first conceding that the medieval monastery represented "Another world,"
but then claiming that "this present poor distressed world might get some profit
by looking wisely into it, instead of foolishly."[33] Such remarks built on Carlyle's
earlier contention, in his 1839 essay on Chartism, that medieval nobles were not
just "governors" but "guides of the Lower Classes," at a time when "*Cash Payment*
had not then grown to be the universal sole nexus of man to man; it was something other than money that the high then expected from the low ..."[34] In a related
but more obviously nostalgic way, the Young Englanders looked back to an earlier
England: Disraeli lamented in his 1845 novel *Sybil, or the Two Nations*, that "there
is no community in England" and proposed the medievalising of the aristocracy
as a solution.[35] Another prominent Young Englander, Lord John Manners, focused
on the Church in *A Plea for National Holy-Days* (1843), which, "in ruder but more
humble times than these, arrested the sword of war by her blessed truce of God."
Only that same Church "will restore to us ... the frankness and good humour, the
strength and the glory of the old English character."[36]

In an alarming world of riots and demonstrations, of railway lines spreading
out across the country, some quite sophisticated thinkers saw solace in the past.
Why had such vast sums been spent on building the railways, Ruskin wondered,
and on creating "a large class of men, the railway navvies, especially reckless,
unmanageable, and dangerous"? He asked his readers to imagine the same men
employed on "building beautiful houses and churches," suggesting that there was
at least as much "mechanical ingenuity ... required to build a cathedral as to cut
a tunnel or contrive a locomotive."[37]

In their different ways Ruskin, Carlyle, Manners and Disraeli yearn for some
kind of return of the Middle Ages. For Carlyle and Disraeli it was not, as it would
later be for others, a matter of turning back the clock and winding back the industrial revolution. It was more that certain medieval values were needed to soften
the society that had grown up around industry. For others, less concerned with
urban elite culture and certainly not interested in jousting, the Middle Ages were
past and gone, yet still making their presence felt in a way that could not be
ignored. The *Manifesto of the Communist Party*, published in German in 1848 and
in English two years later, does regret some aspects of the end of the Middle Ages:

> The bourgeoisie, wherever it has got the upper hand, has put an end to
> all feudal, patriarchal, idyllic relations. It has pitilessly torn asunder the
> motley feudal ties that bound man to his "natural superiors", and has left
> remaining no other nexus between man and man than naked self-interest,

---

[33] Carlyle, *Past and Present*, in Shelston, ed., *Thomas Carlyle: Selected Writings*, 267; see
further Chandler, *Dream of Order*, 122–51.
[34] Carlyle, "Chartism," in Shelston, ed., *Thomas Carlyle: Selected Writings*, 193.
[35] Disraeli, *Sybil*, 64.
[36] Manners, *A Plea for National Holy-Days*, 26.
[37] Ruskin, *The Seven Lamps of Architecture*, 195.

than callous "cash payment." It has drowned the most heavenly ecstasies of religious fervour, of chivalrous enthusiasm, of philistine sentimentalism, in the icy water of egotistical calculation. It has resolved personal worth into exchange value ...[38]

This well known passage does not, however, open out into general praise for the Middle Ages in the *Manifesto* or later works by Marx and Engels. As Stephen H. Rigby has pointed out, in later writings Marx and Engels make the opposite argument: that it is under feudalism that "the reality of exploitation is most apparent," while under capitalism, coerced labour is obscured.[39] Proletarian revolution explicitly looks ahead, implying that there is no going back. "For Marx and Engels," Chris Waters writes, "there was no returning to the past."[40]

Yet revolutionary socialism would not always be able to let go of those "motley feudal ties" – as the career of the socialist William Morris shows most clearly. Waters notes that many socialists were caught up in nostalgia and would focus on specific periods within the medieval whole which they regarded as having been particularly propitious (148–49). It is unsurprising that many working-class people also looked back rather than forward, to more natural relations imagined to have existed in the past than to a conjectured post-revolutionary future, so that working-class medievalism, as Charles Dellheim describes it, often focused on an imagined lost world of rights and liberties. The "Norman Yoke" thesis (which saw the supposed rights and liberties of the Anglo-Saxon state as having been taken away by the Normans) was often popular in the nineteenth century. The radical social commentator William Cobbett used medievalism in support of "his vision of productive, independent workers in a cooperative society."[41]

Working-class appropriations of medievalism cannot, however, be written off solely as nostalgia for a past that never was. Antimodernism in general was never "wholly regressive," as Jackson Lears observes: "On the contrary, far from encouraging escapist nostalgia, anti-modern sentiments not only promoted eloquent protest against the limits of liberalism but also helped to shape new modes of cultural authority for the oncoming twentieth century."[42] Of medievalism more specifically, Dellheim notes that it was "a plastic language." The past could be used in ways sophisticated and unsophisticated. Early nineteenth-century working-class responses to technological innovation included what was known as Luddism, the destruction of mechanised weaving devices perceived to threaten jobs. But there were more subtle reactions as well. The device known as the gig-mill, by mechanising part of the clothmaking process, threatened to diminish the status of the croppers (elite clothworkers). It was, as E. P. Thompson reminds, "an old invention"; under a statute of the time of Edward VI, its use had been prohibited. Hence, when it was reintroduced in Yorkshire in the late eighteenth century,

---

[38] Marx and Engels, *Manifesto of the Communist Party*, 70.
[39] Rigby, "Historical Materialism," 479.
[40] Waters, "Marxism, Medievalism and Popular Culture," 149.
[41] Dellheim, "Interpreting Victorian Medievalism," 45.
[42] Lears, *No Place of Grace*, 6.

croppers formed themselves into organisations and appealed to the sixteenth-century statute. "However obsolete the statute of Edward VI ... may have been," Thompson notes, "it is important that the croppers were aware of it and held that protection against displacement by machinery was not only their 'right' but also their *constitutional* right."[43] Drawing on the mid sixteenth century as it does, this is perhaps not strictly an invocation of medievalism (though in the nine-teenth century, a sharp distinction was not always made between the late Middle Ages and Tudor times). But it does show another side to nostalgia for the distant historical past, a somewhat more hardheaded approach to the possibilities the late Middle Ages might afford.

Hence by the time the crowds began queueing up to enter the Great Exhibi-tion to see Pugin's Mediaeval Court, the legacy of the Middle Ages was already a complicated one. Clearly, the medieval period had become a resource on which very different kinds of people could draw to quite different ends. The 1840s had produced a contradictory sense of the medieval: for some the Middle Ages was becoming synonymous with tournament, pageantry and romantic love, for others, with feudal oppression. The word "medieval" itself had come into being to refer to a time past and gone, but the new noun *medievalism* referred to a manifestation of the medieval in the present day. As the adjective, too, was soon contaminated with that sense, the Middle Ages and modernity came to exist once more, as it were, side by side. In a way that recalls the late sixteenth century, it became possible to imagine that the Middle Ages might return.

Some saw this possible return as desirable; for others, it was a scarcely imagi-nable evil. Almost everyone, of course, was selective. Carlyle might wish for a feudalisation of industrial relations in *Past and Present*, but he was scathing about what he calls Puseyism (but which others were calling *mediaevalism*): "O Heavens, what shall we say of Puseyism, in comparison to Twelfth-Century Catholicism? Little or nothing; for indeed it is a matter to strike one dumb."[44] Reviewing the Mediaeval Court in the *Gentleman's Magazine*, C. B. could see some value in the Gothic style, but objected to the mere simulation of medieval art. "We should gladly have welcomed in the Crystal Palace such a mediaeval court as would have shewn of what mediaeval art really is capable," he wrote; "how suitable also it is, or rather how suitable it is capable of being made, to ourselves as a national style." But he objected to the idea that anyone wanted "to be surrounded by mere copies of what the men of the middle ages actually did." C. B.'s deeper concern involves some familiar fears about the Catholic past (probably, in this case, animated by the fact that Pugin was a Catholic convert): the Court "ought to have exemplified the middle ages in their progress," he wrote, and should not "have been a mere Romanist display." C. B. called for "an equally comprehensive and equally prac-tical illustration of the application of Gothic art to the purposes of our Protestant ecclesiastical architecture."[45]

---

[43] Thompson, *The Making of the English Working Class*, 575.

[44] *Past and Present*, 275.

[45] C. B., "On Mediaeval Art," 581, 582. For a detailed description of the contents of the Court, and other anti-Catholic reaction to it, see Wedgwood, "The Mediæval Court."

Walter Benjamin wrote of such World's Fairs as the Great Exhibition that they "are places of pilgrimage to the commodity fetish."[46] Despite its deep historical roots, there is a strong sense in which modern British medievalism really begins here in the 1840s, where it was born under the sign of the commodity fetish. It was at this moment that a straightforwardly linear imagining of history, which had been projected with the coinage of the neologism *medieval*, became a paradoxical imagining of history, expressed by the neologism "medievalism," and haunted by the idea of a returned Middle Ages. From this time on, the medieval could be imagined as both distant and present, locked in a past historical era yet likely to reappear at any moment.

Looking Back and Forth

It is not surprising that when in the 1880s and 1890s the time travel narrative first became significant as a genre, it was almost from the beginning obsessed with the Middle Ages. It is true that some of the very earliest literary time travellers showed little interest in the past but went forward into the future, like the main characters in Edward Bellamy's *Looking Backward* (1888), William Morris's *News from Nowhere* (1890), and H. G. Wells's *The Time Machine* (1895). Yet even then, the future can look like the Middle Ages, as the dreamer finds in *News from Nowhere*, in which the future communist utopian England looks a lot like the fourteenth century with the grimmer parts removed and the Houses of Parliament converted to a Dung Market. It was not long before time travellers went back, and when they did that, it was usually to the Middle Ages, as in Morris's *A Dream of John Ball* (1887) and Mark Twain's *A Connecticut Yankee in King Arthur's Court* (1889) – a tradition more recently perpetuated in Michael Crichton's *Timeline* (1999).

One straightforward way of reading the time-travel narrative is by seeing *time* as a metaphor for place. *News from Nowhere* is not really about the future so much as it is a cry of political anguish about England in the late nineteenth-century present. By then, there were already senses in which medievalism could be regarded as haunting the margins of the civilised world. One of the fundamental moves made by cultures that regard themselves as being in a more advanced state than others is what Johannes Fabian calls the "*denial of coevalness*," through which other cultures are imagined as less developed and hence as belonging to a different time.[47] In newspaper coverage of an outbreak of disease in Russia in 1879, for example, a writer contrasts the handling of epidemics in modern Britain and a Russia which was still, he thought, "medieval." This led him to "other and more serious evils" engendered by "Russian mediaevalism," such as the "dirt and discomfort" in which the peasants live, ensuring high infant mortality.[48] From this British writer's standpoint in the world's major industrial power, looking at a peasant-based economy, it was simple enough to state – apparently without meaning it as a metaphor – that the Middle Ages actually continued in Russia.

---

[46] Benjamin, "Paris, the Capital of the Nineteenth Century," 7.
[47] Fabian, *Time and the Other*, 31.
[48] "The Russian Epidemic."

Clearly this was not a desirable medievalism; it was the past that an industrial nation could congratulate itself on having escaped. What is interesting is that in the idea of the medieval as a *time* in the past – which by definition cannot come back – there is nevertheless the residual fear that the medieval is also a *place* not too far away, whose inhabitants might not stay in that place. This is familiar to us today; one of the fears behind the current wave of anti-immigration sentiment in western European nations is this same belief that people from Africa, or the Islamic world, or Central Europe, are not coeval with us. When it is suggested that "they need to learn our ways," this is perhaps less fearful of their different cultures – the cultures westerners fly around the world to observe, after all – than expressive of the belief that they need to modernise. As Kathleen Davis and Nadia Altschul write of this nexus between time and territory, "European colonizers established their superiority in temporal terms by mapping colonial lands and people as backward in time and, in many cases, as still living in the Middle Ages ... Colonizing nations could thus see themselves as both fully understanding the position of the colonies – better than the colonies themselves – and as the most appropriate tutors in the mission of 'civilizing' these lands."[49]

By the late nineteenth century there was already a strong tradition of portraying the Middle Ages as a time that could be visited. The Eglinton Tournament was the first large-scale, self-conscious medieval re-enactment. It is less well known that in 1849, the tournament was re-enacted in Chelsea's Cremorne Gardens. The idea of *visiting* the Middle Ages was already understood in London by the time of the Great Exhibition of 1851, which opened the period up to the masses, doing so in a way that framed the Mediaeval Court as a place as well as a time. Contemporary accounts treated the exhibition as a form of narrative, recreating for the reader the experience of passing through the various exhibits. In *Chambers's Edinburgh Journal*, the writer first describes exhibits from the West Indies, Canada, Australia and New Zealand, announcing, "we are pleased with our colonial brethren, and give them great credit for their industry and enterprise." Then he moves on: "Next, after the colonies, comes the mediaeval court..."[50] As John Ganim has noted, such descriptions, along with the exhibition's catalogue itself, equate *colonial space*, as represented by the West Indies or Africa, the Indian Court and the Turkish Court, with the *time* represented by the Mediaeval Court.[51] Ganim neatly captures the conceptual chiasmus here: "If the medieval past of the European host countries was sometimes represented as if it were a colonized past, the present of the colonies was often presented as if it were the Middle Ages."[52]

Viewers passed, then, from representations of places they had not seen, to a time they had not seen. Both sets of exhibits operated as simulacra placing viewers in those places/times, in which they experienced the colonies/Middle Ages in what we would now call hyperreal form. In later exhibitions, as Ganim notes, this nexus of medieval place and time became standard. The World's Fairs of the

---

49   Davis and Altschul, "Introduction: The Idea of 'the Middle Ages' Outside Europe," 2.
50   "A Glance at the Exhibition," 337.
51   Ganim, *Medievalism and Orientalism*, 99.
52   Ganim, *Medievalism and Orientalism*, 102–3.

second half of the nineteenth century often linked themselves to medieval trade fairs. They would sometimes represent the vanished past of the city in which they were located; an exhibit of "Old London," at the International Health Exhibition of 1884 was designed to contrast the unhealthy past with present conveniences, but in fact became "enormously popular as a themed exhibit on its own."[53] Similarly "Vieux Paris," at the Paris International Exhibition of 1900, offered a hyperreal version of the medieval remnants of Paris which had been demolished less than half a century before as part of Haussman's redesign of the city.

Medievalism in this form represents a *vanished* past. Its manifestations could therefore be regarded as involving a form of traumatic intervention. This view is most closely associated with the work of Kathleen Biddick, one of the first to describe the reciprocal and often antagonistic relationship between medievalism and medieval studies. For her, the professionalisation of medieval studies saw the traumatic expulsion of what we now call medievalism to the exterior. The spread of the neo-gothic in Britain after Rickman's *An Attempt to Discriminate the Styles of Architecture* was "an intensive and ubiquitously material internal colonization of England, its Gothicization."[54] Biddick is writing specifically of ecclesiastical neo-gothic here, but the remark could be extended to the uncanny return of the medieval past of Europe's cities in hyperreal form: the way in which such exhibits as Vieux Paris recalled the vanished medieval streets.

Yet, as the very popularity of Vieux Paris and the Mediaeval Court suggests, there is much in late nineteenth-century European medievalism that argues for it as widening access to the past, as a *democratisation* of time by comparison with the aristocratic Eglinton Tournament at the beginning of Victoria's reign. The Eglinton Tournament, though in fact well attended, was held in Ayrshire, far from metropolitan centres. Its reenactment in Chelsea a decade later, and the ease with which middle-class Victorian visitors moved among medievalist exhibits in 1851, suggests that nineteenth-century medievalism rapidly become more plural, less uniformly traumatic, than Biddick allows.

Certainly, there were people who objected to the internal colonisation that was neo-gothic: I have already cited the *Athenaeum's* consistent railing against "ultra-medievalism." But such critiques also often came from those *sympathetic* to medieval gothic: the kind of concern displayed by the *Athenaeum's* writer, in the face of both demolitions and ill-advised restoration, led to the formation of the Society for the Protection of Ancient Buildings (SPAB) in 1877. Similarly, C. B's response to Pugin's Mediaeval Court suggests that it was possible to deplore the return of "Romanism" while at the same time seeing the potential for neo-gothic as a *native*, essentially English style. This and other exhibitions of the second half of the century suggest that just as some were concerned to preserve the real thing, many others, rather than lamenting the disappearance of real gothic, accepted the medieval as their own heritage and were pleased to see its return in sanitised form.

[53] Ganim, *Medievalism and Orientalism*, 104, see also 98.
[54] Biddick, *The Shock of Medievalism*, 29.

Indeed, the SPAB was established by such people as William Morris and John Ruskin who actively *espoused* neo-gothic. For Ruskin neo-gothic, far from being a traumatic imposition, was a kind of coming home. Noting, in *The Stones of Venice*, the history of the word *gothic* as a term of abuse, Ruskin says that there is nevertheless no need to find a new term:

> As far as the epithet was used scornfully, it was used falsely; but there is no reproach in the word, rightly understood; on the contrary, there is a profound truth, which the instinct of mankind almost unconsciously recognizes. It is true, greatly and deeply true, that the architecture of the North is rude and wild; but it is not true, that, for this reason, we are to condemn it, or despise. Far otherwise: I believe it is in this very character that it deserves our profoundest reverence.[55]

Trauma, then, tells only one part of the story of medievalism, and possibly a relatively small part. Medievalism, as I have described it here, was *always* on the margin, exterior to mainstream scholarship. Morris's *News from Nowhere* depicts revolutionary trauma in the future; in the 1950s, the workers at last rise up against the British government. Ultimately what results is a kind of late medieval utopia, but with certain key aspects of the Middle Ages removed. The Morris of *The Earthly Paradise* who had urged the forgetting of contemporary London, "overhung with smoke," in favour of a dream of Chaucer's London, "small, and white, and clean," had changed the terms on which a return to the Middle Ages was desirable.[56] He now depicted a renewed medieval period, one without the cash nexus or feudalism. The utopia he depicted was far from perfect, but he nevertheless envisaged that return as lying on the far side of trauma; the medievalised future was, itself, a form of coming home for the man wearied by the nineteenth century.

The strange dream vision that Morris wrote in 1887, *A Dream of John Ball*, makes his ambivalences clear. In this narrative a dreamer – he is quite clearly a version of Morris himself – finds himself in a Kentish village on the eve of the 1381 rebellion, listening to John Ball preaching the night before the rebels' march to London. After a brief skirmish in which the local lord's forces are defeated with several casualties, the dreamer spends most of the night in conversation with people, especially John Ball himself. Whereas the dreamer in *News from Nowhere* is constantly but unsuccessfully trying to avoid giving away the fact that he is from the past, the same figure in *John Ball* is clearly recognised as different, and is taken for a seer and visionary. This makes it a more uncomfortable book; the dreamer and the reader know that the revolt will end in death and failure. In reluctantly predicting this for John Ball himself, the dreamer goes on to promise that the injustices of feudalism will, nevertheless, soon come to an end. But in doing that, he can only go on to concede that still greater injustices will succeed feudalism. It

[55] Ruskin, "The Nature of Gothic," 155.
[56] See preceding chapter, p. 28.

is a highly teleological dream vision which has no utopian endpoint; the trauma is *[handwritten: always focus on present]*
not in the medievalism, but the relentless harshness of Morris's modernity.

John Ball is the less read of the two dream visions Morris wrote late in life, and it is in many ways the more troubling text. At one stage it takes on an almost Borgesian ambivalence, with the hint that not only is the dreamer dreaming of John Ball, but that John Ball is dreaming of the dreamer. Their long conversation takes place in a church over the bodies of those killed in the earlier skirmish, as the fourteenth century slowly fades around the dreamer, the dawning day filling the church with light and gradually drawing him back to his own present. Both *John Ball* and *News from Nowhere* are elegiac: the dreamer brings to his dreams not simply near-despair about the polity of his own day, but a sense of personal wounding. In *News from Nowhere* his wistful longings after Ellen are perhaps echoes of Morris's own failed marriage. The innocence of the vision in *The Earthly Paradise* is gone. Both the late dream visions depict the queering of time itself: in *News from Nowhere*, time folds back on itself, the future turning back into the Middle Ages, while in *John Ball*, the fourteenth-century church acts as a portal between the two times. But, as the dream visions of Chaucer himself show (and Chaucer was clearly Morris's model), dreamers wake, usually to a sense of loss and the iterative, melancholy task of relating what they have just experienced.

These instances – the exhibits, the asynchronous time of the dream vision – complicate *time* with *place*. The medieval is a time, but one which for such figures as Morris becomes the object of an intense yearning. From about the time of the Great Exhibition and *The Stones of Venice* onward, a split between the two fundamentally different ideas of the Middle Ages I discussed in the introduction became evident. On the one hand, the grotesque Middle Ages – with its origins in sixteenth-century thought – simply continued so as to remain, as we have seen, a resource for gothic imagery of all kinds. But on the other, the romantic Middle Ages (and its close relation, the civic Middle Ages), was increasingly influential as the image of a time of beauty, romance, and poetry was established. And while for many, of course, the Middle Ages could not be reduced to either stereotype, it was nevertheless from this time in particular that the two concepts would establish themselves in popular consciousness.[57]

For obvious reasons, the romantic concept of the Middle Ages intensified the idea that the period might be thought as a *place* one could recreate and revisit. One outcome today of the romantic Middle Ages is the Society for Creative Anachronism (SCA) and the 30,000 members it claims. Through re-enacting, members express the desire to *inhabit* a medievalised space. More closely examined, re-enactors arguably wish not so much to return to a time as to make it present to themselves, actively participating in a recreation of themselves and their surrounds as medieval. History and heritage, as Jerome de Groot puts it, become "something to be consumed as an experiential leisure form."[58] The SCA's website

---

[57] See further, on this opposition, Simpson, "The Rule of Medieval Imagination."
[58] De Groot, *Consuming History*, 119.

states: "welcome to the current middle ages ... how may we help you?"[59] Put like this, the period sounds like a cheerful franchise restaurant, ready to serve.

Yet the grotesque Middle Ages also invites visitors. The writer who in 1879 decried Russian medievalism was perhaps not suggesting that people should experience it for themselves, but London's unhealthy medieval past, as we have seen, was a draw at the International Health Exhibition. Such exhibitions, like the circus and the fair before them, always have an element that is designed to frighten. The denial of coevalness was in this regard a titillating hint that past times, with all their unsanitary and brutal horrors, might be found just the other side of a curtain. Today, this is still realised in York's viking museum, the Jorvik Viking Centre, in which the visitor passes through a modern museum space exhibiting artefacts retrieved from the York excavations, before stepping through a doorway and taking a seat in a moving float which then runs through reconstructed street scenes from viking-era York. The sounds, sights and – most grotesquely – smells of the early medieval past are recreated. While there is an emphasis on viking craft and social organisation, there is no backing away from the less savoury aspects. There is a starving beggar asking for food in Old Norse, and in the museum's most notorious piece of grotesque ultra-realism, a man trying to get some privacy for a bowel movement.[60]

For some, the denial of coevalness is an invitation to go in and make changes. Many civilised nineteenth-century Britons felt that if one could detect a backward and medieval past in Africa, then surely the only thing to do was to go to there and drag it out of the Middle Ages. For the romantic re-enactor and the coloniser alike, time eventually turns into space. We think of nostalgia as a longing for the past but the term originally expressed a sickness arising from a longing for a place: for home. In 1756 it was given as a synonym for *Heimweh*, the pain felt for home. Only later did nostalgia take on its sense of longing for the past. Time and place are difficult to separate – this chapter has repeatedly failed to keep them entirely apart. As the next chapter will show, time becomes a *place* that is no longer so very distant, but one that can be visited. It might be friendly, it might be threatening, but either way, you can make it your own.

[59] www.sca.org. See further Cramer, *Medieval Fantasy as Performance*, 43–44.
[60] On Jorvik and the role of odour in medievalist tourism see further D'Arcens, "Laughing in the Face of the Past."

3

This Way to the Middle Ages: The Spaces of Medievalism

THE DREAM VISION encodes the impossibility of visiting the Middle Ages. When we stand, as tourists, before the cathedral of Notre Dame in Paris, we are encouraged to think that what we are doing is visiting the Middle Ages. We go to a medieval cathedral of the gothic era: "[T]he illusion of permanence and connectedness with the past is almost perfect," as Richard Utz writes.[1] In fact this is almost as illusory as the travels undertaken by William Morris's melancholic dreamers. When we walk in that vast nave, we move amid a palimpsest of all historical eras. We may go down into the crypt, where the origins of a church from earliest Christian times can be seen; we may go up the tower and admire the gargoyles, many of which were added in a nineteenth-century restoration after revolutionary desecration; we can attempt to distinguish, among the sculptures, those that are medieval from those that replace originals destroyed in the Revolution. Notre Dame, like all such places, exists in a historical continuum. But since the nineteenth century, we have been encouraged to think of it as a gothic church, the "noblest of all," as Ruskin called it.[2] Evidently, gothic is its primary architectural idiom. But it can only be maintained in that idiom by extensive renovation in modern times.

Similarly, the Old Town of Warsaw was, before World War II, a palimpsestic ensemble of buildings. Established in the thirteenth century, the Old Town features a range of buildings of all periods from the Gothic through to the Baroque. It is now a UNESCO World Heritage site. Yet these buildings are almost entirely reconstructions. In 1944, in reprisal for the Warsaw Uprising, Nazi troops destroyed 85 per cent of the Old Town. After the war, the Poles set about rebuilding and over two decades, reconstructed it. So today the late medieval cathedral of St John offers a more extreme example of renovation than Notre Dame, as it has been almost entirely rebuilt.

---

[1]   See Utz, "'There Are Places We Remember,'" 101.
[2]   Ruskin, *The Seven Lamps of Architecture*, 2nd edn, xiv.

3   Château de Guédelon. Photograph: A. Bernau.

UNESCO, of course, recognises this. The heritage listing fulfils, in particular, two of UNESCO's ten criteria: (ii) "to exhibit an important interchange of human values, over a span of time or within a cultural area of the world, on developments in architecture or technology, monumental arts, town-planning or landscape design," and (vi) "to be directly or tangibly associated with events or living traditions, with ideas, or with beliefs, with artistic and literary works of outstanding universal significance." In relation to the latter criterion, it is recognised that:

> The historic centre of Warsaw is an exceptional example of the comprehensive reconstruction of a city that had been deliberately and totally destroyed. The foundation of the material reconstruction was the inner strength and determination of the nation, which brought about the reconstruction of the heritage on a unique scale in the history of the world.

The reconstruction of the historic centre so that it is identical with the original symbolizes the will to ensure the survival of one of the prime settings
of Polish culture and illustrates, in an exemplary fashion, the restoration
techniques of the second half of the 20th century.[3]

In this frank acknowledgement that the site is not by ordinary measures
authentic, what is proposed is that a major historical rupture, involving destruction and reconstruction, has not altered the essentially historical and continuous
character of a site. While we might legitimately wonder whether every stone is
back in place and everything really as it was, this is not a criterion; a continuous
history is taken by UNESCO as its major criterion of authenticity, as is, perhaps
more contentiously, "the inner strength and determination of the nation." The site
has retained what Walter Benjamin would call its "aura"; its authenticity "is the
essence of all that is transmissible from its beginning, ranging from its substantive
duration to its testimony to the history which it has experienced."[4]

Such criteria suggest that it is unlikely, conversely, that a World Heritage Listing
will ever be given to the Château de Guédelon in the *département* of Yonne in
northern Burgundy (Figure 3). This thirteenth-century castle, originally constructed
for the Seigneur Guilbert, is being painstakingly built using medieval construction techniques. Craftsmen – stonemasons, smiths, carpenters, ropemakers – use
medieval methods to produce the building's raw materials. The mortar is made of
lime and sand produced on the site. Roof tiles are made from a claypit and then
fired in a kiln, both also on the site. Nothing is permitted that cannot be verified in
thirteenth-century texts. But Guédelon is, nevertheless, a complete fiction. It was
begun in 1998 at the instigation of a local landowner, Michel Guyot, who wanted
to experiment with medieval building techniques. The Seigneur Guilbert, its puta-
tive original owner, is also a fiction, invented to give the castle a history.[5] There is
a heavy emphasis on authenticity of materials and techniques, but no claim to be
doing anything other than *inventing* a neomedieval site.

Just as nobody is concealing the fact of the Warsaw Old Town's destruction,
nobody is claiming that the Château de Guédelon is anything other than a modern
fabrication. By consensus, the former has an authenticity that the latter does not.
Yet the Old Town's aura must be detected through the evident fact of its rebuilding
and when we visit such sites there is, *in the instant in which we experience them*,
simply no difference between them. Both would appear to be hyperreal in Jean
Baudrillard's sense, in which "The very definition of the real becomes: *that of
which it is possible to give an equivalent reproduction*."[6] What separates them is
the visitor's consciousness that the Old Town has a history, belongs to a nation,
exists through time and therefore has the aura of authenticity, while Guédelon has
no history other than that which commenced with its invention in 1998. These

3 http://whc.unesco.org/en/list/30, accessed 6 April 2011.
4 Benjamin, "The Work of Art in the Age of Mechanical Reproduction," 215.
5 http://guedelon.fr. See also Schofield, "France's new medieval castle". See further Utz,
"'There Are Places We Remember,'" 106–7.
6 Baudrillard, "The Orders of Simulacra," 146.

things have to be learnt to be appreciated, however, and a visitor who does not know the facts might conceivably find Guédelon stimulatingly historical and the Old Town a fake.

By common consent, a pure simulacrum such as Guédelon is without authenticity not because it is a modern construction, but because it lacks history. It has endured fleetingly through time as one man's brainchild rather than the expression of a nation's will. But in *neither* case can we experience the history; we only know, in the case of Warsaw, that history has occurred. UNESCO would, presumably, resist any contention that the Old Town is a simulacrum. Its continuous history and, crucially, its expression as the will of a nation combine to suggest that it does not matter whether the buildings themselves have always been intact. The cathedral of St John simply *is*, then, a medieval cathedral in a way that Guédelon will never be a medieval castle.

What we actually visit, I suggest, when we go to medieval places, is the contemporary version of a historical site which we can only experience in its modernity. That modernity might, it is true, involve something that has barely been touched since the Middle Ages (Tintagel castle in Cornwall); it might involve reconstruction, whether partial (Notre Dame de Paris), substantial (the citadel of Carcassonne) or near-total (Warsaw's Old Town), or it might involve something entirely invented (Guédelon). Making similar arguments about the discontinuities in the histories of medieval artefacts, Stephanie Trigg observes that "Most medieval buildings and religious establishments do not survive unmodified as medieval buildings, of course; they have distinctive histories of discontinuity, disruption, and violent destruction." For Trigg, in a meditation on the different purposes different kinds of visitors to cathedrals might have, this leads to the conclusion that "Whether we like it or not, there is no 'pure' medieval; there is only medievalism."[7]

This is a fact that is frequently skirted around in both scholarship and tourism. There is a strong tendency at touristic sites to fix on a certain time as *the* period from which a given artefact dates. In the Languedoc *département* of Aude in southern France, castles are invariably *Cathar* castles – as if their existence as strongholds occurred only in the relatively brief part of the Middle Ages in which the Cathar heresy was significant in the Languedoc. Notre Dame in Paris and the cathedral of Chartres are *the* quintessential gothic cathedrals. At the same time, though, to visit Notre Dame thoroughly the discerning tourist needs to be apprised of the fact that its origins are much older; it has to be characterised as both a gothic church, and not a gothic church. London's Westminster Abbey, while similarly characterised as a gothic church, is even more clearly a palimpsest, with its origins in the time of Edward the Confessor, its major reconstruction by Henry III in the thirteenth century, the Flamboyant Gothic chapel built by Henry VII at the end of the Middle Ages, and its spires added by Nicholas Hawksmoor in the eighteenth century.

Yet despite the reality of the medieval church's existence through time, there is a tendency to take such places as expressive of a particular moment. Proust's

---

[7] Trigg, "Walking through Cathedrals," 12, 33.

narrator Marcel satirises this tendency when, in *In Search of Lost Time*, he mocks architects who, like Viollet-le-Duc, "fancying that they can detect, beneath a Renaissance rood-screen and an eighteenth-century altar, traces of a Romanesque choir, restore the whole church to the state in which it must have been in the twelfth century."[8] Marcel himself espouses a very different model of time when he describes the church of Saint-Hilaire in Combray. If Combray is, famously, summoned up by a tea-soaked crumb of a madeleine, it is also epitomised in a ten-page description of its church:

> an edifice occupying, so to speak, a four-dimensional space – the name of the fourth being Time – extending through the centuries its ancient nave, which, bay after bay, chapel after chapel, seemed to stretch across and conquer not merely a few yards of soil, but each successive epoch from which it emerged triumphant, hiding the rugged barbarities of the eleventh century in the thickness of its walls …; raising up into the Square a tower which had looked down on Saint Louis, and seemed to see him still; and thrusting down with its crypt into a Merovingian darkness … (72)[9]

This four-dimensional aspect of medieval monuments is tacitly acknowledged at tourist destinations, at the same time as it is in a sense covered up in the service of saying that a given edifice is gothic, or romanesque, or Merovingian. Not many places are as conveniently transhistorical as the abbey church of Mont Saint-Michel, which features a romanesque nave and a gothic choir which was added when the original collapsed (reminding us that medieval builders themselves were relentlessly unsentimental modernisers).

This chapter examines the things that happen when medieval sites of various kinds are visited, thinking about the implications of the persistence of the Middle Ages in both real and hyperreal forms. What do scholars and tourists think they are experiencing? In what forms does tourism exploit the medieval? In what ways does the medieval exploit tourism? What is the difference between the real medieval and the invented; can we always tell which is which, and does it matter if we cannot? The chapter roughly follows a trajectory from the real to the hyperreal, the authentic to the invented.

The Middle Ages on Sixpence a Day: The Nineteenth-Century Tourist

In 1844, when the word "medievalism" was freshly in use in anti-Catholic polemic, the Great Western Railway reached Oxford, one of the United Kingdom's most medieval cities. In August of the same year, the Railway Act required the railway companies to offer one train a day on all routes with the cheap third-class rate of a penny a mile.[10] At the same time, it was possible to travel from London to Paris

---

8 Proust, *In Search of Lost Time*, 198.
9 For a full analysis of this famous passage, see Emery, *Romancing the Cathedral*, 139–41.
10 http://www.railwaysarchive.co.uk/documents/HMG_Act_Reg1844.pdf

by steamer and diligence in twenty to thirty hours, for a minimum fare of £2 8s –
with a guidebook in hand to explain how to do it.[11] The era of mass travel was at
hand, and after nearly half a century of burgeoning study of the Middle Ages, it is
not surprising that medieval edifices and artefacts now took their place alongside
the classical ruins and Old Masters of the aristocratic Grand Tour.

This almost immediately occasioned travel writing in a nostalgic mode. In *Bentley's Miscellany* in 1847 the travel writer "Odard" lamented the rise of factories
around the Norman city of Rouen and wistfully described the "spirit of Mediaevalism" awaiting its doom in Rouen cathedral.[12] In this, a very early use of the
word "medievalism," Odard is actually wrenching it away from the pejorative sense
with which it had first appeared a few years before and using it positively, for
perhaps the first time in print. By staging the contrast between industrialism and
a positively envisioned medievalism, Odard anticipated some more famous travellers to the medieval. In his essay "The Nature of Gothic" in the second volume
of *The Stones of Venice*, John Ruskin too sees the Gothic as in part a matter of
spirit. Understanding gothic is not simply a question of identifying pointed arches,
vaulted roofs and flying buttresses, Ruskin writes, but of finding those places in
which such elements "come together so as to have life." Various elements must
be present for the gothic style to exist: "It is not enough that it has the Form, if
it have not also the power and life. It is not enough that it has the Power, if it
have not the form." Gothic is particular to northern Europeans, a "grey, shadowy,
many-pinnacled image of the Gothic spirit within us."[13]

Later still, in his classic narrative of travel and medievalism, *Mont-Saint-Michel
and Chartres* (1904), Henry Adams opens his account by picturing the tourist
looking out over Normandy from the highest point of the Mont Saint-Michel,
considering the likelihood of that tourist's having Norman blood, and slips into
the first person so as to occupy the Norman past: "we of the eleventh century,
hard-headed, close-fisted, grasping, shrewd, as we were, and as Normans are still
said to be, stood more fully in the centre of the world's movement than our English
descendants ever did."[14] Time and space briefly mingle for Adams in this passage;
standing in one of the spaces of medievalism allows him to eclipse time and to
place himself imaginatively in the medieval period, to belong to it and *be* of it.
As Kim Moreland writes, to Adams, unlike Mark Twain, "The twelfth century was
not wholly Other."[15]

Within Britain, tourists, who might have Thomas Rickman's book on the styles
of gothic architecture in one hand, found fresh interest in England's medieval
cathedrals or among the colleges of the ancient universities. Writing in 1870 about

---

[11]   The figures are from *Hand-Book for Travellers in France*, xix–xxi, part of a series
of guide books commenced in 1836. An earlier guide from 1836, Henry Gally Knight's *An
Architectural Tour in Normandy*, was comprehensive on, but confined to, the architecture;
John Murray's new series fulfilled the role of a modern travel guide.

[12]   Odard, "A Sentimental Journey through Normandy," 399.

[13]   Ruskin, "The Nature of Gothic," 152, 153.

[14]   Adams, *Mont-Saint-Michel and Chartres*, 9.

[15]   Moreland, *The Medievalist Impulse in American Literature*, 78.

the charms of Magdalen College, Oxford, a journalist in the London newspaper *The Graphic* notes that it is "rendered infinitely more attractive by the air of medi-aevalism that seems to overhang the whole place."[16] Magdalen – founded in 1458, built from 1467 – is indeed medieval. But by choosing the term medieval*ism*, the author leaves open just what exactly it is the visitor is attracted by. Medieval*ism* in its sense of reinvention was also available to the same visitors, who might have discerned in All Souls College the precocious, early eighteenth-century neo-gothic of Nicholas Hawskmoor (an architect more readily associated with neo-classical Palladian design).

Those first trains to Oxford in 1844 also coincided with medievalism in a different, more modern and precise sense. The newly minted word referred, as we have seen, to the reinvention of Catholicism, the Oxford Movement. In 1856, a writer in *The Examiner* critical of the failure of reforms of Oxford University stated:

> Oxford may yet do noble work in the world … but she will not do it while her hands are thus fettered. She may shake off her external mediaevalism, she may be deprived of her exclusiveness, she may amend the framework of her institutions, but if any real good is to be done, reform must not stop here.[17]

When this writer refers to the need to "shake off her external mediaevalism" he is unlikely to be suggesting that Oxford should be rebuilt in a modern style, but is instead alluding to something more nebulous: an attitude, a stance (which probably includes the Anglo-Catholicism of the Oxford Movement). In 1895, the novelist Thomas Hardy displays acute awareness of this context in his final novel, *Jude the Obscure*. When Sue Bridehead tells Jude, "The mediaevalism of Christ-minster must go," readers would have understood "Christminster" as a fictional version of Oxford and, particularly given that Jude himself is at the time immersed in the writings of leading figures in the Oxford Movement, J. H. Newman and E. B. Pusey, they would have seen that Sue is attacking the Movement. But Sue also concedes, "at times one couldn't help having a sneaking liking for the traditions of the old faith, as preserved by a section of thinkers there in touching and simple sincerity" (words which presage her own eventual return to the Church).[18]

Hence as a city Oxford could obviously be the target of visits to the medieval; it was *the* medieval city of England, offering some of the most unequivocally medieval scenery to be found. As much of its architecture was not ecclesiastical, it had been relatively well preserved from iconoclasm. And yet, as the centre of the Oxford Movement, the city was also in another sense already offering what was – to some – an inauthentic Middle Ages. Oxford mingled two different kinds of medievalism which were not always, perhaps, readily distinguished from one another by contemporaries. It is, incontestably, a city displaying its real medieval

[16] "October Term at Oxford, 1870," 446.
[17] "Oxford Tutors – What Are They?" 242.
[18] Hardy, *Jude the Obscure*, 185.

fabric everywhere, but as contemporary commentators show, and as Hardy recalls at the end of the century, it is also a place where the strange temporality of medievalism is at play, always confusing what can be said to be *truly* medieval.

The Occult Middle Ages: Southern French Villages

The Languedoc region in the south of France, stretching from the Rhône in the east to the Pyrénées in the west, is historically a poor relation of Provence – climatically and geologically similar, its development has been held back by poverty and population decline. In recent times, however, it has become an increasingly popular destination with a rapidly growing reputation for wine, gastronomy, and outdoor leisure pursuits. As its popularity grows, the region is increasingly unified by the idea of the *pays d'oc* – the region of the Occitanian language. This was the southern French of the Middle Ages, the language of the troubadour poets of the eleventh and twelfth centuries, distinct from the northern *langue d'oïl*. It still survives in places as a dialect, but is most evident, all over the Languedoc, in modern road signs indicating place names. Very many Languedoc villages now feature two names, one of them the standard French, the other the same name in Occitan. In the past few years the idea of the *pays d'oc* has become increasingly prominent; the flag of the region, featuring a red cross on a yellow background, is now more common than the French *tricouleur*.

Although, like Provence, the region was of course an important part of the Roman empire, it has fewer Roman remains than its neighbour. It is marked by all eras of history, from the Roman onwards: the remarkable *canal du midi* that traverses it from Toulouse to the Rhône was built in the late seventeenth century; there are traces of the silk industry that prospered in the eighteenth and nineteenth centuries; the vineyards were largely a product of the nineteenth century, and many of the fine houses date from that period. Nevertheless it is the *medieval* character of the region more than any other that supplies an underlying, unifying mythology. The major cities, such as Béziers, Montpellier, and Narbonne, feature medieval cathedrals; the countless villages usually have a medieval church at or near their centres and sometimes the ruins of a castle. Superficially, the villages, with their houses in stone and terracotta-tiled roofs, have a medieval look – even though most of them have undergone continuous rebuilding over the centuries.

Perhaps the most powerful historical aspect of the region that roots it in the Middle Ages, however, is the prominence in cultural memory of the early thirteenth-century Albigensian crusade. The devastation wrought on the region by the forces of the northern French monarchy and the papacy, on the grounds of Languedocien adherence to the heresy of Catharism, is today "remembered" as an enduring injustice. Catharism appears in various guises all over the region, from "Cathar castles" and memorials to immolated heretics, to a local drink made by a winery in the Saint-Chinian appellation, *catharoise*. The *pays cathare* is a brand.

In important ways, the Languedoc offers its own brand of the Middle Ages, placed slightly obliquely to outsiders' views of the period. The Middle Ages of the *langue d'oc* is very much the romantic Middle Ages – this is the birthplace, after all, of the troubadour lyrics and courtly love. But there is also a more domesticated and ordinary Middle Ages, famously revealed by Emmanuel Le Roy Ladurie's *Montaillou* (English translation, 1980), a book based on the heresy-trial testimony of early fourteenth-century Cathars. The chief force of the Cathar connection, unsurprisingly, is to bring the grotesque Middle Ages into play, by invoking the persecution of Cathars at the hands of the French monarchy, and their burning at Minerve, Béziers, and Montségur, reminding us of the evil medieval practices of the past.

In this narrative the Cathars themselves are actually romantic: representations of their persecution are instances of the productive hybridising of grotesque and romantic Middle Ages. The persecution narrative is a particularly focused form of the grotesque Middle Ages, a variant we can place as an occult, deviant Middle Ages. It was promoted in the bestselling 1982 work, *The Holy Blood and the Holy Grail*, by Michael Baigent, Richard Leigh, and Henry Lincoln, but reached its apogee in a book heavily reliant on the earlier work: Dan Brown's extraordinarily successful *The Da Vinci Code* (2003). Kate Mosse's *Labyrinth* (2005) provides another iteration. These books work off the suggestion that something was going on in the Languedoc in the Middle Ages: something the authorities did not want us to know. One of the myriad aspects of the grotesque Middle Ages is the conspiracy theory: in *The Da Vinci Code*, taking a cue from *The Holy Blood and the Holy Grail*, the deviant Middle Ages actually offers the *real* story, but one that has been suppressed by the authorities. Here, the Middle Ages is back in its old, sixteenth-century role as mysterious Other to modernity, yet it is a positively valorised Other. The grotesque character of this Middle Ages arises from the oppressions carried out by officials; it is the conspiracy theory which conveys a simpler truth.

Visitors to the region can participate in some quite different kinds of Middle Ages, according to their disposition. But whatever they do – sampling local goat's cheese, kayaking down the Orb river, as well as visiting Cathar castles – these activities are all *medievalised*, conducted under the sign of the Middle Ages.

The village of Saint-Guilhem-le-Désert, in the valley of Gellone in the Hérault *département*, is a UNESCO World Heritage site, with a history going back to 804 when, after a lifetime of active soldiery and noble leadership at the court of Charlemagne, Guillaume, a grandson of the Frankish king Charles Martel, founded a monastery there. Two years later, Guillaume joined the new foundation as a monk himself and later became leader of the remote community (Guilhem being the Occitan form of Guillaume). A successful community for centuries, Saint-Guilhem survived the early depredations of the wars of religion, but was later pillaged and fell into decrepitude. It was to some extent renovated and restored to use by Maurist Benedictines in the second half of the seventeenth century. Its cloister was partially demolished in the nineteenth century and while some dispersed pieces of sculpture from it have been located – on the façades of houses in nearby towns, for example – the bulk of the cloister was carted away and passed through the hands of various dealers until, on the Quai Voltaire in Paris, it was bought by the American George Grey Barnard. He had it shipped back to New York, where it was reconstructed in the first version of his Cloisters museum, opened in 1914.

Like so many French churches and monasteries, Saint-Guilhem now stands restored and is a major tourist destination. While much of its cloister remains in north Manhattan, what was left in the monastery itself has been renovated, and in the monastery's museum there is an anastylose – a reconstruction of parts of the cloister on the basis of work done with the materials in the Cloisters. Hence, the museum offers exact and very convincing facsimiles of elements of the cloister outside as it is supposed to have existed, while to see the real thing, the tourist must go to New York.

Saint-Guilhem, then, exhibits some of the complexities involved in modern medievalist tourism. It is, without any question, an authentic remnant of the Middle Ages. In its restored state, it is now in part recreated as a place to go to mass. It is also, of course, recreated as a museum and as such, the main reason why the village attracts thousands of visitors. The church is by origin romanesque. Like any such place, it cannot be seen entirely as it was in any one moment of history, but rather as a palimpsest with the markings of different periods of history on it. As is often the style in France, it is scraped back to the stone, and in places beyond the stone: the visitor is allowed at points to see into the architecture, as it were, where excavations have been left open and are visible through glass screens.

Hence although we can appreciate Saint-Guilhem as essentially romanesque, like most such churches in France, one thing it does *not* do is to present the appearance it probably had in the Middle Ages: it has lost most of the statuary it would once have had, and such items as reliquaries have become exhibits behind glass with instructive plaques, rather than functional parts of the church. Above all, there is no colour, no paint, none of the gaudiness which was the fashion in many if not most medieval churches. As Tison Pugh and Angela Weisl put it, "our understanding of this art is inherently created by the ravages of time, rather than the experience of the material that its original audience would have enjoyed."[19] This colourfulness is clear from some of the statuary preserved from the abbey of Cluny at the Musée du Moyen-Âge in Paris, for example, on which extensive traces of paint remain. Some recent restoration projects are helping to change the impression that tourists are given: the rediscovered and restored early frescoes in the abbey church at Saint-Savin in the Poitou region, for example; another very recent discovery beneath layers of limewash is the story of St George and the Dragon in St Cadoc's church in the small village of Llancarfan in the Vale of Glamorgan. But Saint-Guilhem and other restored churches in France reproduce medieval monasticism in a guise of austerity, asceticism, and restraint, values which sit well with, for example, that musical form closely associated with the French church – Gregorian chant – which every few years re-emerges to produce an unlikely chart-topper.

Saint-Guilhem certainly wants to offer, at some level, the opportunity to function *as* a church, and in that guise it invites the worshipper in. As a building, however, it wants to be seen in a longer *durée*, one which begins in 804, continues through the Middle Ages, then largely skips the Wars of Religion. And of course if the tourist *really* wants to see Saint-Guilhem, that can only be done first by viewing

[19] Pugh and Weisl, *Medievalisms*, 114.

the church and what is left of its cloister; then by seeing the simulacral anastylose in the museum; then by going to New York, where the viewer can stand in the middle of a cloister looking out between columns and arches, some of which are original, some modern fabrications, on to the glittering waters of the Hudson.[20]

This particular piece of the medieval has been dispersed through time and space, the times of its dispersal and recollection corresponding with the rise and fall of interest in the Middle Ages. For a great deal of its history, from the Wars of Religion onward, most of what happened to Saint-Guilhem could be regarded as destructive, the final indignity being the assemblage of a newly pristine cloister in Manhattan while the original crumbled to pieces. But the very destruction itself then becomes, in a short time, an element of its importance as a site. It has achieved what Dean MacCannell calls the first phase of "sight sacralization," when as a "sight" or thing to be viewed it was "marked off from similar objects as worthy of preservation."[21] Preservation and the sacralisation that comes with it are boosted by prior acts of destruction.

Saint-Guilhem also signals in its name another, often vital, aspect of contemporary tourism. The Occitan form of "Guillaume" announces its *regional* character. The non-French-speaking visitor to the region will slowly pick up the fact that many of the inscriptions are not in standard French. For visitors from outside France, who might not be able to spot the linguistic difference, this aspect will gradually be made clear. For those with some competence in French, and of course any Francophone visitors, Saint-Guilhem, like most attractions in the Languedoc, clearly signals its otherness, its non-French character. It is not only overtly historical in the way it represents not a shard but a stretch of history, but also quite defiantly sets itself up as *not* purely a piece of French history.

A few miles northwest of Saint-Guilhem this is even more evident in the village of La Couvertoirade. This village's origins are probably associated with those of Saint-Guilhem, as it is first mentioned in an eleventh-century charter from the abbey. Like Saint-Guilhem, it is designated one of "les plus beaux villages de France."[22] La Couvertoirade is a walled town, once inhabited by the order of Templar knights and, after that order's dissolution in the early fourteenth century, by the Knights Hospitaller. Today, it consists of a small village (in which ordinary people still live), an impressive circuit of walls, and a church.[23] It is located on the plain of Larzac, and although it is a few minutes' drive from an *autoroute*, its own position is quiet and relatively isolated. As a tourist, it is possible simply to walk in through the main gate and wander through the few streets. The main attraction is a paying one, and involves going into the barbican behind the walls, where there are displays, book sales, some account of the town, and access to the walls and church. The recommendation, on buying a ticket, is that the tourist pass upstairs from the main entrance, where a film about the town runs on a loop and a few exhibits are to be seen. From there, the circuit of the walls can be walked.

[20] On the Cloisters Museum as medievalism, see further Utzig, "(Re)casting the Past."
[21] MacCannell, *The Tourist*, 44.
[22] http://www.les-plus-beaux-villages-de-france.org/en
[23] A very good sense of the site can be gained from www.lacouvertoirade.com

La Couvertoirade is also "La Cobertoirada" – the Occitan name takes equal place on signs associated with the town. The plaque on the church of Saint-Christophe similarly describes the building in Occitan, without an equivalent description in standard French. While Occitan is still spoken by a minority in present-day Languedoc, few native speakers of modern French would read Occitan with any great facility, while those who do speak it would almost certainly also read modern French. For the tourist with a smattering of French, Occitan adds a fresh level of difficulty, and in the absence of modern French signage, simply obscures the message. Bilingual signs, and signs in the local language, ostensibly act to enfranchise a local, perhaps indigenous population. But in such situations, the real effect is more obviously a *dis*enfranchisement: both non-French and northern French tourists are being told that there is something here at which they can only look and not fully comprehend. This is all part of the visit: the otherness and distance of the sacralised sight. Indeed some of its sacrality resides in the marker itself, as MacCannell calls the informational plaque. The function of Occitan on a marker is not simply or even principally to give access to a tourist sight, but to characterise it even in the moment in which it appears to obscure it.

The paid visit at La Couvertoirade makes much of the association with both the Templars and Hospitallers. While the town has impeccable medieval credentials, with a considerable amount of extant medieval fabric, there is a mystique surrounding the Templars in particular, who popularly represent the Middle Ages in its occult guise. The brutal suppression of the Templars early in the fourteenth century was accompanied by the circulation of propaganda about their supposed satanic and deviant practices. This, intended at the time to discredit them, now functions of course as an attraction, a re-instilling of a mysterious and Gothic character into the order.

Despite the fact that La Couvertoirade was indeed a Templar site, the film that the tourist encounters at the outset of the visit is, somewhat confusingly, a faded documentary about sheep herding in the recent past, involving an extended interview with a shepherd who took part in the transhumance (the annual migration of the flocks between pastures, sometimes over considerable distances). This is presented very much as a past way of life, the shepherd himself saying that although his own father was a shepherd before him, he feels that the vocation will end with him, as the life is too hard.

The film, in its touristic context, is then concerned with a common trope of tourism: the vanishing way of life. It is about the past, but the relatively recent past. On leaving La Couvertoirade tourists can go and eat a local sheep's milk cheese from the Larzac plain, knowing a little more than they previously did about how it is produced. But why the association with the Middle Ages? Why make La Couvertoirade and the Templars the context for sheep herding, rather than anywhere else *without* medieval connections? There is a slippage here, a very vague assumption that sheep herding, important in the twentieth century, was also important to the local economy in the twelfth, thirteenth and fourteenth centuries. This is not a gothic medieval past, but a pastoral version of the romantic Middle Ages: the medieval past opens the touristic site up to all kinds of other pasts and other vanished ways of life become imbricated with the medieval. History is flattened: the life of the shepherd, which can be viewed on film, is part of a recent yet also remote past. The recent past of the transhumance *might as well be* medieval; both are the matter of elegy, both contrast with how we are living now. All history is medieval.

Hence, to drive away from La Couvertoirade and rejoin the *autoroute* is to have engaged in a potentially broad set of relations with the medieval past. In the largest sense, this is medieval history, the visitable medieval past, the visible remnants that are all we can see of the Middle Ages. But in a narrower sense, and because this is a heavily managed form of the Middle Ages, the site offers an intensified, hyper-medievalism: the occult medievalism of the Templars, of Occitan and the *pays d'oc.*

Although the Cathars are not explicitly memorialised at La Couvertoirade, the village does offer the same kind of intense localism which elsewhere is negotiated through the creation of a sense of grievance based on the massacres of the orig-inal Cathars in the Albigensian Crusade. The town of Minerve, in the Languedoc *département* of Aude, was a Cathar stronghold successfully subdued by Simon de Montfort in 1210. There are two inscriptions recording the event. One, dating from the nineteenth or perhaps the eighteenth century, states, "Here, for the Cathar faith 180 *Parfaits* were killed by the flames" (the *parfaits* or *perfecti* were the Cathar elite, their equivalent of priests). The other, more modern, says simply, "Als Catars 1210." During my visit in the late 1990s, a local guide was equivocal on the exact number of Cathars who died, but was very clear about the injustice that had been done.[24] The town's central street is named the rue des Martyrs. In such places the grotesque Middle Ages comes up against the romantic Middle Ages: an austere romanesque church in a dramatic setting (Minerve is at the confluence of two rivers that have cut deep gorges to either side of the town) is promoted as beau-tiful, but inescapably also as commemorating a violent past which, by implication, we are glad, ourselves, to have escaped.

Tintagel, AD 500–2014: Towards a Theory of Touristic Capital

Tintagel, on the north coast of Cornwall, is the site of a ruined thirteenth-century castle, dramatically located on a clifftop above an often wild sea. The antiquary John Leland saw it in the early sixteenth century, when it was evidently already in very poor shape. Today the ruins are bare vestiges and it is clear that this was also true when tourists began visiting the site in the mid nineteenth century. In the early Middle Ages, the area was part of a trade network; the existing castle, from the thirteenth century, was once the stronghold of Richard of Cornwall, brother of Henry III. Strategically, it was unimportant in the late Middle Ages and given its ruinous state, there has not been much to visit at Tintagel for centuries. Visi-tors today can see the bare outlines of a castle and a few ruined walls. There are not many identifiable features remaining; one that *is* visible is what may well be Britain's airiest medieval latrine.

---

[24] Leading scholars now hold the construction of a deep-rooted dualist heresy in late medieval Europe (by both contemporaries and modern scholars) to be largely an invention. See Moore, *The War on Heresy.*

The site is, however, famous and much-visited. Its status derives from its place in legend as the castle in which King Arthur was conceived. It was also usually taken as Arthur's birthplace though Geoffrey of Monmouth, who seems to have invented the legend, does not explicitly state this. Geoffrey apparently knew what he was talking about, however, in his tale of how Uther Pendragon besieges Duke Gorlois for love of his duchess Ygraine, gains access to her through Merlin's aid, and begets Arthur: in his account the castle is described, accurately enough, as being "high above the sea, which surrounds it on all sides ... there is no other way in except that offered by a narrow isthmus of rock."[25] In the thirteenth century, Henry III's brother Richard, earl of Cornwall, rebuilt the castle; for him it seems to have operated as an opportunity to present "himself as the heir to Arthur in a ready-made fantasy castle" for reasons of "political image rather than any practical need."[26] In the fifteenth century, Thomas Malory in his turn began his own Arthurian work with Ygraine at Tintagel, though without much detail.

The topography of the real Tintagel fits with the image in Geoffrey of a defensible coastal fortress, while wild seas and a rugged coastline provide the atmosphere of dark-age, Arthurian Britain. Today, the village of Tintagel is a tourist destination for which the Arthur story provides the economic lifeblood. Its reputation as an Arthurian site has been growing since about the middle of the nineteenth century. In 1777, Thomas Warton clearly regarded it as a romantic setting in his poem "The Grave of King Arthur."

> O'er Cornwall's cliffs the tempest roar'd,
> High the screaming sea-mew soar'd;
> On Tintaggel's topmost tower
> Darksom fell the sleety shower;
> Round the rough castle shrilly sung
> The whirling blast, and wildly flung
> On each tall rampart's thundering side
> The surges of the tumbling tide ...[27]

But at the beginning of the nineteenth century King Arthur's stock was in fact low. The most famous English retelling of his story, that of Malory as printed by William Caxton in 1485 and last reprinted in 1634, was by then difficult to obtain, at least for those without means. The poet Robert Southey, whose family was not well-off, recalled that as a schoolboy, he "possessed a wretchedly imperfect copy" of the 1634 edition.[28] Many readers would have known of Arthur through late ballads, often parodic and scurrilous like "The Boy and the Mantle," to be found in Thomas Percy's *Reliques*, rather than through Malory's tale of noble deeds of chivalry.

[25] Geoffrey of Monmouth, *The History of the Kings of Britain*, 206.
[26] Rouse and Rushton, "Arthurian Geography," 226.
[27] Thomas Warton, "The Grave of King Arthur," 1777.
[28] Parins, *Malory: The Critical Heritage*, 99.

There was widespread acceptance of a *historical* Arthur, but that made the legendary Arthur problematic. Sharon Turner, in his 1799 *History of the Anglo-Saxons*, attempted to distinguish "the Arthur of tradition from the Arthur of history," rather optimistically imagining that a real Arthur, stripped of the legends, would retain "fame ample enough to interest the judicious, and to perpetuate his honourable memory."[29] Francis Palgrave, in his *Rise and Progress of the English Commonwealth* (1832), stated that "[w]e can neither doubt the existence of this Chieftain, nor believe in the achievements which have been ascribed to him."[30]

In this context as in other spheres of medieval studies the immediate post-Napoleonic years were productive, bringing about a rapid reorientation of the understanding of Arthur in history, legend and literature. In 1816–17, three new editions of Malory's prose work appeared in rapid succession. One, in Walker's British Classics series, bore the title *The History of the Renowned Prince Arthur*, while another, probably edited by an antiquarian named Joseph Haslewood, was entitled *La Mort D'Arthur*. Both of these were in the small duodecimo format and relatively cheap. In 1817 a third edition appeared, this one a much more lavish two-volume quarto, introduced by Southey and bearing the title *The Byrth, Lyf, and Actes of Kyng Arthur*. In 1817 readers had waited nearly two hundred years for an edition of Malory and then three came all at once.[31]

In the next two decades, the burgeoning romance scholarship unearthed numerous Arthurian verse romances, producing some important source material: Nennius' Latin *Historia Britonum*, the earliest Arthurian source, published with a translation in 1819, and Geoffrey of Monmouth's Latin chronicle *Historia Regum Britanniae*, perhaps the most important source of all, published by J. A. Giles in 1842 – the same year in which Tennyson published "Morte D'arthur," the embryo from which his epic *Idylls of the King* grew.

Nevertheless, when in 1854 *Sharpe's London Magazine of Entertainment and Instruction* ran a story on Tintagel, its author was unimpressed by the history of Arthur and displayed more interest in the annual cattle fair at nearby Trevenna and the mechanism by which ore was shipped from a mine close to Tintagel. Even the scenery did not impress him, as he approvingly cited another visitor who had remarked on the site's "unqualified desolation," its "one wide and wild scene of troubled ocean, barren country, and horrid rocks." It was a place that "chilled the tourist," he continued, saying that the view "was enough to give one the tooth-ache."[32]

Yet within a few years, the site's association with Arthurian legend had been cemented and its "horrid rocks" and "barren country" transformed into the pictur-esque and romantic wilderness Warton had envisaged. In 1861, a journalist signing himself E. T. found "The grandeur of the scenery" to be "indescribable," and laced

[29] Turner, *The History of the Anglo-Saxons*, vii.
[30] Quoted in Bryden, *Reinventing King Arthur*, 26.
[31] On the Arthurian revival see Taylor and Brewer, *The Return of King Arthur*, especially chapter 1: "The Return of Arthur: Nineteenth-Century British Medievalism and Arthurian Tradition."
[32] "Tintagel Castle," *Sharpe's London Magazine*, 174.

his account with stories of local curiosities. This writer was clearly interested in Arthur and, if not accepting his historical existence unequivocally, was prepared to repeat various legends, beginning with Warton's poem. But it was Tennyson who at the time was becoming the greatest influence, as E. T. acknowledged: "[O]f all existing Arthurian romances, none can boast of such refinement and purity as the sweet fancies of the author of the 'Idylls,' who has invested the pure King and his court with a beauty and interest they never before possessed."[33]

Before long Tintagel came to frame Arthur's entire life, as it was thought that his final battle with Mordred had occurred not far away from his supposed birth-place. In 1875 another writer on the site unequivocally located it as Arthur's castle, where he was born, from which he went forth to conquer Saxons, Picts, and Scots, to which he returned and was killed in battle. "The feats of arms attributed to Arthur in legendary song are simply incredible, and even ridiculous," says this writer, "but the moral tone of his heroic deeds is invariably correct. He always promotes truth and gentleness, and punishes sin." This author does concede that the legend belongs to the site rather than the ruined castle itself, because "Not a trace exists of Arthurian structure." And like many another writer on this topic, he remains a little uncertain over the historical reality of Arthur. But he wrote: "We do not seek to dispel the glamour of Arthurian romance. Only let it be romance, resting on the somewhat insecure foundation of fact vouched by old Geoffrey of Monmouth."[34] At the time enormously boosted by the poet laureate's ever-growing *Idylls of the King*, Arthur's legend was on the rise and Tintagel on its way to being secured as a prime Arthurian location.

In the 1850s and 1860s, then, Tintagel was going through the first phase of "sight sacralization," and was being "marked off from similar objects as worthy of pres-ervation." While it was Tennyson's poetry, above all, that contributed to Arthur's reputation generally, Tintagel itself was relatively de-emphasised in his work. Its association with lustful behaviour and magically induced adultery was the kind of thing Tennyson removed from the legend, and Tintagel was more important in a rival poet's work. The story of Tristram and Iseult was also associated with the site, which some held to have been the seat of King Mark of Cornwall (the hapless husband of Iseult). In his romantic and dramatic telling, Algernon Swin-burne completed the transformation of the formerly toothache-inducing wilder-ness. Swinburne, who actually knew the north Cornwall coast, described "the wind-hollowed heights and gusty bays / Of sheer Tintagel, fair with famous days," its "towers washed round with rolling foam / And storied halls wherethrough sea-music rang."[35]

The impetus given by Victorian poetry is now largely forgotten at Tintagel; in time, a range of related activities accreted around the tourist attraction, securing its status. One major development occurred in the 1930s, when an eccentric retired

---

[33] E. T., "A Visit to Tintagel," 553, 557.

[34] "Tintagel Castle," *Leisure Hour*, 282.

[35] Swinburne, *Tristram of Lyonesse*, 13, 76; for a more accessible version see the Camelot Project at the University of Rochester, http://d.lib.rochester.edu/camelot/text/swinburne-tristram-of-lyonesse

businessman and Arthurian, Frederic Thomas Glasscock, constructed his Great Halls, featuring some remarkable stained glass telling the story of Arthur. Glasscock envisaged his halls as the centre of a worldwide Arthurian fellowship, but when he died shortly after the completion of his work, the Great Halls fell into abeyance, later to be revived as a tourist attraction in the 1990s.[36] Today, the visitor finds such additional features as an Arthurian laser show. The ripples of Arthurianism spread outwards, and so such loosely related New-Age ventures as a shop selling crystals were once to be found in the main street. Inevitably, the shop was called Merlin's Cave; today Merlin (who often did his best work when hidden from view) plies his trade solely on the internet ("Online shopping at it's best!"), where not only jewellery, crystals and minerals are on offer, but Merlin t-shirts, hypnosis downloads and a daily horoscope.[37] Everything in Tintagel justifies itself in relation to Arthurian legend: one of the pubs, for example, features a menu of Excaliburgers. Tintagel has become, in MacCannell's formulation, a "cultural production that almost magically generates capital continuously, often without consuming any energy for itself."[38]

MacCannell's study, however, tends to assume that tourism focuses on a sight or attraction, something that is actually there. As he notes, there are some locations where something happened in the past (such as the Bonnie and Clyde shootout) but left no trace of itself. In such places, what he calls the sight's "marker" dominates. The marker might be as simple as a plaque relating what happened, but it might be more extensive: Tennyson's *Idylls of the King* has the status of a marker in relation to Tintagel, as it relates what supposedly took place. Jerome de Groot suggests, of such sites from which the original attraction has disappeared, that the kind of history performed by the visitor "views the site as a palimpsest, a series of maps and spatial encounters overlaid on one another. You have to imagine what happened here, or engage in some kind of psychogeographical decoding of the site."[39]

However, as it seems safe to say that Arthur was not conceived at Tintagel, not born there, did not die there and in any case did not rule a united Britain; as the ruins of a castle that has nothing to do with Arthur crumble away, it becomes more evident that Tintagel is a site where *nothing* happened and there is almost *nothing* to see. This is a prime case of the marker obliterating the sight. It is a wild and atmospheric stretch of coastline, but it is hardly unique in that. People visit Tintagel chiefly because of literary and legendary associations, then, and it is a site invested with a kind of numinousness which it shares with other sites where there *are* things to see – the ruins of Glastonbury Abbey, the supposed burial site of Arthur not too far away in Somerset, for example – but which clearly is not based on what is actually *there*.

---

[36] I owe my knowledge of this to Tamas Beregi's fascinating doctoral dissertation, "Nostalgia for a Golden Age: Arthurian Legends in Twentieth-Century Visual Culture."

[37] http://www.cafepress.com/merlinscavenet. Accessed 4 February 2014.

[38] MacCannell, *The Tourist*, 29.

[39] De Groot, *Consuming History*, 113.

To account for this, psychogeography is certainly a factor. But we need a theory of what could be called touristic capital: that quality of a place which raises its value in the eyes of the tourist. The most obvious way in which this might happen is through the sheer monumentality and indisputable historical associations of a site – the cathedral of Notre Dame in Paris would be an example of this. But as Tintagel shows, there are other forms of capital, derived from literary and legendary associations, which confer value on the site. Such associations, in some cases, even work to confer value on sites that are evidently and self-confessedly inauthentic. In present-day Norwich, one of the major tourist attractions is the cell of the celebrated early fifteenth-century anchoress, Julian of Norwich. The cell is – as is made clear in the exhibit itself – entirely a reconstruction of an anchorhold which was pulled down in the Reformation, its precise location now a subject of dispute. But this does nothing to dim its popularity and, as Sarah Salih notes, "visitors almost always treat the reconstructed space as a real site," aware that it *is* a reconstruction, but going away in the belief that they have in some sense visited Julian's cell.[40] The fact that Julian *was* once somewhere in the environs of the reconstruction as an anchoress confers value on the otherwise inauthentic site.

Such a site as this cannot have an *aura*, in Benjamin's sense. And yet the aura of authenticity is precisely what seems to be conferred by the once present, now absent, original. MacCannell reverses Benjamin's concept, arguing that "The work becomes 'authentic' only after the first copy of it is produced. The reproductions *are* the aura, and the ritual, far from being a point of origin, *derives* from the relationship between the original object and its socially constructed importance" (48).

This touristic capital can in turn produce actual capital. The controversial practice in England of putting turnstiles at the entrances to cathedrals is one result. What is levied from the tourist is called a "donation," but one which, unpaid, means the tourist is not allowed in. Worshippers, on the other hand, are welcomed in for free. Hence, at the turnstile a judgement is made about those who are drawn by touristic capital and should therefore be mulcted, and those who are there for the spiritual capital, whose transaction remains private. Even so, extreme pressure is placed on some cathedrals as result of the conflicting demands, as Stephanie Trigg notes, provoking a variety of responses.[41] In France, entry to cathedrals remains free. As a result there is a more or less year-round queue to get into Notre Dame in Paris, where a battery of machines allow visitors to spend their money the moment they are inside, on guide books, cards, and tickets to tours.

Local authorities, understandably, can be very interested in creating touristic capital in order to generate the financial kind. In the case of Notre Dame, they do not have to work very hard: Notre Dame is famous as a medieval cathedral, as being at the centre of Paris, as being central to Victor Hugo's novel of the same name, and the film of the novel. It is famous as a great example of the authentic Middle Ages; it is famously inauthentic, with its celebrated gargoyles supplied in the nineteenth century by Viollet-le-Duc. It is famous, finally, for being famous.

---

[40] Salih, "Julian in Norwich," 156.
[41] Trigg, "Walking through Cathedrals."

4 Old St Mary's cathedral, Sydney, in the 1830s, with indigenous Australians. State Library of New South Wales.

What is peculiar is that while there is no sign that interest in it is slackening, it is now an example of an all but unvisitable site. It is certainly difficult to imagine worshipping in it. But it is also difficult to move around and see: to be in Notre Dame today is, quite simply, to be in the middle of a large, mixed and noisy crowd, filming, taking pictures, talking, and doing all the things that people in crowds do. At that point, the forms of capital, touristic and spiritual, that drew people there in the first place have surely begun to seep away. People are then there simply because other people are there.

The case of Tintagel is rather different, showing that the growth of touristic capital can be a largely spontaneous process, beyond the control of local authorities – though local authorities will step in at a certain point, building restraining rails, ensuring health and safety, constructing a paying car park, and authorising the opening of commercial premises. The aura can, nevertheless, similarly take over the entirety of the site and its environs in every aspect. As a village, Tintagel is overwhelmed by Arthur tourism, and has no other purpose. Every aspect of the place is Arthurian. Even sitting down to lunch, contemplating a menu of Excaliburgers, the visitor must try to work out why a Guinevere comes with beetroot, while a Lancelot has extra cheese.

St Mary's Cathedral, Sydney

Bennelong Point, a small projection into Sydney Harbour today in the heart of the city, was once the location of a hut which was the dwelling place of Woollarawarre Bennelong. Bennelong was the indigenous Australian who at the time of the first white settlement was captured by the first governor of the colony of New

5 Old St Mary's cathedral, Sydney, after fire of 1865. State Library of New South Wales.

6 St Mary's cathedral, Sydney, around 1935, substantially complete. State Library of New South Wales.

South Wales, Captain Arthur Phillip, and became a mediator between the whites and the local aboriginal groups. Bennelong eventually went back with Phillip to London at the end of the governorship, where he adopted European dress and manners before returning to Australia in 1795 and dying, ill and alcoholic, in 1813. Today, the point is occupied by Australia's most famous building, the Sydney Opera House, a temple to high-modernist architecture. Its Danish architect, Jørn Utzon, travelled widely and absorbed lessons from Mayan and Islamic architecture before he designed the Opera House, which, since its much-delayed opening in 1973 has become one of the country's most recognisable images, a status it owes in large part to its uncompromising modernist outward form, its shattering of any expectations about how a concert hall should look.

As a monument, then, the Opera House is seemingly devoid of any reference to the pasts of either European Antiquity or the Middle Ages. Behind it are European science, which drove Captain James Cook and Sir Joseph Banks to the shores of Australia in the first place, and European ideas about criminality that led to the sailing of Arthur Phillip's First Fleet, the establishment of the first penal colony, and its subsidiary mission of making contact with the natives. It was, then, the European Enlightenment which ensured that Bennelong and his companion Colby would be lured down a river, captured, and enforcedly befriended by Phillip. From Enlightenment to Modernism, Bennelong Point seems to register an Australian story entirely free of neo-medievalist associations.

A short walk uphill, however, to a site about ten minutes away, reveals the inevitability that as Australia's white history unfolded in the nineteenth century, it too was caught up in the medievalism that was sweeping the colonial power, Britain. St Mary's cathedral, the centre of the Australian Catholic Church, has its origins in a chapel built on what was then the edge of the town of Sydney near the convict barracks, commenced in 1821. Though nothing remains of this original chapel, we know that it was built in a naive gothic style (Figure 4); major extensions to it in order to create a cathedral were carried out in the 1850s according to designs by Augustus Pugin. This building was largely destroyed by fire in 1865 (Figure 5) and the present church was then designed and built by William Wilkinson Wardell. A disciple of Pugin, Wardell had emigrated to Australia in 1858 as inspector-general of public works in Victoria, and was responsible for some of Australia's most notable neo-gothic buildings.

Like any real medieval cathedral St Mary's was constructed over a long period of time. While the northern section was completed and dedicated in 1882, the central tower was not complete until 1900, the cathedral not consecrated until 1905, while the nave was finished and the cathedral, still not yet quite complete, officially opened in 1928 (Figure 6). Even then work continued, with a crypt constructed in the 1960s. Finally the spires – designed by Wardell but not constructed – were added in time for the Sydney Olympic Games in 2000.[42]

---

[42] See Randles, "Rebuilding the Middle Ages"; Wardell's biography in *ODNB*, http://www.oxforddnb.com/view/article/38106, accessed 25 February 2014; the cathedral's website at www.stmaryscathedral.org.au; Andrews, *Australian Gothic*, 70–72.

7 Sydney Opera House, interior. Photograph Jack Atley.

St Mary's cathedral then not only medievalises space, by bringing the familiar form of thirteenth-century English gothic to Sydney, but medievalises time, given the sheer length of the chronological span across which the process of its construction dominated this space. The building of the crypt in the 1960s consolidated the space; archbishops dead and buried elsewhere were moved to the new crypt, as if more thoroughly to present the space as one orthodox in its medieval character, and to overcome any lingering doubts as to the appropriateness of the form in Australia.

This medievalising of space is, of course, only an outward appearance. When the spires were erected in 2000 for a time they offered a strangely incongruous sight: beneath the Piles Creek sandstone cladding which is visible today there are glittering steel substructures which, for the several months during which they were visible, presented a science-fictionalised vision of the cathedral, as if George Lucas, who was also in town at the time completing his second Star Wars trilogy, had been transported back in time to collaborate with Pugin and Wardell. For those months in the year 2000, the cathedral stood exposed in its inauthentic simulacral character. With the cladding now in place, its simulation is effectively resumed. The spires complete not only the cathedral itself but our sense of the truly medieval timespan of its construction. It is properly medieval.

To *medievalise* a space is to colonise it. The picture of the first church on the site, as Sarah Randles notes, illustrates this, as it depicts aboriginal figures in its foreground, showing "the indigenous owners of the land ... dispossessed and supplanted by a culture whose buildings embody the past of another country." But as Randles also notes, Pugin's Australian churches were explicitly intended to colonise for Catholicism. Hence St Mary's cathedral "can also be read as part of the Irish struggle against British colonialism, even as it participated in the colonization of the new country."[43]

St Mary's is an exact simulacrum, a hyperreal structure, its reproduction of the thirteenth-century pointed style more perfect than anything usually found in an actual thirteenth-century church. It is not necessary to have witnessed the steel framework beneath the spires to know that the building was constructed with the most modern techniques at any given time. It is so perfect a reproduction that it is, to the medievalist, evidently a fake. But not the medievalist alone, because there are no tourists at St Mary's either, no throngs filing dutifully down its nave, filming every niche, every saint. Insofar as St Mary's has any numinousness, it is simply as a Catholic church in which mass is celebrated and weddings and funerals conducted. Strangely, St Mary's is able to function as a medieval church far more straightforwardly than Notre Dame in Paris or Salisbury cathedral in Wiltshire, because the tourists are down at the Opera House, absorbing the numinousness of what has become a far more sacred site than St Mary's cathedral.

Obviously tourists do not come to Australia for the Middle Ages. Even so, the medieval lurks in surprising places. Despite the Mayan and Islamic influences he himself acknowledged, Utzon also, in 1965, referred to his Opera House as a kind of gothic cathedral. Bracingly unconventional as the building's exterior is, anyone who has seen the *interior* of the Opera House would find the statement easy enough to comprehend (Figure 7). The building is notoriously problematic as a concert space. One journalist has suggested that the celebrated shells of the Opera House "are three-dimensional gothic arches generat[ing] huge outward thrust." "The Opera House is really a gothic cathedral," the journalist continued, but "sans buttresses." The shells are pinned together by an "enormous tie-beam" underground, which is one of the architectural reasons why the orchestra pit is, famously, very small and completely inadequate.[44] The Opera House is subject to all kinds of difficulties as a result of breaches of occupational health and safety guidelines, with complaints from musicians crammed into its orchestra pit. Modernism was not supposed to be like this, but rather to marry form and function. The phantom at the Opera House is a return of its gothic repressed.

Katine: Putting the Medieval Right

St Mary's cathedral medievalises the space on which it sits and colonises it, while the Opera House too points back to a repression of the colonist's Middle Ages. I want in this final example to visit a place that has an even more tenuous relationship with the European Middle Ages but one which has also been subject to the medievalist's colonising gaze. It is the least likely of any of the places discussed here to be visited by the western tourist and indeed has no tourist amenities of any kind. And yet when this remote region of Africa was first regularly discussed a

---

[43] Randles, "Rebuilding the Middle Ages," 153.
[44] Farrelly, "Icon sets the tone for everything but music."

few years ago, its physical distance was routinely construed as if it were a distance in time.

In October 2007, *The Guardian* newspaper – a liberal, London-based broadsheet – began a three-year campaign under which it would seek to improve the lives of the inhabitants of a poor region in northern Uganda called Katine. The campaign was announced in a front-page article in the Saturday edition, written by the paper's editor, Alan Rusbridger, with a headline that asked, "Can we, together, lift one village out of the Middle Ages?" He began with the observation that "With the right flight connections, a journey from the 21st century to the 14th century can take just over 12 hours."[45] Rusbridger's metaphor elaborated an idea suggested by the economist Paul Collier in his 2007 book, *The Bottom Billion*. Collier states, of the poor countries concentrated in Africa and Central Asia, that they "coexist with the twenty-first century, but their reality is the fourteenth century: civil war, plague, ignorance." He adds that the poorest billion people in the world "are living and dying in fourteenth-century conditions."[46] Rusbridger cited Collier in noting that Katine had had its share of civil war, plague, and ignorance. He conceded that the "experiment will not be uncontroversial: little to do with aid or development is. The first, and most obvious, question is, why intervene at all in a way of life that has changed little in hundreds of years?"

Starting out with a grotesque Middle Ages, Rusbridger implies that the fourteenth century to which Katine is condemned is a result of the outside agency that brings, or keeps the region in, the medieval conditions of civil war, plague, and ignorance. By the end of the article, however, there is more than a hint of an ongoing, timeless and perhaps romantic Middle Ages ("a way of life that has changed little in hundreds of years"). Either way, this is a surprisingly clear case (for a liberal newspaper) of the anthropological move critiqued by Johannes Fabian as the "*denial of coevalness*," by which he means "*a persistent and systematic tendency to place the referent(s) of anthropology in a Time other than the present of the producer of anthropological discourse.*"[47] As Dipesh Chakrabarty glosses this, the trope means that "it could always be said with reason that some people were less modern than others, and that the former needed a period of preparation and waiting before they could be recognized as full participants in political modernity."[48] In practice this not-quite-modernity often resolves itself as the construction of a medieval period, as Kathleen Davis and Nadia Altschul explain: "European colonizers established their superiority in temporal terms by mapping colonial lands and people as backward in time and, in many cases, as still living in the Middle Ages."[49]

[45] *The Guardian*, Saturday 20 October 2007.
[46] Collier, *The Bottom Billion*, 3.
[47] Fabian, *Time and the Other*, 31. See also Ganim, "Native Studies: Orientalism and Medievalism."
[48] Chakrabarty, *Provincializing Europe*, 9.
[49] Davis and Altschul, "Introduction: The Idea of 'The Middle Ages' Outside Europe," 2.

The Guardian, with its origins in nineteenth-century dissenting traditions in Manchester, is today well known as a liberal newspaper. The denial of coevalness involved in its construction of Katine seemed an unusual step for the paper. In the days following the article's appearance, readers reacted in different though fairly predictable ways. Some wrote the experiment off as renewed colonialism; some, in a related strain, lamented the central presence in the initiative, as sponsor, of Barclay's Bank. Others applauded. And some, even while positive, objected to the use of Collier's medieval metaphor. Paddy Masefield in Devon – one who regarded the initiative as a new colonialism – noted of the summary of life in Katine: "you boldly state this is a middle-ages lifestyle. To me it has more in common with post-civil-war Bosnia, Cambodia or Berlin in 1946 – the absolute basics of survival with little cause to believe in any stability." Another wrote:

> It is disappointing to see that the Guardian, in pursuing a credible initiative in Uganda, has got caught up in the rhetoric of labelling life in Katine as akin to a 14th-century existence.
> This does no favours for people trying to cope with the fallout of colonialism, misdirected investment, corporate greed and rapacious plundering.

Maureen Mackintosh and Doreen Massey, from the Open University's Faculty of Social Sciences, developed their objections to the use of the metaphor more fully, drawing on a personal anecdote involving a Senegalese farmer who had lived in England and fought in France in World War II. "We are all of the 21st century," they concluded. "It helps understanding to know that."[50]

In the years that followed the campaign's announcement a great deal was achieved for the inhabitants of Katine and among the possible objections to an initiative such as this, those of medievalists over the use of their period as a metaphor should surely come very low. We use "social-moral universals" in bad faith but to good ends, as Chakrabarty argues.[51] There *are* nevertheless potentially enormous problems, as Mackintosh and Massey begin to indicate, in the denial of coevalness. One is simply that while we might assume that African villagers are in the Middle Ages things might prove, as in their anecdote, rather more complicated. More importantly, after five hundred years of denigration of the Middle Ages by modernity, the metaphor can never be neutral. It is impossible to impute medievalism to African villagers without also implying a teleology which inevitably places them as backward. As Fabian puts it, "What makes the savage significant to the evolutionist's Time is that he lives in another Time" (27). We propose that *we* are in a modernity that *they* have failed to reach.

In short, by collapsing time into space Rusbridger's article starkly aligned the binaries modern/medieval, western/African, civilised/barbaric. Actively engaging with the longstanding status of the medieval as a metaphor for barbarism, Collier

---

[50] *The Guardian*, Wednesday 24 October 2007, letters section; see http://www.theguardian.com/news/2007/oct/24/leadersandreply.mainsection2.

[51] Chakrabarty, "Historicism and Its Supplements: A Note on a Predicament Shared by Medieval and Postcolonial Studies," Davis and Altschul, 117.

and Rusbridger are in effect only finding a slightly more distanced way of saying *these Africans are backward*. When they add to that the suggestion, *And we are going to lift them out of it*, it is impossible not to see, as some of the letter writers objected, a new colonialism very similar in its attitudes to the old. Even more damagingly, the narrative by which "the African unmodern came to operate under the sign of medievalism" was associated, as Simon Gikandi argues, with the slave trade and imperial expansion, both of which were associated with the "residual medievalism" which Europeans discerned in Africa.[52]

Collier and others might respond to this by saying that in the fourteenth century there really *was* "civil war, plague, ignorance." Here, the professional medievalist does arguably have a role. Historical reality is not neutral, but has been loaded by centuries of perceptions and those are particularly complex in the case of medievalism, as we have seen. Of course it would be beside the point here to delay, keeping African villagers hungry while demanding that the *Guardian* get its sense of the Middle Ages right. But history is not doing the work that the *Guardian* requires of it here, which means that it is worth pointing out that there were many other aspects to the fourteenth century than civil war, plague and ignorance and that, conversely, those features exist in all eras. The fourteenth century cannot function as an absolute comparison but as a metaphor, one which in the context can only be paternalist and colonialist. Used in relation to Uganda by a former colonial master, it proposes that a job begun in the colonial period now needs to be completed. The denial of coevalness implies that western Europe got out of the Middle Ages, and that everyone else who has not will want the help of Europe to do so. This mobilises the trope of "the West and the Rest," in Niall Ferguson's egregious adaptation of a phrase originally used by Marshall Sahlins.[53]

No doubt self-consciously (but not self-consciously enough), the *Guardian* used the Middle Ages in an anachronistic sense, engaging with its strange temporality. As we have seen, the word "medieval" entered the language early in the nineteenth century as a straightforward period term in response to a new awareness of the Middle Ages and consequent need for verbal precision and economy. "Medievalism," by contrast, appeared in the 1840s already loaded with the paradoxical and anachronistic sense of something that was both past and present. These chronological and anachronistic uses, however, are not always easy to separate. In the chronological use, the Middle Ages is a *time* in the past, clearly separated from the time of modernity. This is a time nevertheless which many, from Ruskin to re-enactors, have found it desirable to imagine inhabiting. Alternatively, in the anachronistic sense the Middle Ages inhabits modernity – whether through revival or survival is not always easy to say. The Katine example underlines the way in which the Middle Ages is that which has never gone away, that which continues timelessly to threaten civilisation from whatever margin it inhabits. That which, finally, needs to be eradicated.[54]

[52] Gikandi, "Africa and the Signs of Medievalism," 370, 371.
[53] Ferguson, *Civilization*; see Sahlins, *Culture and Practical Reason*.
[54] See Upton, "'Authentic' Anxieties."

*

Just like the word "mediaevalism" in the mid-nineteenth century, all of these places allow a slippage of meaning, between real Middle Ages and hyperreal, reinvented Middle Ages. Pugin's Mediaeval Court and Julian's cell seem, unlike the cathedral of Rouen, to be entirely invented. Some sites mingle the two categories of medieval and medievalism: most notoriously, perhaps, in the nineteenth-century restorations of medieval French buildings by Viollet-le-Duc. For many, the witch-hat towers of the citadel of Carcassonne and the gargoyles of Notre Dame de Paris are *the* image of medieval France, even though both were supplied by Viollet-le-Duc.[55] As I have contended, even the real medieval can never be visited. We can only go to historical palimpsests. It is difficult, even in an apparently unrenovated medieval church, to reach out and touch a stone that might have been placed there by a medieval stonemason without wondering whether someone else has moved it in the centuries since, whether somebody else has marked it with history. We visit the Middle Ages only in our dreams.

[55] Camille, *The Gargoyles of Notre-Dame.*

4

On Being Medieval: Medievalist Selves and Societies

J.-K. Huysmans' 1898 novel, *The Cathedral* (*La Cathédrale*), presents the ruminations of Durtal as he seeks spiritual calm in the cathedral of Notre Dame de Chartres. Aided by two priests, Durtal examines the cathedral in all its aspects. The novel consists chiefly of his responses to it, and a depiction of his inner states as he agonises over whether he should adopt the monastic life or not. At the end, Durtal departs from Chartres, with many misgivings, for Solesmes, where he plans to consider the life of a Benedictine monk.

The Cathedral is a largely meditative novel in which almost nothing happens. The characters are limited to Durtal, two priests, and a housekeeper. Dialogue is not common, and lengthy descriptions of parts of the cathedral and Christian symbolism form the bulk of the work. It was, nevertheless, a bestseller in France when it appeared at the end of the nineteenth century. It appealed to a conservative Catholic element in French society at the time of the Dreyfus affair and the debates which would culminate with the legal espousal of state secularism in 1905. For Elizabeth Emery, its success is explicable by the appeal it held in a context of *fin-de-siècle* discontent in France. Huysmans (like Zola), as Emery explains, "contrast[s] the 'good' Gothic cathedral of Chartres with the 'bad' Sacré-Coeur," the latter a church which arose out of politics and civil war and a "commercial bourgeois foundation."[1]

Unsurprisingly, given the centrality to it of Chartres cathedral, and the Virgin Mary to whom the church is dedicated, the vision the novel projects is a strikingly *medieval* one. Neither Durtal nor, it would seem, his creator were at all interested in anything that had happened to the cathedral in Chartres *after* the Middle Ages. In fact the Renaissance is repeatedly decried as a historical and ethical Fall. For Durtal, only medieval art has value:

---

[1]   Emery, *Romancing the Cathedral*, 32, 33.

As soon as the sensuality of the Renaissance revealed itself, the Paraclete fled and mortal sin in stone could flaunt itself at will. It contaminated the buildings that it completed, defiled the churches whose purity of form it violated; this, along with the licentiousness of sculpture and painting, was the great deflowering of the cathedrals.

This time the Spirit of Prayer was really dead; everything collapsed. The Renaissance, vaunted so highly by historians in the wake of Michelet, marked the end of the mystical soul, the end of monumental theology, the death of religious art, of all great art in France.[2]

Elsewhere, the Renaissance is referred to as the time of a new paganism. After the Renaissance, things only worsen and the present, Durtal's own time, is depicted as being empty of any spirituality or meaning.

Such sentiments are likely to appear unusual to modern readers who, whether they know it or not, are post-Michelet, post-Burckhardt, and thoroughly imbued with the positive sense of the Renaissance. For many people today, it is an uncontested assumption that *Renaissance* art represents one of the pinnacles of artistic achievement; it is a commonplace that the discovery of perspective, among other things, was a renaissance innovation which moved art along in its development. Huysmans' novel recalls the possibility of a quite different view, in which medieval art is superior, and the Renaissance merely the beginning of the end. When the guide points out to Durtal three sculptural figures which are thought of as masterpieces, he strenuously objects: "That's going too far … they look sullen, and the drapery is too cold – the arrangement of their robes is like that of Greek togas; they have a vague whiff of the Renaissance about them already" (231).

For many of the thousands of original readers of *The Cathedral*, these were clearly appealing ideas. The novel's success stands as a corrective to the state of things in Britain. While in Protestant England in the 1840s, renewed Catholicism was condemned as a neo-medievalism, in Catholic France in the 1890s, a neo-medieval Catholicism is seen as a desirable good that can actually be realised. The novel itself leaves no doubt that it is not simply Catholicism, but Catholicism as a survival from the Middle Ages, that is valued. The novel's drama – to the extent that there is one – is not simply over Durtal's selection of the cloister, but the choice of an essentially medieval life over a modern one. Durtal's meditations make it clear that he seeks not simply to pursue the monastic life in modernity, but in some sense to be returned to a medieval way of being. Observing a choirboy at mass in the cathedral's crypt, Durtal reflects on the "willingness on the part of Our Lady to mould these little urchins dedicated to her service, to make them different to others, restoring them, in the middle of the nineteenth century, to the ardent chastity, the primitive fervour of the Middle Ages" (76). While Durtal has a great deal of trepidation about espousing the Benedictine Rule, there is no doubt that he believes this to be the highest thing he could do.

Hence Durtal, a fictional character, expresses the yearning to live as a medieval person. The chief means by which this might be possible is of course still

---

[2]   Huysmans, *The Cathedral*, 115.

theoretically available today: an individual may join a monastery, following a rule that originated in the early Middle Ages, perhaps even within a medieval building. Small numbers of men and women choose this life, thereby entering a life that has not changed in its essentials since the Middle Ages. But there are many less extreme ways of espousing a medieval self than this, which it is the purpose of this chapter to explore.

The example of Durtal is also a useful corrective to the broad assumption that still exists in the English-speaking world of reformed churches: there is no embarrassment about the Middle Ages in *The Cathedral*. Like most European countries, France had experienced iconoclastic damage to its medieval heritage, during both the Wars of Religion and the French Revolution and although there was not one single event to parallel the Dissolution of the monasteries in England, many French monastic houses were degraded before the Revolution. But with a long-standing Catholic tradition, France never had the overwhelming ideological basis for rejecting the Middle Ages that was laid down in Britain. Huysmans did not have to overcome centuries of anticatholicism in advancing a thesis that medievalism – in this case, a medievalising of the self – could be essentially *liberating*.

The novel is obviously in one sense extreme – not everyone responded to *fin-de-siècle* ennui by wishing to join a monastery. But in other ways it espouses quite reasonable preferences – such as that for medieval art over later art – and deals with common dilemmas – the relationship between the life of contemplation and the life of action in the world. Who would really want to "live medievally"? Is it really possible to find solutions to the problems of living in modernity, in medievalism? This chapter examines these questions, thinking in particular about whether medievalism can ever truly be liberating. A great deal of the work in medievalism studies over the past three decades has focused on the ideological character of medievalism, very often finding medievalism to be an agent of one or another form of repression. Hence, medievalism is often seen as the work of colonists seeking to imprint the past of an old country on a colonised land; it is the work of the rich, seeking to keep the poor in their place; it is the work of modern philanthropists who unwittingly deny coevalness to other nations; it involves the traumatic destruction of rich authenticity and the substitution of the empty hyperrealities of modern capitalism.

Yet every summer in Europe and North America, thousands of people choose to attend medieval-themed events. Around the world there are hundreds of reenactment groups whose members choose to spend part of their time in the guise or personae of medieval people.[3] Such people master various medieval techniques – for making clothing, for example, artefacts, and armour. Others undertake pilgrimages, thousands each year making their way, for example, to the medieval pilgrimage site, Santiago de Compostella in north-western Spain. For these reenactors, medievalism might be leisure. It might be spiritual pursuit. It might also

---

[3]   See for example the list at http://www.histrenact.co.uk/societies/medieval/societies.php.

be a paying concern. This chapter is about what Pugh and Weisl call "experiential medievalisms."[4]

Reenactment has only recently been taken seriously in the discipline of historical studies, which now considers it as a form of affective history.[5] Since the beginnings of modern reenactment in the counterculture of the 1960s, the practice has expanded so that while, at one end of a spectrum, it verges on "fantasy role-playing in its elastic appropriation of both the real and imagined past," it is also a serious pursuit which on another part of the spectrum is indistinguishable from education and closely tied to practices of archaeology.[6] In film and television, both drama and documentary have become reliant on reenactors, while the prevalence of living history in museums also extends the process by which something that began as a kind of anti-history is now thoroughly imbricated with more official practices of history. The fundamental question here is that of whether medievalism can ever appear in the opposite guise to that assumed in most medieval studies. Is there a liberatory medievalism?

Are We Medieval Yet? Towards Medievalist Society

The first reenactor was Don Quixote de la Mancha, the fictional knight of Cervantes' *The Adventures of Don Quixote* (1605, 1615; first English translation 1612). In his novel, Cervantes satirises the idea that the medieval past can be recreated. Don Quixote, his head filled with stories from romance, sets out to occupy the role of a medieval knight errant. His reenactment extends so far that, with comic inappropriateness, he sees inns as castles, peasant women as noble ladies, monks as felon knights. Nevertheless, it is occasionally clear that Don Quixote does not believe he is an actual knight in the medieval past; he understands rather that he is a reenactor of a kind, living in an age of iron, which it is his task to restore to a golden age.[7] But Don Quixote's fundamental misperceptions mean that this task is impossible: as the world around him for the most part refuses to join in his reenactment, the past can never be conjured up except through misrecognition. The knight fights giants, but everyone else sees they are windmills; he wears a golden helm that everyone knows to be a barber's basin.

The historical novel of a later period, by contrast, assumed that realism was possible and that the past could be envisioned in the pages of a book. The model established by Walter Scott's *Ivanhoe* (1819), Victor Hugo's *Notre Dame de Paris* (1831), and Edward Bulwer Lytton's *The Last of the Barons* (1843) was of extensively researched novels related by sententious and authoritative narrators who make it clear they speak from modernity. While pronouncing authoritatively on precisely

---

4 Pugh and Weisl, *Medievalisms*, 122.
5 See the foundational essays in a special issue of *Criticism* 46.3 in 2004, especially Agnew, "Introduction: What Is Reenactment?"; see also Agnew, "History's Affective Turn"; During, "Mimic Toil."
6 Agnew, "Introduction: What Is Reenactment?" 328.
7 See Part I, chapter 20. I have written about this at greater length in "Said in Jest: Who's Laughing at the Middle Ages (and When?)" *postmedieval* 5.2 (2014): 126–39.

how things were in twelfth-century England, fifteenth-century Paris, or fifteenth-century England, each narrator emphasises that the past is a place that cannot be visited, making narratorial intrusions to keep the reader aware of the irretrievable pastness of what is being read. Scott often deployed a spoof-antiquarian narrator who intervened between reader and text (as is the case in his second medievalist novel, *Quentin Durward* [1823]). In *Notre Dame de Paris*, Hugo's narrator will typically say to the reader such things as, "America had not yet been discovered," while Bulwer Lytton will underline historical distance with such statements as: "What we call Patriotism, in the high and catholic acceptation of the word, was little if at all understood in days when passion, pride, and interest were motives little softened by reflection and education ..."[8] The Middle Ages is necessarily a historically remote spectacle.

Nevertheless the effect of the real produced by such novels and their successors proposes the capacity to reconstruct the Middle Ages and hence in turn to *reenact* the period. When *Ivanhoe* reached the stage and the circus, people were then able to visit its world and in effect witness its Middle Ages. In 1839, the novel inspired the large-scale tournament reenactment at Eglinton. Through the later tradition of medieval tourism, and the inevitable inclusion of medieval scenes in the World's Fairs of the second half of the century (considered in chapter 2), people became habituated to the idea that medievalist spaces such as those of Pugin's Mediaeval Court could be visited. For some, an idea of "living medievally" arose. In the 1840s, the accusation of "medievalism" aimed at High Church Anglicanism and Anglo-Catholicism effectively proposed that some people were already medieval. Once that is said, it seemed to open the way to further explorations of ways in which modern people could be medieval. Carlyle, Disraeli, and Ruskin all in their own ways more or less explicitly propose some sort of return to the medieval self.

Jean-Baptiste de la Curne de Sainte-Palaye, whose work is as so often foundational here, wrote the enormously influential *Mémoires sur l'ancienne chevalerie*, initially as a series of works published in the 1740s which were then published together in 1751 and translated into English in 1784. As Lionel Gossman elucidates, chivalry was not, for Sainte-Palaye, a guide to conduct. Instead, Sainte-Palaye rendered chivalry in a fashion appropriate for the Enlightenment scholar. The fifth and last of his *mémoires* on chivalry, for example, "was designed to dispel any suspicion that he might value past times higher than his own." Sainte-Palaye reminded the reader that at the same time that chivalry flourished, so too did debauchery, brigandage and barbarism; his "standards and values remained resolutely those of the unheroic nobility of his own time, the new aristocracy of the monarchical state – urbanity, civilized behaviour, law and order, comfort, enlightenment and, latterly, the good of humanity."[9] Sainte-Palaye, Gossman concludes, "was neither a precocious romantic who somehow strayed into the wrong century nor was he a dyed-in-the-wool conservative still dreaming of the vanished glories of the old blood nobility and scornful of the new aristocracy" (279).

[8]   Bulwer Lytton, *The Last of the Barons*, 1:45.
[9]   See the account and penetrating critique in Gossman, *Medievalism and the Ideologies of the Enlightenment*, 273–96; quotations on 278.

Sainte-Palaye's work was enormously influential on ideas of the Middle Ages throughout Europe. The influence of his book on chivalry in particular was strong, especially in England and Scotland. Gossman claims that Edmund Gibbon's account of chivalry was "entirely based" on Sainte-Palaye's and the Frenchman's work on chivalry and popularisation of the medieval chronicler Jean Froissart was well known to the circle of British scholars that included Richard Hurd, Thomas Warton, Thomas Percy, Thomas Gray, and William Mason (330). In Germany, Sainte-Palaye's ideas came to Gottfried Herder and through him influenced the entire generation of German romantics (and, after them, Walter Scott) (331–32).

As Gossman notes, however, "The nineteenth century thinker or poet, whatever the class of society of the nation for which he spoke, was inevitably in a quite different relation to the Middle Ages from that of the thinker or poet of the Enlightenment" (332). One effect of this can be seen in a post-romantic immersion in the Middle Ages which the Enlightenment Sainte-Palaye would never have sanctioned (or perhaps even have understood). One early English text to engage with chivalry, and through it to present an idea of living medievally, was Kenelm Henry Digby's *The Broad Stone of Honour*, first published in 1822 with the subtitle "Rules for the Gentlemen of England" and again in an expanded version (soon after its author's conversion to Catholicism) in 1826–29 with the subtitle "The True Sense and Practice of Chivalry." Digby's central idea, repeated at ever increasing length, is the exemplary character of the romances of chivalry and their use-value as conduct books for the present. The key to the romances could be distilled into a single word: chivalry. Digby aimed "to shew that chivalry, in some form or other, is coeval with human society, and that it must continue to exist with it till the end of time," and that "under the influence of the Christian religion, it is infinitely ennobled ..." Chivalry itself "is only a name for that general spirit or state of mind which disposes men to heroic and generous actions, and keeps them conversant with all that is beautiful and sublime in the intellectual and moral world."[10] The principal technique of *The Broad Stone of Honour* is to retell stories of chivalry, for the most part quixotically unconcerned about any considerations of literary artifice which might compromise the romances' claims to mimesis. In Digby's hands even the most fanciful romances offer imitable behaviour; although, as he concedes, they are not to be taken as entirely realistic, they nevertheless express the religious feeling that induces good behaviour.

In presenting the idea that medieval chivalry can be adopted in the nineteenth century as a salve for particularly modern ills, Digby offers, albeit in an extreme and improbable form, the same kind of remedy that would later be proposed by Carlyle and Disraeli. Like them, Digby is deeply concerned by the problem of class relations. His book, he proposes, "is directed unto all noble princes, lords, and gentlemen, who delight in honour and in virtue, which are the true ornaments of gentle blood." Even in the first version of his work, Digby advanced a concern that many later writers would adopt: the problem of the middle classes. For Digby, as Mark Girouard points out, the gentleman and the peasant tended to know their

[10] Digby, *The Broad Stone of Honour* (1877, 1876), 1:108, 109.

places and appropriate behaviour. "[T]here is even a peculiar connection," Digby suggested, "a sympathy of feeling and affection, a kind of fellowship, which is instantly felt and recognized by both, between these [lower-class men] and the highest order, that of gentlemen." The problem lies elsewhere: "it is the middle which is the region of disorder and confusion and tempest. The natural extremes of high and low are serene and untroubled."[11] In this mode of medievalism, chivalry has been co-opted in the service of a normative nineteenth-century sense of hierarchy, an image which would then be reinforced by the aristocratic pageantry of the Eglinton Tournament.

Yet not all such returns to the medieval need be regarded as driven by conservative, anti-bourgeois nostalgia. Charles Dellheim has said that "it is assumed too readily that medievalism was simply a conservative revolt against modernity." Medievalism could also be a celebration of more libertarian virtues: such radicals as John Bright and Richard Cobden, Dellheim argues, invoked the end of feudality in calling for a repeal of Corn Laws. "If conservative medievalists were enraptured by a 'dream of order'," Dellheim writes, "their liberal counterparts were inspired by a vision of liberty." The spread of neo-gothic town halls in the north of England in the second half of the nineteenth century, for example, is not easily explained as an appeal to conservative ideas of feudalism. Buildings such as Manchester's town hall were built by middle-class civic leaders – precisely those self-made men decried proleptically by Digby – who "reinterpreted the symbolic meanings of Gothic to celebrate the values and achievements of liberal, industrial civilization."[12] The adoption of gothic by Manchester's leaders had less to do with *feudal* ideas of the Middle Ages than with the image of such free medieval cities as those of the Hanseatic League. Among Ford Madox Brown's famous murals in Manchester Town Hall is a depiction of the establishment of the Flemish weavers in Manchester – apparently as part of a myth of origins for Manchester's textiles trade – that clearly has more to do with mercantilism than deeds of arms.

In 1876–77, Digby published a compendious five-volume version of *The Broad Stone of Honour*. At the same time, the Manchester Town Hall was completed in Alfred Waterhouse's sumptuous neo-gothic style. Digby's book advocated a form of living medievally, using chivalry as exemplary of a good life, while the civic building implied a form of medieval practice: civic business was henceforth (and still is) conducted in elaborate neo-gothic halls. Such buildings as the Manchester Town Hall were built by and to a large extent for the newly enriched urban bourgeoisie: precisely that fraction excluded from the Digby version of chivalry. Why did the bourgeoisie, like conservative nobility, embrace the high medievalism of neo-gothic? For some there is a contradiction here, in the linkage between middle-class confidence and "submissiveness to the standards of the aristocratic class."[13]

[11] Digby, *Broad Stone of Honour* (1823), xxvii-viii, 16–17; see also Girouard, *The Return to Camelot*, 65.

[12] Dellheim, "Interpreting Victorian Medievalism," 41, 48, 49, 52. See, in the same collection, Waters, "Marxism, Medievalism and Popular Culture" which also influences my remarks here.

[13] Webb, "The Bradford Wool Exchange," 53.

The northern neo-gothic town halls might better be reinterpreted as attempting to wrest the medieval-chivalric vision away from Digby and his followers, in the direction of a middle-class reappropriation of what was (as Dellheim puts it) "a plastic language" (54). They are the result of an attempt to medievalise some aspects, at least, of modern society. The middle classes, excluded from an early romantic-aristocratic medievalism, now reappropriate it in a new idiom.

The northern town halls then stand for a confident modernity. The main tower of Manchester's town hall was visible for miles around, competing with but entirely distinct from the dozens of factory chimneys which surrounded it as the visible marker of the industrial wealth the town itself was built on. It was this tower rather than the relatively low-lying cathedral which visitors would have seen as they approached by road or stepped out of Manchester Central Railway station. The town hall allowed civic business to be transacted in medievalist surroundings, bringing beauty into the notoriously filthy, smoke-filled city. At the same time, that form of beauty stopped at the edge of the town hall. It was not envisaged that a whole city should be built that way. Waterhouse's commissions in Manchester meant that medievalism impinged only on the large outlines of life, as the transactions of commerce were registered in the Town Hall, legal matters enacted in the Assize Courts (Great Ducie St, 1859–64), education conducted at Owens College (Oxford Rd, 1869–98), and prisoners consigned to Strangeways (1868).[14] But there was no sense that life, in between the major events signalled by such buildings, should be "medievalised."

John Ruskin was explicitly critical of this. Addressing the manufacturers of Bradford who proposed to build an exchange in a gothic style, he said:

> I notice that among all the new buildings which cover your once wild hills, churches and schools are mixed in due, that is to say, large proportion, with your mills and mansions; and I notice also that the churches and schools are almost always Gothic, and the mansions and mills are never Gothic? Will you allow me to ask precisely the meaning of this? For, remember, it is peculiarly a modern phenomenon. When Gothic was invented, houses were Gothic as well as churches; and when the Italian style superseded the Gothic, churches were Italian as well as houses … But now you live under one school of architecture, and worship under another … am I to understand that you consider Gothic a pre-eminently sacred and beautiful mode of building, and which you think, like fine frankincense, should be mixed for the tabernacle only, and reserved for your religious services? For if this be the feeling, though it may seem at first as if it were graceful and reverent, you will find that, at the root of the matter, it signifies neither more nor less than that you have separated your religion from your life.

Ruskin concluded that "every great national architecture has been the result and

---

[14] See the image of the now destroyed Assize Courts at http://www.victorianweb.org/art/architecture/waterhouse/5.html.

exponent of a great national religion. You can't have bits of it here, bits there – you must have it everywhere, or nowhere."[15]

Bits of it here and bits there was precisely what the modern city wanted from medievalism. Inevitably, others of a more Ruskinian bent envisaged a more thoroughly medievalised society. In his 1890 work *News from Nowhere*, William Morris described a medievalist society both very distant from the conservative aristocratic Middle Ages and the more partial modern Middle Ages. Evidently, Morris believed in and even practised certain forms of return to the medieval: he thought medievalist architecture and furniture, and medieval patterns of behaviour, to be desirable. The extent to which *News from Nowhere* really prescribes a medievalised polity is debatable. Though it is often taken as a utopian text it is as much a melancholy elegy for the present as it is a utopian prescription for the future.

One of Morris's successors, however, was unequivocal about the benefits to modern society of a return to the medieval. Ralph Adams Cram's *Walled Towns* (1919) is nothing less than a manifesto for neo-medievalist society. Cram is best remembered today as a successful architect, the man behind the neo-gothic cathedral of St John the Divine in New York.[16] His route to medievalism was a well trodden one: in his father's library, he read Ruskin and Carlyle, and he later travelled to Europe, becoming interested in the Middle Ages and converting to High Church Anglicanism. He wrote medievalist verse dramas and attempted an Arthurian epic.[17] In later life between the wars, Cram was a writer and critic. Surveying the ruins of post-war Europe in his 1919 polemic, Cram proclaimed that there was no future in the modern way of industrialism and democracy, nor in the emergent communism of the Soviet bloc. Instead, it was the walled medieval town and the cloister that provided the example of a deindustrialised society based on renewed community.

Cram's conviction was based on an idiosyncratic reading of western history, which interlinked the periodic historical renewals of monasticism with the historical phases of social development. As the Roman empire lost its influence, the early monasteries also declined; with the Carolingian renaissance, monasteries regained ground. Now, in 1919, Cram suggests, the world faces "a new Dark Ages" and the threat of "new hordes of Huns and Vandals."[18] He stated:

> there is now, corporately, no evidence of anything but a general breakdown of ideals, and either an accelerating plunge into something a few degrees worse than barbarism, with the Dark Ages as its inevitable issue, or an equally fatal return to the altogether hopeless, indeed the pestilential, standards and methods of the fruition of modernism in the world-before-the-war. (23)

[15] Ruskin, "Traffic," 328, 332.
[16] On this cathedral and Cram's role in ensuring its Gothic character, see Emery, "Postcolonial Gothic."
[17] See Oberg, "Ralph Adams Cram: Last Knight of the Gothic Quest."
[18] Cram, *Walled Towns*, 17.

In response, Cram suggests, it is not his intention to outline a new utopia, before going on to do precisely that. He notes that in his time there has been a revival in monasticism. The curve of civilisation was on a downward trend, he argues, and it is now up to human civilisation to decide whether a new Dark Ages would be entered, or a new beginning (34). What Cram believed was about to take place was a new form of polity "in which the human family is made the unit." Monasticism would continue to exist, he suggested, but additionally, "there will be groups of natural families, father, mother and children, entering into a communal but not by any means 'communistic' life, within those Walled Towns they will create for themselves, in the midst of the world but not of it" (36). With the walled town as his template, Cram went on to describe in some detail how such communities might be set up. They would be places whose members would hold the same religious belief (it does not matter what the belief is, but it is important it be held in common), and live in a preindustrial, communitarian manner.

The influence of Morris and Ruskin on Cram's thinking is clear. Decrying the fact that "about half the working male population in Europe and America is engaged in producing or marketing things which add nothing to the virtue, the real welfare, or the joy in life of man" (42), Cram echoes Morris as well as the Ruskin of *The Seven Lamps of Architecture*. But his debt to these figures is largely suppressed. Morris's avowed socialism no longer accorded with Cram's vehement anti-Bolshevism and he emphasises instead what he calls the "sacramentalism" of his vision, seeing his walled communities as quasi-monastic institutions. There is some sleight of hand here; what he actually describes are religio-political communities which function along medievalist political lines, with gilds and elected authorities. There is no sense in which they are based on monasticism. While monasteries are models for walled communities of a kind, what Cram proposes is more extensive: a religious city-state.

Like many such nostrums for broken societies, even at its most fanciful Cram's work has moments of seductive clarity. Many early twenty-first century readers are susceptible to the charms of a vision of quiet civic harmony, an undemanding religion, cashless trade and a world powered by wind and water; many readers in the 1920s could remember a world that looked a little like that. At other moments, however, Cram's is a frightening dystopic vision. It is never made clear why the towns should be *walled*; for Cram it seems to be enough that medieval towns were walled, so their modern counterparts should be as well. He never mentions, but leaves to the imagination, a society in which it will be necessary to shut the gates from time to time against the barbarians who are inevitably at them. It is not difficult to see that, as he had outlined at the beginning of the book, Cram really does fear a new Dark Ages, in which it will be the lucky ones who are able to retreat behind their ramparts.

Detached from reality as the book might seem, Cram nevertheless apparently wrote out of a sense of conviction. And, though it is easy to see his work as one of the last dying exhalations of Victorian medievalism, it could just as easily be regarded as the first of a line of prescriptive texts that continue to appear down to the present day. In the United Kingdom, the Prime Minister David Cameron came to power in 2010 with a vision of what he called "the Big Society," which was largely based on the work of the theology lecturer turned political commentator, Phillip Blond, in his book *Red Tory*. While Blond is careful to avoid anything like even the veiled dystopianism of *Walled Towns*, and indeed tries to avoid the Middle Ages altogether, inevitably he looks back to an idealised past. Blond's heroes are paternal statesmen and thinkers (so long as they are practical rather than philosophical): "honourable statesmen like Disraeli and Gladstone"; William Cobbett, Thomas Carlyle and John Ruskin, and those "Anglican Tory gentry" who, in the eighteenth century, "defended the prosperity of the poor, their education and even their religious enthusiasm against the modish Whig aristocrats."[19]

Blond is not specifically medievalist in this book but there is a strong medievalist heritage in the list of figures he coopts for a benign conservatism. There is certainly a vision of a Merrie England in both Blond's work and Cameron's articulation of it: that place of cooperation and harmony that always existed a little way in the past. Like a long line of conservative commentators going back to Disraeli and Carlyle, Blond recognises the problems created by industrialism. Unlike them, he also has to negotiate the problems posed by *post*-industrialism. His response, though it carefully evades the nostalgia of Ruskin and Morris, is recognisably in a medievalist lineage: with Disraeli and Carlyle, Blond does not want to reverse time by saying that industrialism should not have happened. He is, rather, saying all would be well if we had what we have, and what we used to have as well: a smaller and more caring capitalism, with more things run by cooperatives. These cooperatives – the department store chain John Lewis, with its share-owning employees, is often held up as a model – would be run by their own stakeholders: schools set up by parents, for example.

In a perceptive review of the book Jonathan Raban singles out Blond's brief but approving mention of G. K. Chesterton, Hilaire Belloc and the Catholic Distributist League, pointing to the links between the League and the Arts and Crafts movement. In Chesterton's and Belloc's hands, medievalism took a distinctly dystopic turn, as both were admirers of Mussolini's Italy. Blond's influence on the current leader of the British Conservative Party, Raban argues, means that a central element of what the party currently stands for emerges from "Chesterton's and Belloc's homesickness for a rural and small-town life that never existed outside their Arcadian dream of Merrie England."[20] To the extent that this is a medievalist vision, it involves that loosely defined Middle Ages that consists of everything up until the industrial revolution. "In the ancient and medieval worlds," as Blond writes, "and still to some extent during the eighteenth-century enlightenment, politics and education spun round in a virtuous circle."[21] In Prime Minister Cameron's thinking, the Big Society involves the formation of local communities which take over responsibilities from central government and which recreate that virtuous circle. In this respect, "Big Society" is an obvious misnomer; what is imagined is, rather, a series of very small societies: villages and shires in a vision of merrie harmony.

[19] Blond, *Red Tory*, 169, 28.
[20] Raban, "Crankish."
[21] Blond, *Red Tory*, 173.

A very different kind of view of society as neomedievalist is that found in international relations theory. The seminal text in this field, Hedley Bull's *The Anarchical Society: A Study of Order in World Politics* (1977), argued that as traditional nation-state organisation declines, the possibility of a post-national world with a more medieval appearance and organisation is manifested. For Bruce Holsinger, this is a decidedly dystopic view: "neomedievalism is a creation of the modern, Cold War and post-Cold War university. As such, its fate during the War on Terror gives us a frightening lens on to the ultimate co-optability of academic theorizing into a regressive and destructive political culture."[22] More recently, the idea that neomedievalism might offer an analogy for contemporary global organisation has been revived and refined by Jörg Friedrichs, in the context of post-Cold War globalisation. For Friedrichs, the Middle Ages is emblematic of a world system in which allegiances are not necessarily primarily to states, but are more dispersed. In a world in which "the primacy of political relations between sovereign nation-states may be coming to an end," Friedrichs envisages "a less homogeneous configuration" which is analogous with the appearance of western Europe in the eleventh and twelfth centuries.[23]

Friedrichs is certainly not afraid of the Middle Ages, which presented "a world which was neither anarchic nor organized around one discursive and organizational centre." The period "knew major crises," of course, "but the system indisputably went along for centuries" (481). Finally, the concept of a new Middle Ages seems for him to be neither a desirable good nor an evil to be avoided, but a model, just as it was for Bull. As John Ganim explains: "One of the ironies of Bull's reputation as the founder of a 'new Medievalism' is that he sketched the possibility of a new Middle Ages as one of several possible historical solutions to his larger goal, which was the reform of the international order of nation states into something more like a society than like a structure or a game."[24] Friedrichs hopes that "the neomedieval analogy will prove to be a creative and innovative device for further reflections about order in the post-international world." (493). What is less clear, however, is what the model is *for*: if it is not a polity we should be aiming to recreate (and Friedrichs is clear that it is not) then the model seems to be simply heuristic, but without any specific application.

Again and again, then, social commentators of various kinds go not to classical civilisation or even late antique and early medieval civilisation but to the period from the twelfth century to the fourteenth which has so persistently functioned as our cultural and political "other" since the late eighteenth century. In doing so, they draw on one or other of the two great strands of thinking about medievalism, at will. Digby's chivalric ideals are thoroughly invested in a romantic Middle Ages, one which can scarcely envisage any other guise for the period. But several of these versions of the Middle Ages in fact keep the two basic kinds in tension. Hence, Cram's walled cities offer an idealised vision of medieval, preindustrial city states, which become romantic islands in a sea of barbarism. It is also clear that, particu-

[22] Holsinger, *Neomedievalism*, 81.
[23] Friedrichs, "The Meaning of New Medievalism," 482.
[24] Ganim, "Cosmopolitanism, Sovereignty, and Medievalism."

larly in the romantic guise, these Middle Ages are taken in their most extended form, that is right up until the industrial revolution. This version of the Middle Ages – the Blond/Cameron version – wants to appeal to the medieval self in all of us: although we live in industrialised late-capitalist society, deep down (so this theory runs) we would all be better off if we cultivated the guildsman, the peasant, the merchant, the kindly feudal lord, that lies within us all.

Curiously, no one noticed that many people were already doing just that.

The Medievalist Self

Michael Crichton's novel *Timeline* (1999) plays with the ultimate fantasy of medievalist reenactment via a time-travel narrative. A group of present-day university archaeologists investigating a site in southwestern France travel back to 1357. One of them, André Marek, has steeped himself in medieval languages and military skills so that he is able to pass for a real medieval person. When the others return to the present at the end of the novel Marek, who has fallen in love in the fourteenth century, stays behind. The novel's last scene has the other characters, back in the present day, finding his medieval grave and its epitaph, which confirms that he married and went on to lead a good and noble life in the fourteenth century.

Marek is thereby confirmed as the heroic, empowered geek (the figure who lies behind all superheroes). He does such pointless things as learning dead languages and making clothes from past times – only to find that these are actually useful pursuits and help him to get the girl. The novel values scholarship, but only as an activity that seeks to capture authentic origins in such a way that it undoes itself. The best scholarship produces not knowledge about its object, but the very object itself in all its plenitude. There is an exact analogy with Crichton's better known novel *Jurassic Park*, in which the science produces real dinosaurs rather than more writing about dinosaurs. The best scholar becomes the object of inquiry: Marek transforms himself from scholarly reenactor to actual chivalric knight. Reenactment, this novel assumes, is a thinly disguised wish-fulfilment fantasy. Deep down, all reenactors, surely, want to go back to the Middle Ages in a time machine? And scholars want to reenact. Why theorise about dinosaurs if you could grow the real thing? Why speculate about courtly love if you could fall in love with a fourteenth-century person?

All over the world, people are reenacting aspects of the Middle Ages and trying to recreate medieval spaces around themselves. The Château de Guédelon in northern Burgundy has already been described (in chapter 3). In the Cévennes mountains in the *département* of Gard in southern France, "Les Fous de la Sogne" are slowly building themselves a medieval village on some terraces above the road near the village of Aujac.[25] Theirs is an unashamedly amateur and voluntary effort with an emphasis on communitarianism and a fraction of the resources visible in the Château de Guédelon. Medieval tournaments, fairs and building projects all

[25] See http://cevennes.unblog.fr/.

flourish around the world, including many places which did not actually have a Middle Ages.

Reenactment is of course very easy to mock. In his installation *Knights (and other dreams)*, the Bulgarian video artist Nedko Solakov depicts himself in a series of films attempting various activities while dressed in a full suit of plate armour. He takes part in a rather farcical reenactment of the fifteenth-century battle of Varna and, more ludicrously, fulfils a desire to be the drummer in a jazz band (while wearing armour). Another film shows the results of his attempts to launch from his gauntleted wrist, not a falcon but a toy helicopter.[26] Each film points to the absurdity of trying to negotiate the twenty-first century while wearing a full suit of plate armour. In the film of the helicopter launch, Solakov eventually, after yet another failure, bends down to retrieve the toy, only to find that the suit doesn't allow him. He straightens and draws his sword to pick it up that way. Full medieval armour and modern toys will not mix, just as jazz drumming is not best served by late-medieval armour. Solakov's critique is a gentle one and largely directed at himself; as his accompanying materials make clear, it is his own reverie of knighthood that he satirises in *Knights (and other dreams)*.

The suspicion, of course, is of long standing. As Carolyn Dinshaw writes, "Amateur medievalists are routinely derided – by historically minded scholars or even by the general public, under the sway of modernist ideals of historical expertise – as merely nostalgic, naively, uncritically, and irresponsibly yearning for an idealized past as escape from a present felt to be dismal and unpromising."[27] At one time the International Congress on Medieval Studies at Kalamazoo tried to underline the divide by asking the Society for Creative Anachronism (SCA) not to participate in the conference.[28]

The SCA is the best known and for a long time dominant force in reenactment of a specifically medievalist variety. This form of reenactment can be traced back to the founding of the SCA in countercultural Berkeley in 1966. It avowedly began with the model of the Eglinton Tournament in view, somewhat ironically given the latter's association with conservative aristocrats. Two years after its founding, the SCA was incorporated as a non-profit educational organisation and today it claims around 30,000 members and remains an umbrella organisation for hundreds of reenactor groups.[29]

Wendy Erisman characterises the SCA's membership as tending to be middle-class, well educated, affluent, predominantly white, with an even gender balance. On her slightly anecdotal evidence, political attitudes tend to be liberal.[30] The

---

[26] Viewed at dOCUMENTA 13 in Kassel, Germany, September 2012. Some detail can be found at nedkosolakov.net

[27] Dinshaw, *How Soon is Now?*, 34.

[28] Cramer, *Medieval Fantasy as Performance*, 28.

[29] Cramer, *Medieval Fantasy as Performance*, 1–5; on the SCA more broadly see also de Groot, *Consuming History*, 119–22.

[30] Erisman, "Forward into the Past: The Poetics and Politics of Community in Two Historical Re-Creation Groups," 44. By contrast Cramer says that the SCA has become more conservative over the years – though he does concur with Erisman in seeing "a thriving gay community in the SCA." *Medieval Fantasy as Performance*, 107.

origins of the SCA in countercultural California in the 1960s, when Tolkien's *Lord of the Rings* was the bible of American campuses, point to the pivotal role of fantasy literature. Several authors of science fiction and fantasy were among the society's prime movers; one was Marion Zimmer Bradley, later the noted author of the Arthurianist fantasy, *The Mists of Avalon* (1982). Erisman locates the SCA as the inheritor of the *fin-de-siècle* American antimodernism charted by Jackson Lears. She notes that one of the early tournaments in the SCA's history was held specifically as a protest against modernity, and says that "This desire to conquer the incivility and lack of caring of the modern world, to find a better life through ideals of chivalry, courtesy, and honor, is known in the SCA as 'The Dream.'"[31]

The SCA, however, has never been closely involved in reenacting actual events. Rather, it is concerned with events that *could have* happened; in a parallel fashion, the SCA's world map divides up the known world into a slightly skewed, medievalised version. The SCA is not concerned with a Middle Ages that actually *was* so much as one that might have been and in this way it is recognisably in a lineage going back through Tolkien to William Morris's prose romances of the 1890s.[32] Inevitably, the success of the SCA has provoked a different kind of movement, one consisting of hundreds of medieval reenactment societies across Europe, North America, and Australia which are less concerned with the fantasy aspect than with the reenactment and commemoration of actual events. Such groups often demand a higher level of historical verisimilitude than the SCA and are often more directly involved in living history and archaeology.[33] At the grassroots level, a reenactment society might consist of a dozen or so members, focused on a small town or village and conceiving of their grouping as, for example, the retinue of a local lord. Such groups may in turn be affiliated to a larger organisation: in the UK, the Wars of the Roses Federation claims to represent around thirty-five smaller groups.[34] Similar arrangements exist for earlier medieval periods; in the UK, The Vikings, founded in 1971, claims pre-eminence in the period.

One aspect that is common to both SCA and more recent reenactment groups, nevertheless, is the invention of a persona. In the SCA, the creation of a medievalised self – not someone who actually lived, but someone who might have done – is crucial, as the SCA's own guide, *The Known World Handbook*, explains:

> Choosing a persona – deciding who to be – is the single most important process of your first year among us. The persona you choose will be the person you would wish to have been, had you lived sometime between 476 and 1600 C.E. It can be as simple as your SCA name and the time and place of some of your garb, or as complex as a complete role encom-

---

[31] Erisman, "Forward into the Past," 89. Lears, *No Place of Grace.*

[32] On the distinction between "reenactment" and "recreation," see Cramer, *Medieval Fantasy as Performance*, 5–6.

[33] These are not of course exclusively medievalist – in the US, the Civil War period is particularly attractive to reenactors, and in the UK, Sealed Knot is a well known group involved in reenactments of the English civil war. See further De Groot, *Consuming History*, ch. 7.

[34] http://www.et-tu.com/wotrf1/cgi-bin/index.cgi. Accessed 12 June 2012.

passing factors as diverse as deportment, use of language, manners, pursuits, weapons systems, and a complete autobiography – all that goes into creating a new self.[35]

Likewise, in reenactment groups, the invented persona remains important. In a survey of reenactors conducted for this book, some respondents summarised their personae in very general terms: "rich viking lady"; "Widow of a local thegn with small land holding." Many others, however, were more elaborate:

Gyrth Albrechtsohn: an English thegn of some wealth, has proven himself as a warrior and now owns land in the Lincolnshire area. Responsible for a small village of some eight extended families, who work the land and pay their taxes. Also have personal retinue of eight *huscarls* (warrior/body-guards).

I am a *huscarl* and fur trader to my *jarl*. I came from a small village in Farham in Denmark. As a second son I would not get the family farm on my father's death so in my early years I travelled the world trading and raiding. Hence I have some items from as far away as Vinland (fur) and Iceland (my hammer), to silk from Byzantium. I have now settled down and have a small farmstead near my *jarl*.

I am an Ottoman Lady of minor nobility living in Istanbul. Even though the majority of the population is Muslim, I am Christian. I'm married to a prominent and respected yüksek mühendis (degree'd engineer,) who is active in renovating the city. We have one child, a daughter. I have an interest in the arts, horses and hounds, and my stable has several renowned mares.

Rainvaeg of Tunendune, daughter of Aethelwold, is the wife of *hundredealdor* Wulfmaer of Tunendune. She is renowned for her embroideries of garments, hangings and ecclesiastical pieces.

Gender is not necessarily restrictive:

I have two personas: as a woman I portray a camp follower in the Wars of the Roses. I also cross-dress to be a billman in the Lancastrian army.

Some female reenactors specifically seek out groups which allow combat by women. A very small minority of those surveyed denied any interest in personae. One respondent, who had been involved for forty-six years, said:

I haven't adopted any personas. To me personas are a fantasy mechanism that I am not interested in. I am me, and simply participate in a variety of time period reenactments (generally from the Dark Ages to Renaissance) of both formal and informal structure. I prefer participating in a participant-

---

[35] Fisher, "Choosing a Persona," qtd in Erisman, "Forward into the Past," 99. On persona see further Cramer, *Medieval Fantasy as Performance*, 57–63.

only activity as opposed to a spectator-focused activity, and only do the
latter if it provides exceptional opportunities of participation or is educa-
tionally structured for the spectators. I dislike being an entertainer for entertainment's sake.

There are also those who resist the persona even within the SCA. It is clear nevertheless that for reenactors of all kinds the persona, and the idea of inhabiting a
second self drawn from medieval history, is central.

While this is often loosely characterised as a form of escapism, it is important
to note that reenactors draw a clear line between the imagined medieval persona
and their everyday selves and tend not to see much potential for full identification
with their period. Members of reenactment groups (as opposed to SCA members)
tend not to cite fantasy fiction as a great influence and instead they respect the
boundary between medieval and modern, in general expressing high awareness
of the shortcomings of the Middle Ages as a time in which to live. In the survey,
reenactors were asked whether they found any aspects of medieval life superior to
practices of the present day, and conversely which aspects of the present day they
found inferior to the Middle Ages. While some respondents referred approvingly
to the simpler life of the Middle Ages, the slower pace, the sense of community,
and the absence of mobile phones and the internet, all respondents nevertheless routinely stated that there was nothing preferable about life in the Middle
Ages. They repeatedly pointed to modern health and medicine as making the
present day a preferable place in which to be. "Life was hard for the majority of
people," said one, "and it was cheap. Life expectancy was not high, rich people had
more rights than poor." "I don't think I'd be cut out for famine, body parasites,
epidemic, or even just life without shampoo or toothpaste," wrote one UK-based
reenactor with twenty-two years' experience. And as another respondent bluntly
put it, "during the medieval period I would not have survived. I am diabetic with
poor eyesight."

Indeed, despite their obvious attachment to a period in the past, the reenactors'
sense of history is often overtly progressivist and presentist. In response to the
question inviting them to reflect on the aspects of their past period they found
inferior to the present day, reenactors routinely emphasised the superiority of the
present. One who focuses on the mid-fifteenth century replied, "Almost all [aspects
of the past are inferior] from a technological and scientific point of view but that
would be the case with any period other than the present." Another responded,
"Pretty much everything [would have been inferior in the Middle Ages]. We have
never had life so easy (not that that is necessarily a good thing)." Again and again,
respondents noted better medical science and hygiene as superior aspects of the
present day, and stated that medieval daily life would have been very hard. One
reenactor responded to the question about whether any aspect of the Middle Ages
was superior to the present day by saying, "None! You would have to be nuts
to want to really live back then!" On the superior aspects of the present day, he
added: "Life expectancy! Work-life balance. Diet: who wants to live without coffee,
chocolate and potatoes cooked in so many ways?"

This last response, from someone who clearly has a well developed sense of things in the present day that he finds attractive and would not give up, was from a Viking reenactor with twenty-seven years' experience. His and other responses suggest that while reenactment is obviously a deeply affective form of behaviour, there are sharply defined limits to reenactors' identification with the object. Carolyn Dinshaw, in her revalorising of the activities of the amateur, wishes to bring nostalgia back into the centre: "Recent work on medievalism," she says, "has undertaken to make nostalgia a subtle and complex instrument of historical and cultural analysis – rather than the punitive bludgeon that it has been – by demonstrating its complexities and not shying away from paradox or conceptual incoherence."[36] But what we see among the reenactors is a shying away from nostalgia altogether. They tend not to be relativists but historical absolutists: in their view, what we would see today as a hard life would have been experienced in the Middle Ages as a hard life. Far from over-identifying with the object of their study, in very many cases reenactors have a more intellectual and rational basis for what they are doing.

In line with this, while many of them are autodidacts, they are generally committed to learning more about their period. Respondents cited a range of sources they used to learn more about their periods. While they might originally have become aware of the Middle Ages because of a film, experienced reenactors tend to reject feature film and fiction as sources in favour of archives, museums, academic histories, university websites and (often with reservation) television documentaries. In turn, these respondents often gave, as the most rewarding aspect of reenactment, entertaining and talking to the public. A few are led to more mainstream scholarship as a result of their activities: one woman in an American city, with twenty years' experience as a reenactor, wrote: "I never went to college, yet here I am writing major research papers, being judged by my peers, doing basically experiential archaeology ... for the fun of it!"[37]

Far from collapsing subject into object, a large number of reenactors state that, in effect, the Middle Ages has become more strongly marked as a field of inquiry through their participation.

> I have gained a greater understanding of the conflicts of the time and the changing powers through the era. Also, by living amongst the environment, a further insight into how the people of the time actually lived. What they wore, the foods they ate and the resources available to them.

The period is "Much more complex [than I had thought]," wrote another; "arts and religion [were] very important; [there was] much more international trade than I at first thought." Another spoke of having gained "far more respect for [medieval peoples'] work, especially in works of art and literature." While several respondents did not feel their views of the Middle Ages had changed as a result of their

---

[36] *How Soon is Now?*, 35.
[37] Cramer also notes the convergence of SCA activity with academic scholarship. *Medieval Fantasy as Performance*, 28.

activities, this sense of a deepened knowledge was the more typical response. As one defiantly said in this context:

> There is so much more to the period than people think, looking at the earlier Saxon/Viking craftsmanship, jewellery, their trade links with other countries, the discovery and settlement of areas and foundation of other countries. All this proves there was nothing dark about this period.

For many reenactors, of course, the primary purpose of joining a historical reenactment group is simply leisure. Erisman argues of the SCA that membership of it has "far more to do with a longing for community than with a desire to actually experience the past" ("Forward into the Past," 178). Some of the survey respondents spoke of a love of camping and communal weekends away. For others, it is a family activity. A few had met their partners through reenactment. Some had become involved because their children were interested; in other cases, children follow parents into reenactment.

Even more often (for both men and women) it is combat that draws them to reenactment and to their specific periods. About a quarter of all survey respondents, some of them women, emphasised the part that combat plays; one had specifically sought a group that allowed full contact combat for women. Combat is integral to medievalist reenactment and has been since the Eglinton Tournament. While scenes of everyday life have taken their place in living history, battle reenactments have always been central. Both Cramer and Erisman note the preoccupation with combat in the SCA, an organisation in which the "kings" gain their positions through winning combat. Erisman overtly criticises the society's "obsession with rank and hierarchy" which, being based on performance in combat, leads to male dominance ("Forward into the Past," 32).

What both Erisman and Cramer miss is the inevitability of this obsession. It is notable that among reenactors everyone chooses a knight, earl, a prominent viking, a noble lady or an ecclesiastic for their personae. Few adopt the personae of Robin the miller or Wamba the swineherd (still less Alice the peasant's wife). There would be obvious limitations for anyone who did so.

There are some people nevertheless who conceive of a modern existence in explicitly medieval terms, taking the medieval in a liberatory sense. Adina Hamilton has discussed the case of the Crossroads Medieval Village Co-Operative, an enterprise registered as a co-operative in New South Wales, Australia, in 1992.[38] At the time Hamilton was writing in 2005, Crossroads was a collective planning "to build a medieval village on our property at Yass, New South Wales, Australia." This was to include accommodation for sixty people, a replica of a small French castle and "A residential subdivision with a medieval theme." But it was also to establish "A permaculture farm featuring old animal breeds and plant varieties," so that Crossroads involved a convergence of medievalism with ideas of equality and ecology via permaculture (216). In 2013 it is clear that progress has been slow though some building has taken place. A community has been established and

---

[38] Hamilton, "A New Sort of Castle in the Air."

future plans still include the replica castle and village, with a view to recreating the appearance of the period 1400–30.[39]

Certain obvious questions suggest themselves. Why, in rural Australia, need a commune be based on the French province of Berri in the early fifteenth century? Why imitate medieval European buildings under the hot sun of Australia? It is possible to imagine models of community that might be better adjusted to modern Australian conditions than medieval feudalism. An Asian Buddhist monastery (though it would pose problems of gender) might seem more immediately available and climatically appropriate. But as Hamilton suggests, "If ... some contemporary popular medievalism mediates its understanding of the medieval past through the (re-)creation or use of isolated physical or literary objects, rather than a coherently historicized view of the Middle Ages, this does not mean these understandings are themselves incoherent, isolated or fragmented" (218). The medieval period confers coherence on the project as a whole, making it broadly intelligible. It is, apparently, the medieval model that provides the most intelligible and easily decoded template in modern, postcolonial Australia.

This intelligibility is also at work in such medievalist community events as the fair. Colchester, in Essex, boasts an annual "fayre" which takes place each June. Its origins lie with a "History Fayre" which first took place in 1989 to mark the 800th anniversary of the granting of the town's charter. The fayre, which is based on the period of the fifteenth and sixteenth centuries, continued through the 1990s, then became the Oyster Fayre in 2003. In early June 2012, it took place as the tenth annual Colchester Medieval Festival and Oyster Fayre Market.[40]

The Colchester Medieval Festival may well be one of the biggest and best established of such events but it is only one of many that occur every summer across the UK and Europe. A small market already mentioned in chapter 1, in the Cantabrian town of Cabezón de la Sal, is typical of the smaller versions in that while it is advertised as "medieval" its medievalness is actually minimal and signalled chiefly in some decorative touches added to a market which otherwise does precisely the same things as the regular Saturday market in the same town.

Colchester's market appears to offer, by contrast, a strong commitment to reproducing aspects of the Middle Ages and doing so with some authenticity. An archery contest, for example, is clearly based on tales of Robin Hood. Entry conditions are stringent: competitors must use the English longbow and must be members either of an archery club or a medieval reenactment society. They must be costumed in clothing of the period from the fourteenth to the sixteenth century, will be docked points for inauthentic materials, and are requested to wear contact lenses rather than glasses: "Our aim is for authenticity and the public has the right to expect you to look the part."[41]

There are also numerous traders in Colchester. Some stalls reproduce an image of medieval trade: it is possible to buy furniture, musical instruments, and of course

---

[39] http://crossroads.org.au/the-future/.

[40] http://www.oysterfayre.flyer.co.uk/billoffayre.html.

[41] "English Longbow Competition Registration Form," at http://www.oysterfayre.flyer. co.uk/Archersbookingform2012.pdf. Accessed 11 June 2012.

weaponry. For others, the Middle Ages supplies a theme: jewellery in a Viking or otherwise medieval style, for example. Many of the stalls, however, have little or nothing to do with the Middle Ages but represent the kind of thing that accretes around the modern medieval: pottery and ceramics (not necessarily reflecting medieval designs); tarot card readings; "esoteric goods"; fossils and gemstones; olives; homemade fudges, all of it less Middle Age than New Age.

That the organisers of a festival that asks its archers to wear contact lenses are inclusive when it comes to herbs, crystals, and "pagan goods" suggests that something other than medievalist authenticity is at stake. Ralph Adams Cram's medievalist utopia, similarly, is reminiscent of actual practice which Cram might have observed in those sects which, like the Pennsylvania Amish, have withdrawn from the capitalist world. What is being pursued here in the guise of medievalism is, once again, simply preindustrialism. Or rather, the Middle Ages is imagined in a capacious form as running right up to the industrial revolution. A friend of mine, invited to a medievally-themed wedding, objected that he did not have any medieval dress; it was suggested that he must be able to find a shirt with a grandfather collar. Even a bathrobe might signal medievalness, as Carolyn Dinshaw notes.[42] The Colchester fayre is given coherence by the template of the fourteenth and fifteenth centuries, just as Cram creates a late medieval world. But the specific yearning in Colchester as in Cram is not so much for the medieval as for a world powered by wind- and watermills. Cram himself makes it clear that his own model for a medievalist society was his childhood. "Les Fous de la Sogne" are building a medieval village which, in its appearance so far, could just as easily be thought of as a sixteenth-, seventeenth- or eighteenth-century village. The key to it is not really anything very obviously medieval, so much as its evident pre-industrial non-modernity. Back in 1919, Cram drew on living memory; for today's enthusiasts at the medieval fayre, it is more likely to be a memory of the world of their grandparents.

More than any other form of medievalism, experiential medievalisms underline the extent to which the Middle Ages is the convenient other to wherever and whenever we happen to be. The only instances of pure identification with the medievalist self happen in fiction. *Timeline* presents a Middle Ages with many grotesque aspects but its romance plot enables Marek and his band to defeat these various threats in order to create for him a romantic Middle Ages in which he marries the heiress and settles down to a life of chivalric virtue.

For everyone else, negotiations with medievalist selfhood involve the dialectical tension of the gothic-grotesque and the romantic. For reenactors, as the results of the survey repeatedly showed, their use of the Middle Ages involves investment in the attractive elements of a romantic Middle Ages (arts and crafts, rules-based combat, good conduct) with the tacit acknowledgement that, as a period, the Middle Ages was fundamentally gothic and not a place where anyone would really want to be. The popular success of the fantasy-oriented SCA and the more

---

[42] See her *How Soon is Now?*, ix–xii.

historically aware reenactment societies suggests, however, a genuinely liberatory possibility for medievalism of this kind. The terms in which reenactors speak about their involvement generally suggests (as many of them affirmed) a weekend hobby, in which winters are spent working on kit and summers on reenacting. The societies clearly offer communities of a kind that might once have been supplied by a church or a workplace-related group. In the US the SCA has every appearance of a form of secular religion.

There has often been a relationship of mutual distrust between academe and reenactment groups, with academics often unwilling to acknowledge the alternative and amateur routes to knowledge represented by reenactment. Yet standards of imitation and reenactment have risen in the past thirty years and are now supported by, for example, professional makers of armour: Medieval Weaponry in the north-west of England, or the Knight Shop in North Wales. This brings in turn a convergence between reenactment, drama, documentary and the academic world. Makers of film and television now have access to readymade extras who might know more about period detail than they do, and on whom they have come to rely. The academic expert now must share space with autodidacts.

In 170 years since the first great modern tournament at Eglinton there has been a tendency to think of participants as victims of the kind of renewed feudalist ideology promoted by Walter Scott and those Victorian adherents of order who invoked chivalry against a world of advancing technology and working-class rebellion. Yet for many today, it is clear, reenactment is less the conscious or unconscious promotion of a comforting archaic ideology than an ensemble of techniques of the self, whereby individuals fashion alternative selves, continuous with, perhaps regarded as truer than, the selves that go to work in an office each day or run a household. In their different ways, the SCA and reenactment groups now offer forms of association taking the place which might once have been filled by activities sponsored by trade unions, churches, and sports clubs. (Indeed, combat-focused reenactment is itself a kind of sports club.)

Experiential medievalisms, therefore, suggest that a model which is focused on the repressive character of medievalism is outmoded, and even a conceptual model such as that which counterposes "repressive" and "liberatory" medievalisms misses the point: medievalism is one aspect of the way in which, today, a popular turn to history affords individuals a form of self-fashioning that lies outside traditional structures of value.

III
HISTORY AND DISCIPLINE

5

Wemmick's Castle: The Limits of Medievalism

I N THE FIRST two parts of this book, I have made various claims about the
reach and impact of medievalism in a range of contexts, with a particular focus
on the British. I have discussed the way in which medievalism can be traced
back to the immediate post-medieval period itself, as a product of the invention
of the Middle Ages in the sixteenth century. Its major phase in Europe is inex-
tricably associated with the Medieval Revival that began after the middle of the
eighteenth century. In Germany, for example, at the height of the Enlightenment
with its neoclassical impulses, a fresh interest in medievalism was a vital force
behind romanticism. In France, the work of the medievalist Jean-Baptiste de La
Curne de Sainte-Palaye introduced a strand of medieval studies in the time of the
eighteenth-century *philosophes*; in turn, romanticism became the most dynamic
literary movement in Britain of the late eighteenth century and the early nineteenth. As a result, cultural medievalism became a powerful emergent force in the
late eighteenth century, alongside the dominant neoclassicism.

In Britain, romanticism was a transforming force in literature. While literary
medievalism in Britain waned with the fading of the gothic novel in the 1820s and
the deaths of most of the major Romantic poets, medievalism then shifted into
new cultural realms, becoming particularly dominant, for example, in architecture
from the 1840s and making a significant mark in the visual arts in the second
half of the century. Britain led in gothic revivalism but it was taken up in France
with the establishment of the Commission des Monuments Historiques in 1837
and also became a force in post-Napoleonic Germany, taking root across Europe
more generally in the second half of the nineteenth century. In addition, Britain's
colonies – especially India and Australia – were strongly marked by neo-gothic
architecture while America, though it had shaken off colonialism, adopted neo-
gothic anyway.

As I have suggested, the entry into the English language of the adjective and
noun "medieval" and "medievalism," in about 1817 and 1844 respectively, marked
different phases in the understanding of the Middle Ages. The first word, after half
a century or so of medieval revivalism, signalled an attempt to shift away from a
"gothic" Middle Ages and to reconceive the period in more scholarly and objective

terms. The advent of the second word in the 1840s, initially as a term of abuse, signalled, in turn, the inevitable return of that gothic repressed, as the original negative associations of the Middle Ages were energetically redeployed (in, for example, British anti-Catholicism in the 1840s). Yet at the same time, thinkers conservative and radical alike looked back in hope to the medieval period for solutions to contemporary problems.

Towards the end of the century, there was a decisive split as "medieval studies," a formal discipline of study, was consolidated in European universities. What was excluded by medieval studies – which encompassed all such postmedieval phenomena as neo-gothic – would later be redescribed as medievalism and later still, constituted as part of a new "medievalism studies."

So far, the book has tended to suggest that medievalism is a very broad and pervasive phenomenon, found in most places at many different epochs. The very idea of the Middle Ages itself produces medievalism. Evidently, there was also an especially marked and self-conscious phase of medievalism in the late eighteenth century, peaking in the 1850s to the 1870s.

The purpose of this chapter is a simple one. It is to reexamine this standard account in order to describe the *limits* of medievalism. Specifically, I am interested here in two things. One is the relation of *medievalism* to a broader interest in history. It is hard to doubt that nineteenth-century architecture fell under the influence of neo-medieval forms and it is clear that medievalism was expressed in various other forms of cultural production. But is the impact of medievalism in, for example, the novel, poetry, or visual arts comparable with its impact on architecture? This leads to my second concern, the relation of medievalism to what, in a given culture at a given time, is taken for *canonical* art. In discussing what I think to be dominant cultural forms and productions at a given time, I do not intend to refer to inherent cultural value, but rather to the positions taken within a "field of cultural production," in Pierre Bourdieu's terms, the "distinction" accruing to the various cultural productions discussed here.[1] One argument, as we have seen, constructs medievalism as the despised other of medieval studies as the latter formed in the nineteenth century. While this high/low, official/non-official construction might be oversimplifying, it is still worth asking what impact medievalism has had on the arts and whether it has entered into canonicity at any points in its history.

It is evident that medievalism studies, whatever claims it makes for the wider applicability of its findings, is particularly invested in the medievalism of the period 1760–c.1900, with an especial focus on the second half of the nineteenth century (the time of the spread of neo-gothic, of Tennyson, William Morris, the imitators of the Pre-Raphaelites). Important though this phase evidently is to the study of medievalism, my contention here is that across the full history of medievalism and the reception of the Middle Ages, it is anomalous. It is, furthermore, an anomaly that has been taken for the norm. I propose therefore that it is a methodological paradox of medievalism studies that so far it has taken as norma-

---

[1]   Bourdieu, *The Field of Cultural Production*, see 64, 184.

tive what ought in fact to be regarded as aberrant. I will examine this first in relation to medievalism studies, then by looking at some specific examples, with a particular focus on the medievalist novel. My contention is that the Medieval Revival detracts attention from the normative view, which is that the Middle Ages is typically regarded as the childhood of modernity, and medievalist productions as, correspondingly, infantile.

Did Medievalism have a "Boom"?

When the study of medievalism was first established in the late 1970s by Leslie Workman (later with Kathleen Verduin) and the Salzburg group, it was possible to argue that the neomedievalism sparked in the 1760s had been inadequately analysed. The nascent medievalism studies that arose in the 1980s did two things: it placed such well known medievalisms as Pre-Raphaelite art in a new conceptual framework, and it brought some more buried forms of medievalism to light in order to place them in that same framework. Hence, the first issue of *SiM* in 1979 featured essays, predictably enough, on Carlyle's *Past and Present*, Dante in Ruskin's thought, and Morris's *Earthly Paradise*. The remaining essays – on Samuel Johnson's attitudes to the Middle Ages and Hardy's *Tess of the d'Urbervilles* as Arthurian Romance – were far less obvious choices.[2] There are two groups here, the first consisting of what was always vaguely known to be medievalism even if that specific concept was not deployed, and the second, what was never thought to be medievalism and needed the concept to bring it into view.

In the years since, while focusing on central medievalist topics, *SiM* has expanded the object of study, taking the discipline to such unexpected places as an analysis of the queer medievalism of John Kennedy Toole's *A Confederacy of Dunces*.[3] It was implicitly understood from the beginning that if medievalism studies were to be a discipline, it could not restrict itself to the Medieval Revival of 1760–1900 as conventionally understood. To do that would have been simply to give a new name to a field whose contours had already been mapped. Medievalism had to be *more* than the Medieval Revival, or it risked being nothing at all.

In 1979, *SiM* used on its masthead a statement made, apparently in 1859, by Lord Acton:

> Two great principles divide the world, and contend for the mastery, antiquity and the middle ages. These are the two civilisations that have preceded us, the two elements of which ours is composed. All political as well as religious questions reduce themselves practically to this. This is the great dualism that runs through our society.

Evidently this statement, which has remained at the front of every issue since,

---

[2]   See *SiM* 1, no.1 (1979) and its articles: Tomarken, "The Fictions of Romantic Chivalry"; Jann, "The Condition of England Past and Present"; Bidney, "Dante Retailored for the Nineteenth Century"; Boos, "The Medieval Tales of William Morris' The Earthly Paradise"; Clark and Wasserman, "*Tess of the d'Urbervilles* as Arthurian Romance."

[3]   Pugh, "'It's prolly fulla dirty stories."

argues for the *pervasiveness* of medievalism. In his classic 1994 article, "Medievalism and Romanticism," Leslie Workman argued for his belief that medievalism was a field comparable with romanticism. He looked back to Acton when at the end of the article he conceded a lack of parallelism between the two terms under study:

> The problem with medievalism is clearly very different [from those problems raised by the term romanticism]. It is not a period term at all, but an open-ended theme running through postmedieval Europe, a concept which we have barely begun to put to work in the manner suggested by Acton. The fact that it was never a "movement" at all, like Romanticism, does much to explain its neglect in the twentieth century: it is almost too endemic to be recognized.[4]

Workman's very useful observation here is one that he did not see through to its logical conclusion: if medievalism really is an endemic theme or set of themes in European culture, then it can never be made concrete as a single discipline (as the study of romanticism can be). To recognise this fully would have been to undo the whole project. Hence on the one hand, medievalism risks being nothing more than a new name for the Medieval Revival. But on the other, if medievalism is simply everywhere, then its disciplinary coherence is at risk of dissolving. What *really* links Thomas Carlyle with John Kennedy Toole? Can a discipline base itself on something that emerges in such disparate modes and places?

Underlying the very idea of "studies" in medievalism is the possibility of evading precisely this problem. This scholarly genre allows the endless proliferation of micro-studies, none of which ever comes up against the methodological problems of the discipline; as Stephanie Trigg has suggested, "the dominant scholarly genre in the field remains the essay, rather than the monograph."[5] In 2007, the then new editor of *SiM*, Karl Fugelso, rightly noted that "it was high time to ask scholars who have long been associated with *SiM* to address the nature and parameters of our field."[6] But at first, the chief result was to underline the methodological murk surrounding the term. "[T]he term 'medievalism' remains somewhat slippery," wrote one contributor. The term is "maddeningly vague for those who seek in it a clear definition," wrote another. Former editor T. A. Shippey stated of the standard definition, "The trouble ... is that, in its effort to be comprehensive, it lacks clarity; and...it lacks general acceptance and recognition even within the academic world."[7]

This is why, although he conceded that medievalism is endemically diverse, Workman had to act where *SiM* was concerned as if precisely the opposite were true because such diversity would have destroyed any sense of an emerging field. To a large extent, one of the only things that kept "studies in medievalism" together

---

4   Workman, "Medievalism and Romanticism," 33–34.
5   Trigg, rev. of Gallant.
6   Fugelso, Editorial note.
7   Morgan, "Medievalism, Authority, and the Academy," 55; Emery, "Medievalism and the Middle Ages," 77; Shippey, "Medievalisms and Why They Matter," 45.

as a genre was the existence of the journal itself. Without it, an essay on the Pre-Raphaelites would have been sent to an art history journal; an essay on *Tess of the d'Urbervilles* to a Hardy journal, and an essay on *A Confederacy of Dunces* to a journal specialising in the novel or American literature. Exit, medievalism.

One result is a tendency among proponents of medievalism to construct progressivist narratives. It is very easy, of course, to build a picture of a mid nineteenth-century boom in medievalism. Workman stated that by the middle of the nineteenth century, "Medievalism in England was diversifying and seemed to be going from strength to strength, most obviously in art, architecture, and literature."[8] Michael Alexander, in his turn, has suggested that medievalism "boomed" in the nineteenth century.[9] But it is what happened next that is crucial. Alexander concedes that there was a major *fin-de-siècle* hiatus: "Victorian medievalism had lost its vitality before the lives of its remaining practitioners came to an end in the 1890s" (211). This accords with Alice Chandler's view of medievalism in its political form: "the function of medievalism was finished by the 1870s," she suggests, remarking that it was "a transitional philosophy."[10] In the spheres of art and literature, medievalism had lost its impetus by 1900, by which time Morris, Burne-Jones, Tennyson and Ruskin were all dead.

Alexander then argues persuasively for "an Edwardian relaunch of medievalism, a second Medieval Revival" and describes the way in which medievalism mutated into new forms in the early twentieth century (212). Even in the era of high modernism, it can be detected in ways obvious and more hidden:

> 1900 was the year in which medievalism once more became a revival rather than a continuation: a minority movement, not going with the flow of the times, but oppositional in a new way. The old medievalism was fading into artistic wallpaper and stained glass, urban Art Nouveau and vernacular Arts and Crafts. It was just a style. In architecture, the tide of Gothic Revival building had ebbed, leaving much behind it to be wondered at. Poetry and painting had moved from medieval legend to mythology in general. Historical novels set in the Middle Ages were usually boys' adventures stories. On the other hand, knowledge about the Middle Ages had greatly increased. (211)

Alexander's approach has the advantage of breaking any necessary link between the Medieval Revival and medievalism. In this view, long after the romantic Medieval Revival had ended it is possible to trace twentieth-century medievalisms, even in the modernism which is its implicit antithesis.

It is indeed relatively straightforward to show the links of high modernism to medievalism. It is easy to link Pound and Dante or Pound and Anglo-Saxon poetry and impossible to imagine such a central modernist text as T. S. Eliot's *The*

---

[8]   Workman, "Medievalism and Romanticism," 16.
[9]   Alexander, *Medievalism*, 22.
[10]   Chandler, *A Dream of Order*, 183.

Waste Land without its substrate of Arthurian myth.[11] Kathleen Verduin alerts us to medievalism in D. H. Lawrence, while Lucia Boldrini has done the same in relation to James Joyce.[12] In another sphere, twentieth-century cathedrals managed to incorporate both modernism and medievalism, in effect absorbing modernism and surviving beyond it to produce medievalised modernist form: Scott's Liverpool Cathedral and Antonio Gaudí's Sagrada Familia in Barcelona are obvious examples. So it could be said that medievalism outlasted modernism and adapted, eventually to take the place it currently holds in postmodern popular culture, where its presence in a range of cultural forms today is easy to detect – especially in films, computer games, graphic novels, music (from folk to heavy metal), heritage and tourism.

It clearly remains the case, however, that medievalism as a larger phenomenon entered a major hiatus at the end of the Victorian period and did not return to its previous prominence. In the moment that the medievalism of a major modernist is described, that same medievalism only highlights the bewildering variety of competing discourses. It is necessary to know something about the Arthur legend to understand *The Waste Land* – Eliot tells us so himself. But to consider *The Waste Land* a "medievalist" poem, implicitly aligning it with Algernon Swinburne's *Tristram of Lyonesse* or Tennyson's *Idylls*, obviously makes no methodological sense in relation to a work that also draws heavily on Sophocles, Ovid, the Bible, Shakespeare, Donne, Baudelaire, and Verlaine.

This leads to the suspicion that, outside the limits of the Medieval Revival, medievalism is only a minor key, one theme among many. The career of the painter J. W. Waterhouse can be used to highlight the problem. In 2009, the Royal Academy mounted a major retrospective of Waterhouse's work, describing him as "The Modern Pre-Raphaelite." Some of Waterhouse's paintings show him as the clear inheritor of the tradition established by the young Rossetti and Burne-Jones. Waterhouse's *Tristram and Isolde* of 1916 (New York, private collection), depicting the lovers in the moment where they take up the cup with the love philtre, is a pure piece of belated Pre-Raphaelitism. In the same year Waterhouse returned to one of the favourite Pre-Raphaelite scenes, the Lady of Shalott. His *I am Half Sick of Shadows, said the Lady of Shalott* (Art Gallery of Ontario) is a far more sober meditation on Tennyson's poem than the better known *The Lady of Shalott* by William Holman Hunt (1905, Manchester City Art Gallery). Waterhouse had drawn on the Lady of Shalott twice before, and perhaps his most Pre-Raphaelite painting is the one used to promote the exhibition, the 1888 painting of the doomed Lady, her beauty already fading, drifting in her boat towards Camelot and death.

The medievalism of Waterhouse seems then indisputable. Yet even a rapid examination of his output shows that it is no more important than a number of other thematic strands in the painter's work. Like his contemporaries, Waterhouse looked to many aspects of the distant past, real and imagined, for his subjects. In another guise, he was a classicist, well known for such works as *Hylas and the*

---

[11] See also Anderson, "A Language to Translate Into."
[12] Verduin, "Lawrence and the Middle Ages"; Boldrini, ed., *Medieval Joyce.*

Nymphs (1896, Manchester City Art Gallery), *Circe Offering the Cup to Ulysses* (1891, Gallery Oldham) and a host of other works based on classical themes. The career of the historical painter Lawrence Alma-Tadema (in whose work medievalism is relatively rare) shows even more starkly that, at century's end, the range of genre painting encompassed biblical scenes, scenes from antiquity, and orientalism. Late Victorian painting was not particularly concerned with the Middle Ages, but with History itself.

For these various reasons it is now time to *qualify* the picture that has been painted so far. How great an impact on art and thought did medievalism really have? How much, in consequence, can it be regarded as a methodological cornerstone? In this and the following chapter, I aim first to look at the *limits* of medievalism and then at what can be said about the *reach* of medievalism. After three decades of excavation of medievalism, it is time, I argue here, to take a closer look at what exactly we have found.

Medievalist Art and the Canon

Leslie Workman regarded English medievalism as both "diversifying" and "going from strength to strength" by the middle of the nineteenth century. Of course this statement seems to stand up when we consider the Gothic Revival in architecture: at mid century, the best was yet to come, the Houses of Parliament at Westminster not yet complete, the St Pancras station hotel yet to be commenced, the colonial gothic cathedrals of America and Australia yet to be built. In America, Collegiate Gothic was under way; in Germany Cologne cathedral was being completed after a hiatus of several centuries, "the Middle Ages set going again," in Rosemary Hill's resonant phrase, "like a clock that had merely been stopped."[13] In literature, the serial publication of Tennyson's *Idylls of the King* had begun. After the initial disgust provoked by Pre-Raphaelite medievalism, medieval motifs in the visual arts proliferated and by the end of the century would have major outcomes in the Arts and Crafts movement and Aestheticism.

And yet there is another way of looking at it. *Influential* though medievalism would still be in all kinds of diverse ways in anglophone culture, there is a great deal to say that we should be careful about privileging its impact in British culture – even at its height in the mid-nineteenth century. Medievalism of the kind represented by the fashion for romance in the 1830s and 1840s had one important outcome in impelling the development of medieval studies and in turn, a better knowledge of the Middle Ages. But in the late Victorian period much of this energy would be directed toward the institutionalisation of medieval studies, which would become a university discipline by century's end. So far as the broader worlds of art and culture are concerned, medievalism would certainly have an influence – in ways that have often been discussed and which I will summarise below. But as I have indicated by brief examination of the output of Waterhouse, medievalism was just one thread among many in most spheres of

---

[13]   Hill, *God's Architect*, 199.

culture. Outside the realm of architecture, it can be argued, the reign of medievalism was brief indeed. Indeed in many spheres of culture, medievalism was
destined for a decline into disregarded, non-canonical status. In this respect there
are substantial differences between anglophone traditions and traditions elsewhere
and in what follows, I contrast continental European medievalisms with those of
English-speaking culture, in which medievalism largely vanished from the canon
after the mid-Victorian period.

When Tennyson completed his *Idylls of the King* in 1885 he triumphantly
capped a tradition of long poetic narratives based on medieval themes which
had been prominent for more than a century. Among these we could include
Thomas Percy's *Hermit of Warkworth* (1771), Samuel Taylor Coleridge's *Christabel*
(1797–1800), Walter Scott's *The Lord of the Isles* (1815), Edward Bulwer Lytton's *King
Arthur* (1848–49), the collection of works in William Morris's *Defence of Guenevere
and Other Poems* (1858), and Algernon Swinburne's *Tristram of Lyonesse* (1882).
Acclaimed and widely read as many of these texts were in their own time, little of
this verse is read today. The *Idylls* not only capped a tradition, but seemed to end
it. While the decline of this kind of medievalist narrative might have much to do
with the decline of narrative verse itself, the case of the genre that succeeded it in
English tradition, the novel, provides a more complex picture.

The ur-text is of course Scott's *Ivanhoe* (1819), the wildly successful novel of
Wilfrid Ivanhoe's attempts to win his spurs and his girl at the end of the twelfth
century. The novel has a Templar villain, a mad old witch, the siege and destruction of a castle, a great tournament, Richard the Lionheart, and Robin Hood.
As we have already seen, it engendered many stage versions and was probably
a great impetus behind the Eglinton Tournament of 1839. It influenced genera-
tions of novelists, from the early Victorians G. P. R. James, Harrison Ainsworth,
and Edward Bulwer Lytton, to G. A. Henty, Arthur Conan Doyle and Henry
Rider Haggard at the end of the century. In the twentieth century it was filmed
numerous times, especially for television.

Famous and undoubtedly influential as this novel was, it occupies a peculiar
position in *criticism*. Like most of Scott's novels, it has never really been canonical.
Scott's enormous popularity in his own day led to predictions of literary immor-
tality. But conversely, even from early times Scott's very popularity led to doubts
about his likely critical longevity; Thomas Carlyle suggested in 1838 that such
popularity was intrinsically transient. Scott's "enormous appeal had opened up
an awkward gap," Ann Rigney writes, "between contemporary taste and future
longevity, between popularity and critical value that has been growing ever since.
Scott was well loved, but was he great?" By the time of the 1932 centenary of
Scott's death, the one-time Great Unknown had, as Rigney records, become the
Great Unread.[14]

Ivanhoe, in terms of the distinction and cultural capital conferred by the
academy, has had negligible impact. Its great importance in the history of medi-

---

[14] Rigney, *The Afterlives of Walter Scott*, 211. Reviewing this book, John Sutherland notes
how under-represented Scott's novels are in both the Oxford World's Classics and Penguin
Classics series. "Waverley Street," 3.

evalism distorts perceptions of its success in the history of the novel. *Ivanhoe* was not, for the most part, imitated by the canonical nineteenth-century writers – the Brontes, Eliot, Dickens, Thackeray. Rather, Scott's direct followers were prolific writers – such as James, Ainsworth and Bulwer Lytton – who were regarded even by their contemporaries as the pulp fiction writers of their day. Ian Duncan, commenting on *Waverley* in particular, notes, "With Scott, for the first time, the British novel claims fiction as the motive principle" and that "The reader of Scott's novels is brought to recognize the imaginary, aesthetically and socially constructed character of historical reality, in the present as well as in the past."[15] But important as Scott is to the later tradition of the novel and the novel's approach to history, so far as the historical novel in the strict sense is concerned (with the partial exception of the more broadly respected Bulwer Lytton), none of Scott's *direct* imitators enjoyed the status of *litterateur* achieved by Dickens.

It is of equal importance within the history of medievalism that neither Scott nor his literary successors can be thought of as especially preoccupied with the Middle Ages. In part because of the influence of *Ivanhoe* and Scott's more general concern with a world of chivalry and knighthood, he is often taken as a medievalist above all. In fact the early narrative poems with which Scott made his name do not generally venture into the Middle Ages: *The Lay of the Last Minstrel* (1805) is set in the second half of the seventeenth century; *Rokeby* (1813) in the mid seventeenth; *Marmion* (1808) and *The Lady of the Lake* (1810) in the first half of the sixteenth century. *The Bridal of Triermain* (1813) contains an embedded twelfth-century romance but it was not until 1815 and *The Lord of the Isles* that Scott ventured on an unequivocally medieval tale. As a novelist, he produced *Ivanhoe* and then his second medievalist novel, *Quentin Durward*, in 1823. But his major interest through his first decade of writing novels was either in the liminal period of the Tudors and Stuarts between Middle Ages and modernity (*A Legend of Montrose* [1819], *The Monastery* [1820], *The Abbot* [1820]), or the eighteenth-century Jacobite risings (*Waverley*, *The Black Dwarf* [1816], *Old Mortality* [1816], *Rob Roy* [1817], *Redgauntlet* [1824]).

Scott, of course, can hardly be held answerable for this. His work does not claim any exclusive preoccupation with the Middle Ages and moreover, he worked with a far looser sense of the threshold between medieval and early modern than we do today. *The Lay of the Last Minstrel* might be technically a poem about early modernity but it also depicts a version of medieval culture. Scott (in his guise as the antiquarian Laurence Templeton) suggested that the historical past was nearer in Scotland than it was further south: "in England, civilization has been so long complete, that our ideas of our ancestors are only to be gleaned from musty records and chronicles."[16]

But it would nevertheless be a distortion to see Scott as primarily a medievalist. Among his novelist successors, the same is true. With *Rienzi: Last of the Tribunes* (1835) and *The Last of the Barons* (1843), Edward Bulwer Lytton might have

[15] Duncan, "*Waverley*," 179.
[16] Scott, "Dedicatory Epistle to the Rev. Dr Dryasdust, F.A.S." in *Ivanhoe*, 523.

announced himself as Scott's successor. But his most famous novel of the period was *The Last Days of Pompeii* (1834). G. P. R. James and Harrison Ainsworth might occasionally have been interested in the Middle Ages, but were in fact far more preoccupied, like Scott, with the sixteenth and seventeenth centuries. Along with much of Scott's output, therefore, they offer examples of "Tudor-Stuartism" rather than medievalism. They are best described simply as *historical* novelists.

The novelists who accrued most canonical distinction to themselves, meanwhile, such as the Brontes and Dickens, used gothic motifs but avoided the actual Middle Ages. Charlotte Bronte's *Villette* (1853) sets up a tension between its realist tone and, by contrast, certain events which seem to the narrator, Lucy Snowe, to be supernatural in a gothic way. She appears to be subject to haunting by a ghost. At the end, everything is explained in realistic terms: the imagined ghost is no more than an ardent suitor in disguise, for example. Hence Bronte is able to use gothic devices without, finally, sacrificing realism. Something similar is done, to more satirical effect, in Jane Austen's *Northanger Abbey* (1817), while Dickens sprinkles his novels with such gothic characters as the vampiric lawyer Vholes in *Bleak House* and the gargoyle-like dwarf, Quilp, in *The Old Curiosity Shop*.

In such novels, the Middle Ages is at a remove from a remove. Gothic – based on a distant idea of the Middle Ages – is in these works never finally gothic, but always recuperated for realism. The great Victorian realists never committed themselves to the Middle Ages, so that nineteenth-century Britain entirely lacked its version of Victor Hugo's *Notre Dame de Paris*: the acknowledged high-art novel of medievalism. Instead, the most popular Victorian novelist was given to ridiculing the fashion for the Middle Ages. In *Great Expectations*, Pip is taken home by Mr Wemmick, who shows off the house he has designed to look like a castle. Pip records, "it was the smallest house I ever saw; with the queerest gothic windows (by far the greater part of them sham), and a gothic door, almost too small to get in at." The moat dividing Wemmick's private life from the outside world is just four feet wide, yet Wemmick's father proudly believes that "This spot and these beautiful works upon it ought to be kept together by the Nation, after my son's time, for the people's enjoyment."[17]

Rather than a great cathedral and a national classic, the anglophone medievalist novel led to the boys'-own adventure story. In the last third of the nineteenth century, the prolific George Alfred Henty wrote several medievalist tales set across the entire Middle Ages from the Anglo-Saxons to Agincourt. Arthur Conan Doyle published tales of the Hundred Years War, *The White Company* (1891) and *Sir Nigel* (1906), and Henry Rider Haggard turned away from his usual African settings for his saga-based *Eric Brighteyes* (1890). Such works were often explicitly addressed to young male readers – Henty sometimes began his prefaces with "my dear lads." In twentieth-century British fiction this pattern allowed the success of often thoughtful medievalist writing for children by such figures as Rosemary Sutcliff and Henry Treece. Once again, though, medievalism was not a particular

---

[17]   Dickens, *Great Expectations*, 229–30.

preoccupation of any of these writers, so much as history itself. Henty wrote about all periods; Sutcliff was best known for her works about Roman Britain.

This largely realist tradition of medievalist writing is continued today by the heirs of Henty and Conan Doyle: such figures as the prominent historical novelist, Bernard Cornwell, who has written books set during both the Anglo-Saxon period and the Hundred Years War, or Ken Follett, a writer of historical thrillers who produced *The Pillars of the Earth* in 1989 and its more recent sequel *World Without End* in 2008, both set in the fictional English cathedral town of Kingsbridge. There is also a small industry in the medievalist detective novel, in which Ellis Peters' Cadfael books are perhaps the best known (filmed by Central Television in the 1990s), and Ariana Franklin's three Mistress of the Art of Death books a more recent instance.

Paralleling the realist novel and eventually overtaking it in popularity is a strand of medievalist fantasy writing. At the end of the nineteenth century, William Morris experimented with prose romance narratives, trying to give them a new seriousness and imbue them with progressive politics. Directed at an adult readership, the resultant works – *The Well at the World's End* (1896), *The Water of the Wondrous Isles* (1897), and others – had only very specific and limited impact. But Morris had a direct influence on the mid twentieth-century work of C. S. Lewis and J. R. R. Tolkien. Lewis's fantasy works of the 1950s, the Narnia chronicles, did not pretend to be other than children's literature. Tolkien's *The Hobbit* (1937) began life as a children's work; his later epic, *The Lord of the Rings* (1954–55), aspired to, and achieved, an adult audience, still without gaining a general critical acceptance. After Tolkien, a vast literature of more or less medievalist fantasy writing has been produced, of which George R. R. Martin's Song of Fire and Ice series is currently prominent owing to an HBO television series which premiered in the US and Britain in 2011. This strand of fantasy fiction is licensed by the enormous success of Tolkien's work and the readership it created.

Successful as a great deal of this writing has been, it is, self-evidently, almost entirely genre fiction. It is much more difficult to find examples of medievalist novels in the English-speaking world which have fulfilled the usual criteria of high-art literariness and which have been *critical* successes. One of the most obvious is the publishing phenomenon of the 1980s, Umberto Eco's *The Name of the Rose*, set in a monastery in 1327 (and translated from Italian). Actual English-language examples include John Fuller's *Flying to Nowhere* (1983) and Barry Unsworth's *Morality Play* (1995). Fuller's short novel appeared in the same year as the English version of *The Name of the Rose* and peculiarly, it is in outline a version of the same story told by Eco, in which a detective-like visitor comes to a remote abbey where he investigates mysterious deaths. Unsworth's novel, set in the fourteenth century, is about a troupe of players, with a murder plot at its heart. Another recent example of the medievalist novel that had some critical success was Adam Thorpe's *Hodd* (2009), a demythologising version of the Robin Hood story.

As the novels by Eco, Fuller and Unsworth in particular suggest, the high-art medievalist novel – when it appears at all – tends to invoke some old gothic tropes (the cover blurb of *Flying to Nowhere* called it a "modern Gothic novel with spiritual overtones"). The odd consonance between *The Name of the Rose* and *Flying to Nowhere* is unlikely to have been a result of direct influence, but rather the fact that the authors drew on a common store of basic ideas. Whatever their high-art ambitions, *The Name of the Rose, Flying to Nowhere,* and *Morality Play* – just like the Cadfael novels or *Castle of Otranto* – have murder at the heart of their plots. Eco's novel plays most explicitly with the conventions of genre fiction, with its hero, William of Baskerville, obviously echoing Conan Doyle's Sherlock Holmes.

Thorpe's *Hodd* (2009) does not share the detection plot but it does participate in a long tradition going back from *The Name of the Rose* to *Ivanhoe* and *Castle of Otranto*. This is the tradition of the authorising manuscript. In this case, the author Adam Thorpe attributes *Hodd* to an amateur scholar, Francis Belloes, recording how it came to his hands in the form of a printer's proof of a book prepared by Belloes from the manuscript he took out of a crypt in a French church on the Somme. The original text was in Latin, translated by Belloes, and is purportedly a memoir composed late in life by an old monk who as a boy was associated with one Robert Hodd (to whom he was known as Muche). The narrative both does and does not resemble stories of Robin Hood; "Belloes" has translated the original Latin into an archaised modern English; the result reads as pastiche of a nineteenth-century medievalist rather than a medieval work. The text is thickly encrusted with marginalia – not medieval marginalia, but Belloes' own learned notes, through which the occasional personal touch emerges. Belloes is clearly traumatised by his experiences in World War I and lost a close friend with whom he might have been in love. While Belloes is presented convincingly as a learned amateur of the early twentieth century, part of the effect of doing so is created by presenting the Hodd narrative as something which occasionally sounds more like an eighteenth-century confession than any form of medieval narrative. It is a knowingly self-undoing medievalist narrative, in which every page testifies to its constructed and artificial nature.

The one English-language novel that stands out as an exception to this general rule is William Golding's *The Spire* (1964), a novel which uses a medieval setting to explore faith and doubt, hubris and madness, as Dean Jocelin sacrifices everything to his grand plan to construct a massive spire on a cathedral which everyone tells him cannot support the weight. Descriptions initially offer the hint that the novel is in some sense about Salisbury cathedral in Wiltshire, but by the end it is clear that, while the buckling spire still stands, this is not a story of triumph. The novel offers neither the external perspective of a modern narrator (as Scott or Hugo did), nor an intradiegetic narrator who expresses himself in clear modern prose (as in *Morality Tale*), nor the postmodern layering of *Hodd*. Instead Jocelin is made "medieval" through modern novelistic techniques; interior monologues and an increasingly fractured viewpoint convey his breakdown, his pride and eventual loss of faith.

Fuller's and Unsworth's novels were shortlisted for Britain's prestigious MAN Booker Prize, though neither won. Both Golding and Unsworth won the Booker with historical novels, but not their medievalist works. Novels of medievalism have not tended to receive the highest accolades, which makes an instructive contrast with one of the shortest-priced favourites (and eventual winner) for many years, Hilary Mantel's *Wolf Hall* in 2009. Two years later, Mantel's sequel, *Bring up the*

Bodies, leapt straight to the top of fiction bestseller lists on publication in May 2012 and went on to an unprecedented second Booker win, the first time a sequel had won and the first time a British author had won a second Booker.

Wolf Hall and *Bring up the Bodies* are historical novels set in the 1530s, focusing exclusively on the career of Thomas Cromwell. Genuinely popular choices as Booker winners, and widely read despite their bulk, they are interesting as explicitly *anti*-medievalist works. *Wolf Hall* appeared at a time when "Tudorism" seemed to be enjoying a popular resurgence marked by the novels of Philippa Gregory, C. J. Sansom's Tudor-crime Shardlake series (2003–10), two crime novels about Giordano Bruno in England by S. J. Parris (2010–11) and a television series, *The Tudors* (Showtime, 2007–10). This series – like several recent historical dramas – was a reimagining of Tudor history with the sex put back in. It wanted viewers to note the *difference* of Tudor-era people, who were bound by elaborate codes of behaviour that no longer apply. At the same time it projected the idea that underneath the ruffs and the doublets, sixteenth-century people were *like* us, especially in their sexual desires.

Mantel's novel was unlike this, marking itself as *literary* by simple but effective devices: it is written entirely in the present tense, and rigorously focalised through the viewpoint of a single character, Cromwell himself. Like the popular novelists, Mantel acknowledges sexual and emotional worlds. But there is also a great deal which acknowledges the difference between them and us, recreating something that few modern anglophone readers have directly experienced: religious controversy.

Despite the fact that most readers know that Cromwell will ultimately fall and be executed, the novel unequivocally locates Cromwell as its hero, its renaissance man. Cromwell, we are told, was born on the day of the Battle of Bosworth Field – the day the Tudor dynasty took the crown and so, symbolically, the last day of the English Middle Ages. His troubled childhood leads to time spent in Italy; he speaks many languages, he is a biblical scholar, one who knows the truth of the Bible. He has mastered memory systems, he is a diplomat, and anti-war. Cromwell is, in short, a man for all seasons. Thomas More, meanwhile, the original man for all seasons of Robert Bolt's play of the same name (1960), is the novel's unequivocal villain.[18] *Wolf Hall's* revisionism resides in part in portraying More as a persecutor of Protestants (as he was) rather than a humanist and scholar (as he also was). More is the figure who, if allowed to lead, would keep England in superstitious darkness.

Relative to the usual popular understanding of the Tudor period – and indeed of some academic understandings – this is a radical revision. But in order to achieve its revisionist view, *Wolf Hall* in fact repeats many of the stereotypes that pit the medieval against the early modern. Cromwell's task is to lead England, reluctant though it might be, out of the superstitious medieval past. And as Cromwell's is overwhelmingly the only perspective on offer, it is difficult to see the novel as doing anything other than endorsing this historical necessity. At one early point,

---

[18] This point was also made by Penn, "A Man for this Season," 44.

there is a retelling of the medieval Albina myth – a fabulous legend of the foundation of Britain which was popular from the early fourteenth century onwards. At
first it is hard to see who is telling the story and it has the appearance of a fresh
voice within the narrative, as if fable and legend were now to be introduced as
countering discourses to Cromwell's rationalism. But it quickly becomes clear that
the story is being recounted through Cromwell's perspective, as it was told to him
by his mentor Cardinal Wolsey. It is also clear that it is told only to be rejected. The
Albina story is medieval national *legend*, the purpose of which is to be replaced
by early modern national *history*, which *Wolf Hall* depicts in the making. In this
novel, real history begins here, with the Tudors.

On the back of their Booker Prize wins, then, and widespread critical success,
Wolf Hall and *Bring up the Bodies* seem to be already established as modern
literary classics, with a third and final book still to come. Why has no explicitly
medievalist novel in English achieved this? While there are evident difficulties of
representation in bringing medieval culture to the page, similar difficulties are
apparently overcome in *Wolf Hall*. And other European cultures seem effortlessly
to produce versions of the Middle Ages that are acclaimed as high art and in
some cases take on revered national status. Hugo's *Notre Dame de Paris* has been
mentioned; Gustave Flaubert's *Legend of St Julian Hospitator* (published as part of
Trois Contes in 1877) also comes to mind. In Sweden, Sigrid Undset published the
three novels of her fourteenth-century epic, known in English as *Kristin Lavransdatter*, in 1920–22; she later received the Nobel Prize for literature.[19]

In the realm of cinema, the contrast between English-speaking and continental
European worlds is even more stark. Medievalist narrative has been a staple of
film almost since the creation of the medium and recent productions suggest its
popularity is ongoing. A burgeoning critical literature dealing with the phenomenon shows that it is now respectable for medievalists to write on film.[20] Some of
the more noteworthy films in recent memory include Robert Zemeckis's *Beowulf*
(2007), Ridley Scott's *Kingdom of Heaven* (2005), Brian Helgeland's *A Knight's Tale*
(2001), and Mel Gibson's *Braveheart* (1995). Yet, as with the novel, it is difficult to
think of a medievalist film in the English language that has both achieved popularity and accrued sufficient cultural capital to be thought of as canonical. In some
ways the most successful medievalist film in terms of its canonicity is also the least
respectful: the very knowing parody, *Monty Python and the Holy Grail* (dir. Terry
Gilliam and Terry Jones, 1975).

[19] By contrast, however, the great Italian historical novel of 1827 – Alessandro Manzoni's
I promessi sposi (*The Betrothed*) is set during the Thirty Years' War in the first half of
the seventeenth century. It is too soon to say what the impact of still another form of
novelistic medievalism will be: Paul Kingsnorth's *The Wake* (Unbound Books, 2014), set in
the immediate post-Conquest period, is written in a challenging version of Anglo-Saxon.
[20] Harty's *Cinema Arthuriana* (1991) was an early instance and Lindley's "The
Ahistoricism of Medieval Film" regarded as something of a classic. More recently, see Aberth,
A Knight at the Movies; De la Bretèque, *L'Imaginaire médiéval dans le cinéma occidental*;
Bildhauer, *Filming the Middle Ages*; Finke and Shichtman, *Cinematic Illuminations*; Bernau
and Bildhauer, eds., *Medieval Film*; Haydock, *Movie Medievalism*.

Matters are very different in European cinema. There is scarcely a European cinema culture that has not produced avowedly high-art medievalist films, often critically acclaimed, often accorded classic status: in France, Robert Bresson's *Lancelot du Lac* (1974) and Eric Rohmer's *Perceval le Gallois* (1978); in Sweden Ingmar Bergman's *Seventh Seal* (1957) and *Virgin Spring* (1960); in Denmark Carl Theodor Dreyer's *La Passion de Jeanne d'Arc* (1928); in Russia, Sergei Eisenstein's *Alexander Nevsky* (1938) and Andrei Tarkovsky's *Andrei Rublev* (1966). The Icelandic film *Útlaginn* (Ágúst Gudmundsson, 1981), a version of *The Saga of Gisli*, is perhaps also a contender; the various films about feudal Japan by Akira Kurosawa could also be included. So too, curiously enough, can an Italian version of an English classic, Pier Paolo Pasolini's *I racconti di Canterbury* (1972).[21]

Set against this roll call, it is difficult to compare such recent English-language offerings as *Black Death* (2010), a gothic horror of monks and zombies, or *Your Highness* (2011), a sword'n'sorcery spoof which features the line, "This quest sucks." And if those choices from recent cinema unbalance the case somewhat, it is nevertheless very difficult to find an example from Hollywood or British cinema of a medievalist film which, by critical consensus, can be regarded as a high-art success. Medievalist films – even the more serious ones – always seem close to provoking a laugh. By contrast, far more successful as arthouse films are those about the Tudor period, such as Shekhar Kapoor's *Elizabeth* (1998) and *Elizabeth: The Golden Age* (2007). Once again – as has already been discussed in relation to the second of the Elizabeth films in chapter 2 – these narratives are founded on explicitly anti-medievalist positions and hence along with Mantel's novels reinscribe the original Tudor invention of the medieval with a view to repressing it. The contrast with European cinema is a very marked one.

Why this should be is difficult to answer. It is clearly not a problem of historical representation itself, as anglophone cinema has always been successful at representing past historical periods (when they are not the Middle Ages): the Western comes to mind. It is surely not a question of available source material either. Many of the European films listed above are based either on classic texts (*Perceval le Gallois* and *Lancelot du Lac* on medieval romance; *I racconti di Canterbury* on Chaucer), or on specific legendary or historical events (*Alexander Nevsky*, *La Passion de Jeanne d'Arc*). British medieval culture, with a longer vernacular literary tradition than most other European cultures, stretching back to *Beowulf* and forward to the Arthurian cycle, is hardly disadvantaged in this respect. Yet the critically acclaimed Arthurian films are the French versions by Bresson and Rohmer, not John Boorman's *Excalibur* (1981), still less Jerry Zucker's *First Knight* (1995). Metro-Goldwyn-Mayer lavished money and stars on *Knights of the Round Table* (Richard Thorpe, 1953), but the result achieved little critical success.

One possible answer that might explain general attitudes to the recreation of medieval culture in Protestant Britain and America is that the late nineteenth-

---

[21] This is not to deny the existence of another kind of cinema altogether: the Turkish film, *Fetih 1453* (2012), reputedly a very popular celebration of the fall of Constantinople to the Ottoman Turks; Renzo Martinelli's *Barbarossa* (2009), a patriotic tale of northern Italian resistance to the German emperor Barbarossa.

century medieval revival should be regarded as the anomaly, and the anti-medievalism from the Reformation to the Medieval Revival as the norm. The legacy of the Middle Ages – the very circumstances of the period's invention – is such that the Anglo-American cultural tradition has never been sufficiently at ease with that legacy to produce something that sits within recognised canons of high art. In this context Mantel's *Wolf Hall* could be seen as the triumphant restatement of the reformed, Protestant English foundation myth which demonstrates the lasting appeal of this basic anti-medieval position in anglophone culture: checked but never defeated by the medieval revival. *Flying to Nowhere, Morality Play, Hodd* and even *The Spire*, though respectable and critically successful, show by contrast that neither the prizes nor the widespread commercial success come to the medieval setting. In this view, Tennyson's *Idylls of the King* is the last substantial, canonical work of anglophone literary medievalism.

As an explanation this has some appeal. However, other cultures no less strongly based on Protestant reform have clearly managed a much more comfortable relationship with their Middle Ages, as the presence of so many Scandinavian films in the list above would suggest, along with Undset's *Kristin Lavransdatter* and, in still another medium, the predominance of medieval motifs in the operas of the German Richard Wagner: *Rienzi* (1840, more enduring than the Bulwer Lytton novel on which it was based); *Tannhäuser* (1845), *Tristan und Isolde* (1865), *Der Ring des Nibelungen* (1869–76), and *Parsifal* (1882).

A second and related explanation has to do with the specific trajectory of medieval culture in the British and later the American context. This is the consistent *infantilising* of medieval culture, especially literary culture, from the late sixteenth century onwards. As we have seen, sixteenth-century thinkers first condemned the Middle Ages as a *dark* time, then as a *middling* time, conflating the dark and middle characters of the period. Less well charted is a tendency that my account of the medievalist novel has already hinted at: that in which the Middle Ages is seen as the remote *childhood* of modernity, a time when culture was unformed, underdeveloped, at best promising, at worst simply infantile.

The Childhood of Modernity

The presentation of the Middle Ages as a form of childhood, and its productions, consequently, as childish, is a clear development of the later Tudor period. In the 1550s, a great deal of medieval English literature was still available in print, at least to those with the money to purchase the expensive folio and quarto editions of the works of Chaucer, Gower, Langland, and Lydgate all in existence. The Elizabethan period, however, saw a rapid narrowing of the available literature, so that Gower and Langland, for example, would go without fresh editions for 250 years. Chaucer continued to be highly valued, though less as a *medieval* author than as a poet positioned as the first of the moderns.

What remained very popular, however, was medieval romances – especially those concerning Bevis of Hampton and Guy of Warwick – along with *Mandeville's Travels*. These were produced in relatively cheap versions, illustrated with crude woodcuts, with increasingly simplified texts, the language often simply updated to the English of the day.²² *The History of Guy of Warwick* and *Sir Bevis of Hampton* were popular productions in print from around 1500, when the early printers Richard Pynson and Wynkyn de Worde produced versions of each. Later, even in a context in which there were increasing attacks on the immorality of romance, William Copland produced a version of *Guy of Warwick* around 1565 and two impressions of *Bevis* c.1560–65, while Thomas East produced another *Bevis* around 1585. At the same time, the fourteenth-century *Mandeville's Travels* was one of the most frequently printed English medieval texts of the sixteenth century.²³

The reputation of such works was clearly much lower than that of works by Chaucer, Malory, and Lydgate. A host of references makes it clear that courtly taste increasingly disdained (or affected to disdain) such texts as *Bevis* and *Guy*, which had evidently become proverbial for their incredibility. At the beginning of *Henry VIII*, a Shakespeare and Fletcher collaboration of 1612–13, for example, the Duke of Norfolk describes the kings of France and England as vying with one another at the Field of the Cloth of Gold:

> ... they did perform
> Beyond thought's compass – that former fabulous story
> Being now seen possible enough, got credit
> That Bevis was believed.²⁴

A split between courtly and popular culture had by then already been propounded in *The Arte of English Poesie* (1589) by George Puttenham, who lumped together *Bevis*, *Guy* and "such other old Romances or historicall rimes, made purposely for recreation of the common people at Christmasse diners & brideales, and in tauernes & alehouses and such other places of base resort" as the work of "blind harpers or such like tauerne minstrels that giue a fit of mirth for a groat ..." The chief characteristic of such verse is "short distaunces and short measures," which might please the "popular eare," Puttenham continues, but "in our courtly maker we banish them vtterly."²⁵

But as Henry Peacham put it in *The Compleat Gentleman* (1622), "there is no booke so bad, euen Sir Beuis himselfe ... but some commoditie may be gotten by it."²⁶ Evidently many contemporaries agreed, and *Bevis*, *Guy*, and *Mandeville's Travels* survived. They continued to be printed in the seventeenth century and by the eighteenth, along with tales of King Arthur and ballads of Robin Hood, they formed a group of medieval works which shared some common factors: they were all unbelievable; they were all denigrated in official canons of taste; they were all,

²² On romance reading in general see Davis, *Chivalry and Romance in the English Renaissance*, esp. 1–36. I have written at further length about aspects of this textual history in "Whatever Happened to Your Heroes?" and "The Further Travels of Sir John." See also Crane, "The Vogue of *Guy of Warwick*"; Fellows, "*Bevis redivivus*"; Echard, *Printing the Middle Ages*, ch. 2; Richmond, *The Legend of Guy of Warwick*.
²³ See Bennett, *The Rediscovery of Sir John Mandeville*.
²⁴ Shakespeare and Fletcher, *Henry VIII (All is True)*, I.i.35–38.
²⁵ [Puttenham], *The Arte of English Poesie*, 69.
²⁶ Peacham, *The Compleat Gentleman*, 53–54.

nevertheless, evidently popular; they were all available in chapbooks, usually of twenty-four pages printed on the cheapest paper. By the middle of the eighteenth century they ranked among the cheapest literature of lowest prestige.

The rediscovery of the Middle Ages in the late eighteenth century apparently led to a new seriousness and new cultural prestige for the medievalist work. In some cases, that cultural capital has been enduring, as in the case of Keats's poetry, for example. In the nineteenth century, there were concerted attempts to move the genre of medieval romance back into a position of cultural prestige, into literariness. By the end of the century, a more broadly based Middle English literary studies had consolidated itself as a university discipline, providing further symbolic capital for the works it studied.

Clearly, however, old associations were hard to shake. The rise of university English studies coincided with the golden age of British children's writing that occurred after 1870 and the Forster Education Act, which introduced a minimum of compulsory schooling. In their search for subject matter, many of the new children's writers looked to the Middle Ages and the association of writing for children with medieval literature was clearly a natural one in the eyes of many. One of the earliest to see the potential of Chaucer's *Canterbury Tales* for children was Mrs Mary Haweis, who recorded in an 1877 book that she was "encouraged to put together [Chaucer's work for children] ... by noticing how quickly my own little boy learned and understood fragments of early English poetry." Haweis argued that there was a natural affinity between young children and medieval poetry:

> I think that much of the construction and pronunciation of old [ie, Middle] English which seems stiff and obscure to grown up people, appears easy to children, whose crude language is in many ways its counterpart.
>
> The narrative in early English poetry is almost always very simply and clearly expressed, with the same kind of repetition of facts and names which, as every mother knows, is what children most require in story-telling.

In two later works, Haweis continued the theme, remarking in her *Chaucer for Schools* (1881), that "Probably much of the construction and pronunciation of old English which seems stiff and obsolete to grown-up persons, appears easier to children, whose mode of talking is often very like it."[27]

It is true, of course, that at the same time, serious academic attention was also being devoted to Chaucer. The first major modern edition of Chaucer's works – that by W. W. Skeat – appeared in 1894 and represented the culmination of decades of scholarly work. But in *popular* culture the link between medieval literary culture and childhood has been hard to break. This is abundantly clear in the way in which medieval settings and medieval literature have been used and re-used in children's literature and television. The Middle Ages is fertile ground for children's culture in a way unmatched by the Tudor period, or the English Civil Wars, or the eighteenth century.

---

[27] Haweis, *Chaucer for Children*, ix; *Chaucer for Schools*, ix. I here draw on my essay, "Infantilising the Father."

This is partly because of the association between medievalist productions and fantasy, and the perception that fantasy is particularly suitable for children. Nickolas Haydock has commented, about medievalist film, that "[t]he very alterity of the Middle Ages works to make it an especially potent preserve of fantasy, the realm par excellence of the Imaginary."²⁸ But this is true chiefly in the context of *anglophone* cinema; as the survey above suggested, some European cultures (and Japanese cinema, if we include Kurosawa's depictions of feudal Japan) are far more comfortable with a *historical* Middle Ages on film. It is the English-speaking viewer who is more routinely exposed to the idea that the Middle Ages is a realm of fantasy.

I have already argued above that the nineteenth-century medievalist novel eventually had its major outcome in the children's literature of G. A. Henty and his twentieth-century successors. In a somewhat different mode, medievalist fantasy surfaced in *The Hobbit* (1937), the Narnia books of the 1950s (some of them now made into children's films), and the Harry Potter book-and-film phenomenon. Medievalism, in fantasy and realist modes, has also been a staple of children's television. The Robin Hood narrative was made for television in a part-fantastic mode with an adolescent hero, as *Robin of Sherwood* (1984–86) by Richard Carpenter (also responsible for two series about a medieval wizard in modern times, *Catweazle* [1970–71]). Recent offerings suggest this trend is stronger than ever, with the BBC's *Merlin* (depicting the wizard as a boy), running in four series from 2008 to 2012 and, in a grittier historical-realist mode, the BBC's *Robin Hood*, in three series from 2006 to 2009. For a time *Merlin* and *Robin Hood* alternated in the early evening slot on the BBC on Saturdays, aiming at the prized crossover audience of adults and children.

To suggest that there is a tendency to infantilisation of medieval culture here is not to denigrate the books and series in question, nor to suggest that children's literature cannot be a serious form. It is simply to point out a longstanding tendency in which medieval culture is seen as particularly fit for rendering into children's versions. As we have seen in earlier chapters, the Arthur story was heightened by Victorian authors to the point where it was regarded as matter for the self-consciously high art of Tennyson and Swinburne. But the second half of the nineteenth century is actually the anomaly; with few exceptions, from the sixteenth century to the mid nineteenth, the Arthur story was regarded as *unfit* for the high-art treatment, and since the 1890s, it has been regarded as *especially* suited for retelling for children. The underlying post-medieval pattern has simply reasserted itself.

The trajectory of the popular understanding of Chaucer is quite similar. *Outside* academe, Chaucer was regarded as ideal as children's literature, from the work of Mary Haweis in the 1870s and 1880s onward. At least ten different versions of Chaucer for children appeared in London in the first decade of the twentieth century alone; one of them, J. Walker McSpadden's *Stories from Chaucer: Retold from the Canterbury Tales* (1907), was reprinted fourteen times up to 1930.

---

²⁸ Haydock, *Movie Medievalism*, 7.

The result of this tendency towards infantilisation, for any attempt to create contemporary medievalist art, is eloquently represented in the work of a man who was born in the late Victorian period and came to maturity in the Edwardian, a devout Catholic, who read the fantasy romances of William Morris and George MacDonald in his youth and became a medievalist scholar in early adulthood. The ambition of J. R. R. Tolkien in the work he commenced in about 1916 was to fill the void of English mythology. His work began as an attempt to write of grand themes in mythic and epic forms, and was informed in this regard by such national epics as the Finnish *Kalevala*. The direct result was only published posthumously, first as *The Silmarillion* (1977), then in *Unfinished Tales* (1980) and a string of later volumes. It is easy to forget that the works for which Tolkien is world-famous, *The Hobbit* and *The Lord of the Rings*, were by-products, "offshoots," of the much larger and grander design represented in these posthumous publications.[29]

By the mid-1930s, when Tolkien began composing *The Hobbit* for his own children, he naturally enough drew on the mythic world he had been creating, complete with its own languages, for twenty years. He also had *Beowulf* much in mind – he published a famous essay on it in 1937.[30] By adding the Shire and its diminutive inhabitants to the epic world of elvish heroes and mighty villains he had been constructing, he created a kind of dwindled romance mixed with dwindled epic: it is as if the generic mode of Chaucer's *Tale of Sir Thopas* collided with the story-matter of *Beowulf* and *Sir Gawain and the Green Knight*. Hence when the hobbit Bilbo Baggins encounters the dragon Smaug, the Beowulfian enemy is juxtaposed not with a hero but a slightly ridiculous figure with a waistcoat and hairy feet.

This was hardly a problem given that *The Hobbit* originated as an oral story for Tolkien's own children before being taken up as a children's book by the publisher Stanley Unwin. But the sequel that the publishers demanded, and received years later, was a much more adult work. Unlike its precedessor, *The Lord of the Rings* was undeniably a work of epic scope and ambition, meditating on the corrupting effects of power and the possibility of absolute evil. Though Tolkien himself denied any allegorical intention, much of the book was written during World War II, while Tolkien's own experiences in World War I seem to inform some aspects of the narrative.[31] *The Lord of the Rings* aspires to the grandeur only glimpsed in the earlier book.

Tolkien's classic, nevertheless, remains rooted in the small world of the Shire and its diminutive inhabitants. The novel begins, exactly like *The Hobbit*, with a party at Bilbo Baggins' home in the Shire and for many pages the narrative simply retraces the earlier journey east, as far as the Elvish stronghold of Rivendell. In short, Tolkien commenced his new novel as if he knew no other way to begin; as he later commented of the writing process, in about 1938–39 "we had reached Bree, and I had then no more notion than they had of what had become of Gandalf or

[29] Shippey, *J. R. R. Tolkien*, 226. For a compressed summary of the phases of production, see 227–28.

[30] Tolkien, "Beowulf: The Monsters and the Critics."

[31] See, for the allegorical reading, Dodsworth, "Twentieth-Century Lit 1930–1998," 405.

who Strider was; and I had begun to despair of surviving to find out." The truth of the statement is borne out by drafts of the book which, as Shippey points out, show that "When he started writing Tolkien literally had no idea at all of where he was going."[32]

Of course the later story is far darker than the earlier one, even before the Shire has been left. Yet as the Company that is to make the perilous journey to Mordor in order to destroy the Ring leaves Rivendell and the wizard Gandalf takes the decision to pass through the Mines of Moria, the book is still replaying – albeit in heightened, epic form – the earlier novel. The elvish inhabitants of Rivendell no longer sing "O! tril-lil-lil-lolly / the valley is jolly," but speak of deep matters in their own language; a cave in which the characters take shelter from the rain in *The Hobbit* is transmuted, in the later novel, into the ancient underground kingdom of Moria; the earlier goblins, showing distinct traces of their origins in George MacDonald's late Victorian Curdie novels, have mutated into the more threatening orcs, commanded by an ancient, demonic force called a Balrog.

Despite this new epic grandeur, however, the narrative is all along committed to the hobbits, whom even the other characters regard as faintly ridiculous. They are frequently in the way, doing the wrong thing, making noise when noise is not needed, turning up where they are not really wanted. Wizards are wizards; warriors are warriors. But hobbits must grow up, and must *become* heroes. To do this, they must either, like Merry Brandybuck and Peregrin Took, literally grow up (they become taller as a result of drinking Entish water), or they become burdened with wisdom, knowledge, and hardship, like Bilbo and Frodo, so that they can no longer remain in the childish Shire. But while the Shire is shown to be an innocent and childlike world, it is allowed to remain intact at the end of the book, once it has been liberated from the worst designs of the "Big People." The return of the king, Aragorn, to the ancient realm of Gondor ushers in a new epoch. But not for the Shire. While the novel, in a fashion similar to many medieval romances, focuses on the restoration of a central monarchy of ancient bloodlines, this barely affects the Shire. One of the novel's chief narrative projects is to guarantee the continuance of the Shire as the epitome of a rural, craft-based, small-government state, in which the people are left to get on with their own infantile lives. The novel implicitly contrasts those who simply get bigger (Merry, Pippin) and who can remain in the Shire as hobbits, and those who grow up (Bilbo, Frodo, perhaps Sam), who cannot remain in the Shire but must graduate to another realm.

Tolkien's aim to create a serious, grand epic was ultimately frustrated. In his lifetime he never published any of the work he began during World War I and the posthumous publications which represent the epic work tend to be for fans only; even one of his greatest advocates, T. A. Shippey, concedes that "*The Silmarillion* could never be anything but hard to read," while its editor Christopher Tolkien conceded that the publication of the version that appeared in 1977 was "an error."[33]

---

[32] Tolkien, *Tree and Leaf*, unpaginated introductory note; Shippey, *J. R. R. Tolkien*, xxix; see further analysis of the opening sections, 53–68.

[33] Shippey, *The Road to Middle Earth*, 201, qtd in C. Tolkien, *The Book of Lost Tales*, Part I, 1; C. Tolkien quotation, 5.

The Lord of the Rings meanwhile – by some measures one of the most successful novels of the twentieth century – was one which aimed at an epic, medievalist grandeur, yet could only achieve it by recounting the deeds of satirically small people.[34] Tolkien aspired to a high-art vision – nothing less than England's lost mythology – yet even this noted scholar of medieval literature could not avoid building an infantile version of the Middle Ages into his epic. Much as *The Lord of the Rings* strains away from its origins in a children's book, the centrality of the hobbits to the great deeds going on around them means that it is often on the edge of bathos.

This happens in part, perhaps, because Tolkien wanted to hold on to an aspect of the way in which he thought children read. In his essay "On Fairy-Stories," given as a lecture in 1939 as he was writing *The Lord of the Rings* and published as part of the book *Tree and Leaf* in 1964, Tolkien suggested that "the association between children and fairy-stories is an accident of our domestic history," because fairy stories had been relegated to the nursery. He argued that as readers, "Children are capable, of course, of *literary belief*, when the story-maker's art is good enough to produce it."[35] This could be regarded as the willing suspension of disbelief, but Tolkien argued that it went deeper: if the author successfully creates a secondary world the reader, while immersed in that world, *actually* believes. This is stronger than suspension of disbelief, which is a far less engaged form of reading. The implication of this statement is that true reading must always be nostalgic, because it always looks back to the kind of belief of which the child is capable. Adults can only enjoy the marvellous if they *read like children*.

Hobbits, the symbol of an infantilised Middle Ages, nevertheless remain one of Tolkien's most enduring creations: when, in 2004, the skeletal remains of a previously unknown species of diminutive human were discovered on the Indonesian island of Flores, the creature was immediately dubbed the Hobbit. And, despite subsequent classification as *Homo floresiensis*, the Hobbit it has remained: hobbits are the emblem of anything that seems at once infantile and very old.

It is clear that many objections could be raised to the picture presented above. Not all medievalist television is for children: the most recent version of the Arthur story, the Irish/Canadian co-production *Camelot* (Take 5 Productions/Octagon Films, 2011), is an explicitly adult, fully sexualised telling of the tale in a more or less believable Dark-Age setting with the fantasy element muted and intermittent. Not all medievalist fiction, as the examples of *Morality Play*, *Flying to Nowhere*, and *The Spire* suggest, is for reading on the beach. The general tendency, however, is one in which medievalist art forms have fallen outside normative canons of

---

[34] I do not seek to deny that in terms of sales, influence, reach and aesthetic impact *The Lord of the Rings* must be regarded as one of the enormous successes of the history of publishing. Recent criticism has placed increasing emphasis on seeing the author not as the virulent anti-modernist of traditional critical accounts, but as a writer of the twentieth century (in the same sense that Joyce and Proust are writers of the twentieth century) and one particularly influenced by World War I. See further Jackson, "Authoring the Century."

[35] Tolkien, *Tree and Leaf*, 34, 36.

value and medievalist art has not regained the distinction conferred on it in the mid-Victorian period. The canonical status achieved for medievalism in that period in the spheres of art, architecture, and poetry was, as I have argued, the exception – in Britain at least, it was medievalism's brief, shining moment. Subsequently, medievalism was transmuted by modernist poetry, and it is perhaps in contemporary poetry more than anywhere else that its high-art ambitions are fulfilled today: in the verse of Seamus Heaney and Geoffrey Hill, for example, and the creative translations and adaptations (in the wake of Heaney's *Beowulf*) of Simon Armitage (*Sir Gawain and the Green Knight*, the *Alliterative Morte Arthur* with *Pearl* to follow) and Lavinia Greenlaw (*Troilus and Criseyde*).

If medievalism had a boomtime, then, we need to be careful about generalising from it. Doing so creates more problems, methodologically, than it solves. Anything that takes the nineteenth-century revival as a norm runs into problems, as Stephanie Trigg has pointed out:

> And if medievalism means predominantly nineteenth-century revivalism, where medieval culture is regarded as a kind of organic counterpart to the industrial revolution, what can this possibly have in common with either Spenser's romantic re-creation of Chaucerian style in the sixteenth century, for example, or with the post-modernist deployment of medieval fragments and traditions in *Buffy the Vampire Slayer* or *Charmed*, in the twenty-first?[36]

As Trigg's remarks immediately suggest, the nineteenth-century revival is comforting, as we know what it is and can circumscribe it in terms that are familiar to traditional disciplines of study in history, art history, and literature. But it also simply does not answer to the wider history of medievalism. Medievalism studies thus constantly threatens to break apart as the sheer incongruity of its objects of study, from Britomart to Buffy, threatens its disciplinary coherence.

In the final chapter, I will return to the questions raised for the discipline by these considerations. In the next chapter, I take up the suggestion made here that it is in fugitive forms – the forms medievalism takes when it is residual rather than dominant in a culture – that its impact is most pervasive.

[36] Trigg, "Once and Future Medievalism."

6

Realism in the Crypt: The Reach of Medievalism

IN MARCEL PROUST'S *In Search of Lost Time*, set in France of the *fin-de-siècle* and early twentieth century, the sense of time is founded on the Middle Ages. As we have seen in chapter 3, Marcel describes the beloved church at Combray as "an edifice occupying, so to speak, a four-dimensional space – the name of the fourth being Time." He regards both the length of the church's nave and the depth of its crypt as showing the way in which it extends across the centuries: the nave marking "each successive epoch from which it emerged triumphant," and the crypt "thrusting down … into a Merovingian darkness."[1]

The Merovingian period – the time of France's founder-monarchs – is usually the novel's most distant past. Marcel shows little interest in Roman times. For him, the medieval past is that which is also somehow present. The medieval past is palpably *there*: it was the steeple of the church in Combray "that shaped and crowned and consecrated every occupation, every hour of the day, every view in the town" (75). And there exist, in the novel's present, characters who seem to be from the Middle Ages: in the sculptured figures of the church, Marcel thinks he recognises the faces of Combray villagers, while the family's servant Françoise "was wont to hold forth about St Louis as though she herself had known him" (180).

Marcel portrays himself as initially unable to distinguish between the ordered past implied by the Middle Ages and a state of raw nature. Thinking of the coastal village of Balbec as a boy, he records having spoken of it to Swann, "hoping to learn from him whether it was the best point to select for seeing the most violent storms." Swann's reply changes the way he thinks about it when he tells Marcel that the church is still half romanesque, "and so singular that one is tempted to describe it as Persian in its inspiration." This thought delights Marcel, in whom it provokes a meditation:

---

[1] Proust, *In Search of Lost Time*, 72.

And that region which, until then, had seemed to me to be nothing else than a part of immemorial nature, that had remained contemporaneous with the great phenomena of geology – and as remote from human history as the Ocean itself or the Great Bear, with its wild race of fishermen for whom no more than for their whales had there been any Middle Ages – it had been a great joy to me to see it suddenly take its place in the order of the centuries, with a stored consciousness of the Romanesque epoch, and to know that the Gothic trefoil had come to diversify those wild rocks too at the appointed time, like those frail but hardy plants which in the Polar regions, when spring returns, scatter their stars about the eternal snows. And if Gothic art brought to those places and people an identification which otherwise they lacked, they too conferred one upon it in return. I tried to picture how those fishermen had lived, the timid and undreamt-of experiment in social relations which they had attempted there, clustered upon a promontory of the shores of Hell, at the foot of the cliffs of death; and Gothic art seemed to me a more living thing now that, detached from the towns in which until then I had always imagined it, I could see how, in a particular instance, upon a reef of savage rocks, it had taken root and grown until it flowered in a tapering spire.... Thereafter, on delightful, stormy February nights, the wind – breathing into my heart, which it shook no less violently than the chimney of my bedroom, the project of a visit to Balbec – blended in me the desire for Gothic architecture as well as for a storm upon the sea. (463–64)

History happens where the Middle Ages have been, in this novel. His medieval obsessions explain why, in the novel's famous opening paragraph, the boy Marcel bizarrely imagines himself, between sleep and waking, to be a quarrel between medieval monarchs. The medieval is the foundation of all that he has come to know, the France in which he lives. This seminal text of modernity is thoroughly founded in a sense of the medieval past.

Having argued in the previous chapter for the limits of medievalism, in this one I am going to do the opposite. Using the form of the novel, I am going to argue for its pervasiveness. But as the example of *In Search of Lost Time* suggests, this chapter is not about the medievalist novel from *Ivanhoe* to *Quentin Durward*, *The Hunchback of Notre Dame*, and beyond. As has already been discussed, there is certainly a lineage going back to Scott's novel, one which has its inheritors in the popular historical novel today by such figures as Cornwell and Follett. But this chapter will instead argue for the continuing pervasiveness of medievalism by turning to the tradition of the literary novel in English and exploring the ways in which – like *In Search of Lost Time* – that tradition is deeply informed by and obliged to the Middle Ages. I mean by this a more hidden Middle Ages than we find in Scott and his successors, and in many cases a deliberately obscured Middle Ages. I argue here that the Middle Ages emerges even – perhaps particularly – in novels which are otherwise thoroughly invested in their own contemporary moments. Tison Pugh and Angela Weisl write:

If many of these Victorian novelists are not as committed and idealistic in their medievalism as Tennyson, they nonetheless perpetuate the importance of invented medievalisms in literature by recognizing the Middle Ages's duality as a past unto itself and as a past increasingly reinvented by their gothic predecessors and other authors.[2]

This chapter looks at the Victorian novel and beyond to show how medievalism is hidden in unlikely places.[3]

Building on Gothic Foundations: Defoe, Charlotte Bronte, Collins

At the end of a novel better known for its account of life marooned on a desert island, there is a curious passage telling of the castaway's return to England via Spain and France and a perilous passage through the Pyrenees. The conclusion to Daniel Defoe's *Robinson Crusoe* (1719) tells how Crusoe, returned to Europe, crosses the mountains in the depths of winter, where his party is assailed by troops of wolves described as "hellish Creatures."

This section of the novel appears to bear little relation to Crusoe's island sojourn, as if it were only a clumsy spinning out of further suspense before Crusoe finally returns home. But perhaps the main problem with the passage for modern readers is the *absence* of gothic in it. Defoe creates a remote, haunting landscape that does not finally haunt. For readers familiar with the gothicised landscapes of later novels, the passage seems curiously flat. The landscape has no agency, malign or otherwise. There is snow because it is winter. Wolves turn out not to be "hellish," but rather just hungry animals; one traveller who is savaged is unlucky rather than fated. The wolves attack in what seems an anthropomorphically organised way but, as local inhabitants explain when told of the adventure, the travellers' mistake was to surround their own horses (the wolves' real target) and, in all, what occurred "was nothing but what was ordinary in the great forest at the foot of the mountains, especially when the snow lay on the ground."[4]

After *Castle of Otranto* in 1764 inaugurated the gothic novel, expectations of this kind of material changed. It is barely possible to read about wolves in a snowbound forest without suspecting that they are the servants of some higher, gothic agency, as they are in works as diverse as Stoker's *Dracula* (1897), Tolkien's *The Hobbit* (1937), and Angela Carter's "The Company of Wolves" (1979). What is curious to the reader of *Robinson Crusoe* today is the absence of a medievalist aspect, whether in gothic or any other guise.

After the success of the gothic novel in the late eighteenth century and the early nineteenth, the cultivation of the respectable nineteenth-century novel was then in many ways a matter of being seen to get away from gothic while at the same

---

[2]   Pugh and Weisl, *Medievalisms*, 41.

[3]   In the context of the nineteenth-century novel, see further Johnston, *George Eliot and the Discourses of Medievalism*. For a treatment of the American context, see Moreland, *The Medievalist Impulse in American Literature*.

[4]   Defoe, *Robinson Crusoe*, 295.

time getting away *with* gothic. Romance, as it had developed in fiction in the late eighteenth century, did not disappear from it in the nineteenth; indeed as Ian Duncan argues, "Romance is the essential principle of fiction." In the period, "The old commonplace of an antithetical relation between romance and reality, invoked by the novel in its own apologies of origin, produces a new dialectical figure of romance as the fulcrum against which – positioned on its edge, between inside and out – reality can be turned around."[5] Victorian realists practised their medievalism at a remove from a remove, employing a form of gothic (itself overlapping but not entirely coterminous with medievalism) which they could reconcile with realism by explaining it in such a way as to reincorporate it as an apparent element of mimesis. The classic text in this regard is Jane Austen's *Northanger Abbey*, in which gothic elements routinely turn out to be banal and everyday.

Austen parodies gothic for what it is, relentlessly exposing the dialectic of the novel after gothic. Most novelists, however, will embrace the dialectic, achieving a gothic effect while ultimately disavowing any literal haunting. As a result, Victorian novels prove again and again to be built on medieval foundations. In Charlotte Brontë's *Villette* (1853), the girls' school in which Lucy Snowe lives and teaches was supposedly once a convent. Inevitably, so the tradition goes, "something had happened on this site which, rousing fear and inflicting horror, had left to the place the inheritance of a ghost story."[6] A ghostly nun in black and white has sometimes been seen and in the garden there is a stone slab which is said to be the last remnant of a vault in which a girl was buried alive by "a monkish conclave of the drear middle ages ... for some sin against her vow" (148). Lucy, an English Protestant in a Catholic country, ostensibly rejects such superstition. She avoids the nightly reading from a book containing saints' lives:

> What gasconading rascals those saints must have been, if they first boasted these exploits or invented these miracles! These legends, however, were no more than monkish extravagances, over which one laughed inwardly; there were, besides, priestly matters, and the priestcraft of the book was far worse than its monkery. (162–63)

And yet Lucy herself is obsessed with ghosts and haunting and her narration is increasingly unable to distinguish between realistic and haunted realms. Notably, she perceives most of the main characters as ghostlike at one point or another: Paul Emmanuel, her eventual suitor, "seemed a harsh apparition" (179); she meets Dr John, the other main male character, in the garden, "like some ghost, I suppose" (157). The tendency extends to herself; she appears "spectral" after her own illness at the end of volume 1 (237). What transpires in the novel is in some senses a battle for Lucy's soul in which she must fend off the malign Middle Ages. At the climactic point at the end of volume 1 Lucy, ill but also apparently psychologically afflicted in a way she cannot describe, goes to confession with a Catholic priest, whom she tells she is a Protestant. The priest wishes her to visit him again the

---

5   Duncan, *Modern Romance and Transformations of the Novel*, 2.
6   Brontë, *Villette*, 147.

following day but directly afterwards, Lucy collapses completely. As she assures the reader, she would not have kept the appointment in any case, stating that this would have ended with her becoming a nun (and that, as the novel has already made clear, leads to death).

It is no surprise when Lucy encounters the ghostly nun itself. This occurs at a moment of psychological tension when Lucy takes to an abandoned garret in the school to read a letter she has received from Dr John. It seems clear that at this point Lucy is falling in love with him, though she, the narrator, cannot seem to articulate this. It is as she reads the letter that she realises there is another presence in the room: "Say what you will, reader – tell me I was nervous, or mad; affirm that I was unsettled by the excitement of that letter; declare that I dreamed: this I vow – I saw there – in that room – on that night – an image like – a NUN" (351). Lucy's fractured syntax is aimed at demonstrating her veracity but seems only to underline her mental stress. Dr John, hearing about it, is inclined to give a physiological explanation, calling it "a case of spectral illusion" (358).

It is even less surprising when realism is ultimately recuperated, and the ghost is given a simple, even banal, explanation, proving to have been simply the disguised male suitor of one of the girls at the school. The gothic Middle Ages provides the substrate of menace to counterpoint Lucy's morbid state of mind – but ultimately the Middle Ages is safely kept at bay. The past really is past, and can live again only in superstition. But that is precisely Lucy's problem, as she articulates it at another point: "when I thought of past days, I *could* feel. About the present, it was better to be stoical; about the future – such a future as mine – to be dead" (151). The past is, Lucy thinks, all she has. The past is the realm of emotion. But the past kills.

The bulk of the action in *Villette* is set in and around the supposed medieval convent that is now the girls' school, so that the gothic is never far away. By contrast Wilkie Collins's sensation novel of 1862, *No Name*, is constructed so as to avoid for much of its length the gothic subtext that Collins had so successfully deployed in *The Woman in White* (1859–60). Set in the 1840s, its plot turns on questions of the law and inheritance – genuine contemporary topics close to Collins's own concerns as the father of illegitimate children. The narrative is set going by modern technology when Andrew Vanstone becomes its victim, killed in a train accident before he can provide for his daughters in his will. While one daughter accepts her fate and loss of fortune, the other, Magdalen, sets out to reclaim her fortune by any means possible.

The narrative turns upon all kinds of aspects of modernity: efficient postal services, for example; rail travel; trade with the colony in India. It is set in London and in the coastal town, Aldeburgh. Nevertheless, when Magdalen is at her lowest ebb, her quest apparently frustrated, the novel turns to the medieval past. Magdalen, disguised, takes a position as a lady's maid at the country home of Admiral Bartram where she believes an important piece of legal evidence is concealed. The house is an old abbey, St Crux, through which the medieval past forces its way into view in novel. Shown over the house by the admiral's old friend, a threatening ex-seaman named Mazey, Magdalen is told by him:

"The monks lived due south of us, my dear, hundreds of years afore his honour the admiral was born or thought of; and a fine time of it they had, as I've heard. They sang in the church all the morning, and drank grog in the orchard all the afternoon. They slept off their grog on the best of featherbeds; and they fattened on the neighbourhood all the year round. Lucky beggars!"[7]

The relevance to the narrative of this piece of antimonasticism is not immediately clear. It establishes something about Mazey's character; we learn elsewhere that his mind is, indeed, "mazed," befuddled by drink and vague on times and dates. But it also brings into view the anti-Catholicism which, it has been argued, lies behind the sensation novel as a form.[8]

Magdalen does locate the secret deed of trust, but it appears to be locked away from her. Her strength and endurance begin to fail her; she is close to despair when she walks in the grounds and takes a seat "on some ruined fragments" by the entrance to what is left of the church:

In centuries long gone by, the stream of human sin and human suffering had flowed, day after day, to the confessional, over the place where she now sat. Of all the miserable women who had trodden those old stones in the bygone time, no more miserable creature had touched them, than the woman whose feet rested on them now. (538)

This vision of the monastic space is strikingly different from Mazey's earlier conjuring up of contentedly drunken medieval monks. At this low point, Magdalen continues to investigate the abbey's ruins, only in order "to fill up the vacant time, and to keep the thoughts that unnerved her from returning to her mind" (539). As she does so, her foot strikes an object which proves to be a rusty old key. This inspires her with new hope; out of her idle curiosity about the medieval past comes a new direction in her quest for her own identity and it is from this point on that a slow upturn in Magdalen's fortunes begins.

The novel's narrative soon moves away from St Crux. But it leaves the question: why must this pivotal setting be a ruined medieval church? Why does Collins turn away from the contemporary world at this point and towards the distant memory of *medieval* suffering to provide a key? In a slightly more veiled way he had done a similar thing in *The Woman in White*, where the central secret of the narrative lies in a register in a parish church described as falling into ruins. As Susan Griffin comments it is surely a medieval church: "in Collins's ruined church," she proposes, "the structures of anti-Catholicism allow sensationalism to intermix ancient forms and contemporary scandals."[9] Collins is drawn to the medieval ecclesiastical past because Catholicism functions, for him and his readers, as the

---

[7] Collins, *No Name*, 519.
[8] Brantlinger, "What is 'Sensational' about the 'Sensational Novel'?"; Griffin, "The Yellow Mask, the Black Robe, and the Woman in White."
[9] Griffin, "The Yellow Mask, the Black Robe," 67.

place of the uncanny. St Crux allows the irruption of the uncanny in *No Name* as if to secure the novel's "sensational" status.

But St Crux allows Collins more than this. Through it, he brings out a signification that has so far remained inert in the novel. The name "Magdalen" is of course a highly symbolic one, suggesting both proximity to God and the possibility of falling into sin. To this point in the novel Magdalen has lost all claim on her name (as the novel's title emphasises). While her recovery of her own name is the object of the novel's quest, the process also involves a dangerous encounter with some of the deeper aspects of being a "magdalen." It is established at the beginning of the novel that a key aspect of Magdalen's character is that she is a born actor. In Victorian code acting is a profession never far from prostitution; while Magdalen never overtly falls that far, her calculating marriage to her cousin Noel Vanstone in pursuit of her fortune is itself a form of prostitution and "the reader is repeatedly reminded of the connections between Magdalen's name (prostitutes or fallen women were often referred to as 'Magdalens') and her actions."[10] Only in the ruined abbey can the various senses of Magdalen's name emerge in full, showing her to be indeed the most miserable of women. While Mazey sees the Middle Ages as a corrupt time of monastic luxury, we learn here a deeper truth, a miserable Middle Ages that lies behind history, threatening to infect modernity. Magdalen's name inevitably leads up to this point of medieval suffering, at which she almost falls. (Conversely, Magdalen's final redemption is completed by marriage to a good man named Kirke.)

Hence, although the secret trust of the plot could just as easily have been hidden in a suburban London house, this novel of contemporary matters is inexorably drawn to the medieval past: St Crux proves to be crucial indeed in a novel which shows the Middle Ages as a gothic repressed that cannot fail to make a reappearance.

Gothic Surveillance: Charles Dickens

Dickens's *Dombey and Son* was serialised in 1846–48, at the height of the rediscovery of medievalism in Britain. The novel is wary about the march of modernity, notably presenting the railways as troubling monsters of technology. Railway cuttings destroy the dwellings of one set of characters, while another is horrifically run down by a train. But Dickens never espoused 1840s medievalism as an alternative to this fearsome modernity. It is instead generally mocked, as we have already seen in the previous chapter in relation to Wemmick's miniature gothicised house in *Great Expectations*.

Yet medievalism is also a resource which, like his friend and contemporary Collins, Dickens was prepared to draw on, chiefly in the form of gothic. When in *Great Expectations* (1861) Pip visits Miss Havisham for the first time, he walks in the deserted garden and brewery attached to Satis House, trying to avoid Estella.

---

[10]   Pykett, *Wilkie Collins*, 141.

It was in this place, and at this moment, that a strange thing happened to my fancy. I thought it a strange thing then, and I thought it a stranger thing long afterwards. I turned my eyes – a little dimmed by looking up at the frosty light – towards a great wooden beam in a low nook of the building near me on my right hand, and I saw a figure hanging there by the neck. A figure all in yellow white, with but one shoe to the feet; and it hung so, that I could see that the faded trimmings of the dress were like earthy paper, and that the face was Miss Havisham's, with a movement going over the whole countenance as if she were trying to call me.[11]

Pip first runs away from, then towards this figure, only to find – of course – that there is nothing there. It is a proleptic vision of Miss Havisham's later repentance and destruction authorised, within its realist context, by Pip's overwrought psychological state. And yet this vision appears to Pip when his psychological torture by Miss Havisham and Estella has barely begun. It is proleptic not simply of Miss Havisham's fate, but of the state of mind as yet unexperienced which would produce such a vision in Pip. In this regard the vision *ought* to be supernatural. This is a ghost that acts like a ghost, gothic looking like gothic, which never receives the kind of sober explanation that recuperates the haunting of Lucy Snowe for realism. Likewise, when the Clennams' house collapses at the end of *Little Dorrit*, it is *both* like the purgative fall of the house of Usher in Edgar Allan Poe's 1839 story of that name, *and* simply another old house with bad foundations. Throughout his fiction, Dickens offers these moments which, like Jastrow's rabbit-duck image, can be rabbit or duck, realist or gothic, without anything changing.[12]

In Dickens' early work, *The Old Curiosity Shop* (1840–41), however, the medievalism is more wide-ranging, and I focus on it for discussion here. In this novel medievalism initially appears in characteristic gothic guise, in the stunted and evil Daniel Quilp. Often simply referred to as "the dwarf," and also as an "evil spirit," Quilp is clearly a kind of goblin.[13] When he acquires the curiosity shop of the title at the beginning of the narrative, he closes it down, thereby threatening the future existence of those who depend on it, Nell and her grandfather. Driven by the suspicion that some money has been hidden away, Quilp persecutes Nell, eventually pursuing her throughout England.

A prime example of the way in which a largely gothic figure is inserted into a realist context, at times Quilp appears to Nell as if by magic. In chapter 27, Nell is looking at a medieval town gate, which is described as "dark, and grim, and old, and cold," and which features "an empty niche from which some old statue had fallen or been carried away hundreds of years ago" (210–11). At this moment, Quilp

[11] Dickens, *Great Expectations*, 65.
[12] I owe my use of the rabbit-duck illustration to a fine article by Helen Barr, "Religious Practice in Chaucer's *Prioress's Tale*."
[13] Dickens, *The Old Curiosity Shop*, 178. The original illustrations to which I refer appear in the Oxford World's Classics edition and are reproduced here from a copy of the text in the John Rylands Library published by Lippincott and Hall in 1874, and reprinted here with permission of the Director, John Rylands Library, Manchester.

8 *The Old Curiosity Shop*: Nell hides from Quilp beneath a medieval gate. Illustration by Hablot K. Browne. © The University of Manchester

9 *The Old Curiosity Shop*: Nell asleep in the old curiosity shop, by Samuel Williams. © The University of Manchester

reappears, in the shadow of the gate itself: "he seemed to have risen out of the earth." Despite this manifestation as chthonic spirit, moments later the narrator describes Quilp as looking "in the moonlight like some monstrous image that had come down from its niche and was casting a backward glance at its old house" (211). It is this moment that is captured in Hablot K. Browne's illustration, which clearly shows Quilp as if he had leapt down from the niche (Figure 8). Later in the same passage, Quilp is described as a waxwork, extending the range of unliving, simulacral figures to which he is compared. Browne's illustration focuses on Quilp's role as an uncanny gothic sculpture brought to life, an "animated grotesque from among medieval curios," as Jeremy Tambling calls him.[14]

In this passage Quilp fails to see Nell, who successfully avoids his gaze. More usually, he has the role of watching, overseeing (in this respect, he is like a gargoyle), underlining the fact that one of the novel's key themes is surveillance and the knowledge derived from such surveillance. This is often very clear in the original illustrations to the novel, which often develop the theme of surveillance even more explicitly than in Dickens's text. The curiosity shop itself, for example, is depicted as full of figures that seem to be *looking*: suits of armour that appear animate, figurines with watchful eyes. The remarkable illustration in chapter 1 – the only one contributed by Samuel Williams – shows Nell asleep in the shop (19) (Figure 9). She is aged fourteen at this point, but it is a slightly sexualised depiction of the young girl, an effect heightened by the fact that every figure in the curiosity shop appears to be gazing at her as she sleeps. A buddha-like figure which ought to be sitting upright leans forward for a better view; another figure praying at a lectern has its back to Nell but turns to look back over its shoulder. Notably, the moment does not explicitly take place in the text; the picture represents the somewhat lascivious imagining of Nell by the narrator of the early chapters, Master Humphrey, at the same time depicting, in Tambling's words, a "sleep [that] allegorises her death."[15]

The surveillance here, the threatening *looking* to which Nell is subject, is given an early association with old things from the past, such as suits of armour. Soon afterwards it is Quilp who takes the place of chief agent of surveillance. He is shown behind a door, watching, and elsewhere, looking over the unaware Nell and her grandfather. Late in the novel, the association of surveillance with a specifically medieval past is clinched when Nell and her grandfather rediscover the schoolmaster they have been seeking and come to rest after their long journey in the town where he is to teach. Reunited with him, Nell and her grandfather wait in the parish church – depicted in full gothic decrepitude in George Cattermole's illustration (351) (Figure 11) – while the schoolmaster retrieves his keys. There is then a narrative hiatus; succeeding chapters reveal the other things going on at the same moment while Nell sits in the church. In one, the mysterious single gentleman who has himself been seeking Nell (though apparently with good intent) continues to look for her. In another, Quilp plots against them. At the end of this sequence

14 Tambling, *Going Astray*, 92.
15 Tambling, *Going Astray*, 92.

10 *The Old Curiosity Shop*: Nell's new home, by George Cattermole.
© The University of Manchester

11 *The Old Curiosity Shop*: The church, by George Cattermole.
© The University of Manchester

the action returns to Nell in chapter 52, where she and her grandfather have been sitting in the timelessly enduring medieval space.

The schoolmaster now reveals a house which is to be Nell's (Figure 10). This too is a crumbling medieval space and once again Cattermole chooses to heighten the aspect of surveillance in a specifically medieval guise. Two figures by the fireplace in the house are said in the text to be "mutilated" but "still distinguishable for what they had been … like creatures who had outlived their kind, and mourned their own too slow decay" (388). In Cattermole's illustration, inevitably, the two figures seem quite clearly to be looking at Nell as she enters the room. Before she realises that this is to be her home, Nell calls it a place to "learn to die" – it is not necessarily said disapprovingly (389). Despite what appears to be a positive point in the narrative for Nell, with her fortunes on the upswing in a moment of stasis after the travails and near-death of the journey, there is also now a constant sense of death as near by, of wished-for decay. The ensuing days find Nell happy in the churchyard. In chapter 54 she and her grandfather spend time tending it. A small boy tells Nell he does not want her to go and become an angel, alluding to another friend who has died (414).

Most tellingly, within the crumbling gothic church there is a crypt, which Nell takes to sitting in (Figure 12). Again, the illustration is eloquent, showing the effigies of dead crusaders. But these figures no longer carry out surveillance. They are emphatically deceased and here, Nell "was happy, and at rest" (401). Within this crypt there is an ancient well – effectively a crypt within a crypt. This was depicted in another remarkable illustration, the only one contributed to the novel by Daniel Maclise (Figure 13). In it the sexton, obsessed by age and death, shows the well to Nell. Maclise has a full-length Nell appear the picture of apprehensive innocence while the outsized sexton, with a crazed expression and a skull-like head, points with an elongated finger into the pit. In the text the sexton tells how the well once had water, though it is now dry. The past was a time of plenitude, it seems, and the well a dark hole looking back into the past.

Unlike *Dombey and Son* and other later novels, *The Old Curiosity Shop* does not generally depict a rampant modernity. With the notable exception of its frightening vision of the furnaces of Birmingham, there are no charging steam engines, no suburbs demolished in the cause of progress. There is a strong sense of a past which, while it is not so far away, is already passing into some other state, invisible down a black hole. The curiosity shop that gives the novel its title in fact lasts only a short time in the narrative before Quilp shuts it down. But it is an appropriate emblem, in that it offers old things from a past that is still valued, even if those things no longer have an obvious purpose. Throughout the novel the abiding question for Quilp as well as the reader is that of whether Nell and her grandfather might in fact be rich without knowing it. The pursuit by the mysterious single gentleman only heightens this sense that there might be money left over from the shop, and hence that investment in the curious old past can in fact bring wealth.

Is the past valuable? the novel asks. The past is crumbling away, yet it watches over people and cannot be disregarded. And in this novel, that part of the past that is medieval is not subject to the humorous tone Dickens later takes towards the Middle Ages. To the contrary, the most active and malign figure in the novel,

12 *The Old Curiosity Shop*: Nell at rest in the crypt, by George Cattermole.
© The University of Manchester

Quilp, in his role as gargoyle and goblin is a kind of agent of a medieval past which thereby has agency in the present. At the same time, in this narrative characters are learning to live without the medieval past. The curiosity shop is closed, never to be reopened, by a figure who looks like an escapee from among its wares. The past crumbles before characters' eyes, old wells dry up, suits of armour offer no further protection to damsels in distress.

The novel concludes with a famous deathbed scene. Nell dies young and is of course buried in the church where she had spent her final months. Finality is emphasised, as the mourners "saw the vault covered and the stone fixed down" (542). Quilp is already dead by this point. While Nell, too, now fades into the past there is much to hint that she joins the angels (a closing illustration shows her borne up on a cloud by seraphim). But it is difficult to ignore a pervasive attitude to the past in the novel – explicitly based on and always visually represented by the medieval – which depicts the past not as angelic but as always crumbling even as it stays in place to look over the living. Quilp is gone, Nell is gone, but the medieval stays in place, decaying, but undead.

Fig. 13. *The Old Curiosity Shop*: The sexton shows Nell the dry well, by Daniel Maclise. © The University of Manchester

Scholarly Medievalism: Elizabeth (and William) Gaskell

Victorian authors did not necessarily turn to the Middle Ages for the well worn tropes of gothic. Elizabeth Gaskell did write gothic tales, but in her descriptions of the dismal Manchester slums of the late 1830s in *Mary Barton* (1848) she nevertheless avoided gothic metaphor. While she engages extensively with the Middle Ages in this novel, it is not to create a gothic effect. Instead, her novel exhibited what is, for the period, remarkable learning in medieval literature.

In *Mary Barton*, Gaskell's main characters are working-class figures from Lancashire whose speech is represented in dialect. The factory-owning upper-class figures, by contrast, speak in standard grammar and without a marked accent. The latter was the norm for the heroes and heroines of Victorian novels, who are usually given speech unmarked by dialect. If, like Pip in *Great Expectations*, they start out with dialect, they soon learn to shed it. This creates a problem for any novel in which the main figures speak in dialect, because they are inevitably marked as non-normative.

In *Mary Barton* it is the dialect-speaking characters who are central; Gaskell's response to the problem this posed was to turn to medieval language and literature. Throughout the novel, lower-class and regional forms of speech are glossed in footnotes which point to Anglo-Saxon, Middle English or (less often) early modern antecedents. Sometimes a footnote simply explains a dialect word's meaning and etymology. Many, however, go further than that, justifying a particular word or phrase with a citation from a medieval author. Hence when John Barton uses a double negative, a footnote records a double negative from Chaucer's *Miller's Tale*; the word *liever* (meaning "rather") is glossed by reference to *Troilus and Criseyde*; the dialect word *nesh* (meaning "soft") is correctly identified as of Anglo-Saxon origin and supported with a quotation from the Middle English poem *The Court of Love* (wrongly attributed to Chaucer).

As Thomas Recchio suggests, "The purpose of those notes was not to suggest a thematic or imagistic connection between the literature and the dialect; rather, it was to provide a history for working-class speech, illustrating it to be as English as middle-class standard English speech."[16] These notes appeared in the first edition of *Mary Barton* in 1848. In subsequent editions the number of notes and the level of detail increased until, in the fifth edition of 1854 (the last that Gaskell herself oversaw) they were supplemented by two appended lectures written by her husband, the Unitarian minister William Gaskell. Overlaps between lectures and notes strongly suggest that it was William Gaskell who in fact contributed the notes to the novel.[17] Footnotes were common enough in novels of the first half of the nineteenth century. In *Mary Barton*, they serve as an authenticating paratext, a means by which the reader is habituated to the idea that apparently non-normative word forms are not just historical and authentic, but literary. Medieval texts are repeatedly used as warrant for what have become, in mid nineteenth-century Lancashire, dialect words. Gaskell has recourse to Chaucer, the Wycliffite Bible, *Piers Plowman*, and in one instance the chronicle of Robert Mannyng of Brunne.

It is not surprising that Elizabeth and William Gaskell, both well educated, were familiar with Chaucer. Editions of Chaucer were abundant (if not necessarily very scholarly) in the first half of the nineteenth century. The misattribution of *The Court of Love* was not the Gaskells' mistake but a commonplace in the kinds of editions available to them. However, the wider knowledge of medieval literature displayed in *Mary Barton* is unusual for the 1840s. At the time there was a single recent edition of *Piers Plowman*, which had appeared in 1814. More prominent among the citations are works attributed to Wycliffe. The Wycliffite Bible appeared

[16] Gaskell, *Mary Barton*, ed. Recchio, 10 note 2.
[17] Recchio (Gaskell, *Mary Barton*) firmly attributes the notes to William Gaskell.

in a full edition in 1850, but the Gaskells were already drawing on Wycliffe in the 1848 edition. It is logical enough that a trained minister of the Church would have been aware of the work then referred to as the *Apology* of Wyclif, which he possibly read in the Camden Society edition edited by James Henthorn Todd in 1842 as *An Apology for Lollard Doctrines, Attributed to Wicliffe*. He perhaps also drew on H. H. Baber's *The New Testament by John Wiclif*, published in London in 1810. But if it is not surprising that a Unitarian minister had read extensively in the works ascribed to Wyclif, it is more unusual that William Gaskell was familiar with the *Chronicle* of Robert Mannyng. This work was available in an edition by the antiquarian Thomas Hearne published in 1725 and reprinted in 1810; Gaskell probably read it in the excerpts published in the only literary history of medieval poetry at the time, Thomas Warton's *History of English Poetry* (originally published in 1774–81, possibly read by Gaskell in Richard Taylor's revised edition of 1840). A work of little historical value and scarcely any literary influence, Mannyng's *Chronicle* was an unusual thing for anyone but a specialist to have been reading at the time.

Even more surprises lie in the two lectures added to the 1854 edition. In these, William Gaskell essentially supplements his footnotes with a scholarly discussion of the origins of various words. At a time when a comprehensive historical dictionary of English was barely dreamt of Gaskell's etymologies and attributions are certainly sometimes wide of the mark. But his lectures display a remarkable acquaintance with Old English and late medieval literature at a time when there were few shortcuts to such knowledge. In illustration of one point, Gaskell casually refers to the chronicle of Layamon, not just as if he has read it but as if he expects his hearers to know it as well. The chronicle had been published in 1847 by the notable scholar of Middle English, Frederic Madden. But as current scholars of Middle English well know, this vast work has never commanded a wide readership; Gaskell's grasp of it, when no one but a few specialists had even heard of it, is unusual indeed.

These footnotes and the lectures in *Mary Barton* ostensibly demonstrate the author's learning and at the same time culturally enfranchise her characters by conferring authority on their dialects. Elizabeth Gaskell's dilemma in a novel thoroughly sympathetic to the labourers was to present their speech with authenticity, at the same time ensuring that they would not lose by contrast with the orthodox English used by the factory owners, the Carsons. Drawing on her husband's reading and research in medieval literature – impressively extensive for the time – Gaskell presents the non-standard language of the Bartons and Wilsons in the novel in a way that both claims their authenticity as regional types and states a case for theirs as a form of English more authentic than that of their oppressive masters. In fact the claim goes further than that. The addition of William Gaskell's lectures in 1854 completed the process by which it is proposed that it is in the Manchester labourers' speech that an authentic and true English norm is found; implicitly at least, it is the factory owners whose speech is a deviation. William Gaskell's deeper knowledge of medieval literature via such obscure texts as Layamon's *Brut* acts as a challenge to less well informed critics to doubt the heritage of the dialects.

This is then clearly a very different kind of medievalism from the gothic that runs through so much of nineteenth-century realism. In describing the horrors of industrial Manchester Gaskell avoids descending into what was by then well worn Gothic imagery. Instead, she employs a brand of medievalism which shows that the nascent Middle English scholarship of the 1840s was already developing the potential to offer a counter-discourse to the dominant gothic impression of the Middle Ages.

The Ruined Church: Thomas Hardy

Like Gaskell, Thomas Hardy was deeply interested in non-standard dialect and like her, he was sympathetic to the Middle Ages. Hardy used the term "medievalism" more frequently than any other Victorian novelist and debated the questions raised by medievalism more thoroughly than anyone else. As a young man he trained as an architect in a firm specifically involved in the restoration of gothic churches. Later in life, as a member of the Society for the Protection of Ancient Buildings (SPAB), he was emphatically against such renovation. While, like most Victorian novelists, Hardy uses gothic devices in his fiction, he is more thoughtful than most about the Middle Ages. He considers the question of what to do with the medieval past: whether to restore and revive, or whether to leave it as it is. Born in 1840, Hardy was of the first generation for which railways, factories and large industrial cities were simply a fact of life. Repeatedly, his novels display the ambivalence of his era towards the problem of revering the past while trying to live in modernity.[18]

In his early novel, *A Pair of Blue Eyes* (1872–73), Hardy drew on his own experiences as an architect. He is believed to have been writing autobiographically when he described how his character, the young architect Stephen Smith, is sent to a remote Cornish village to draw up plans of renovation for the Gothic church. The resident parson, Swancourt, is an enthusiast for restoration of the church "in the newest style of Gothic art, and full of Christian feeling!"[19] But other characters are ambivalent about medievalist restoration and inhabitants of the village give the sense that the church might be better left as it is. Hardy himself encouraged this idea in the preface he wrote for the novel in Macmillan's 1895 collected edition (by which time he had espoused the cause of the SPAB),[20] where he effectively recants his own past as a restorer, noting that the book had been written "when the craze for indiscriminate church-restoration had just reached the remotest nooks of western England." Remarking on the harmony between the wild coastline and "crude Gothic Art," Hardy suggested that "[t]o restore the carcases of a mediae-

---

[18] This section is an expanded and revised version of material that originally appeared in my essay, "From Mediaeval to Mediaevalism." On Hardy's medievalism see further Elliott, "Hardy and the Middle Ages," and Rogers, "Medievalism in the Last Novels of Thomas Hardy." Elliott writes of "Hardy's delight in the medieval," and both critics take Hardy's view of the Middle Ages to be less ambivalent than I do.

[19] Hardy, *A Pair of Blue Eyes*, 314.

[20] See Rogers, "Medievalism in the Last Novels of Thomas Hardy," 301.

valism whose spirit had fled seemed a not less incongruous act than to set about renovating the adjoining crags themselves."[21]

Smith falls in love with Swancourt's daughter, Elfride (just as, in comparable circumstances, Hardy fell for his future wife Emma Gifford).[22] But the romance does not proceed smoothly, because of a rival lover, Henry Knight, whom Elfride meets when he reviews a medievalist romance, *The Court of Kellyon Castle*, which she has written under a pseudonym. The resultant love-triangle motif, familiar from Arthurian romance, is one Hardy would return to obsessively in some of his greatest novels.[23] Henry Knight is Smith's intellectual mentor; when he discovers Elfride's earlier attachment to Smith, she attempts to reassure him of her love by indicating the tower of the village church as an emblem of solidity. But moments later, that tower falls before their eyes; unknown to them, the "restorers," acting on the plans to which Smith has contributed, have been undermining it.

The gothic metaphors of *A Pair of Blue Eyes* are complex at this point. The church is not simply gothic in the architectural sense but "Gothic" in the eighteenth-century sense, with a crypt which acts as a grim portent of death to come at the novel's conclusion. When the church tower falls it kills a malevolent gossip, Mrs Jethway, and the secret with which she has been threatening the central romance dies with her. Yet it is too late; as we already know by then, the fallen tower has undermined the romance by so evidently failing to stand for romantic solidity between Knight and Elfride. Within the love triangle, both the chivalric Knight and plain Mr Smith will be frustrated; *Elf*ride will remain elusive. Late in the novel it transpires that she is more than just a parson's daughter as she is in fact descended from a branch of the local aristocratic family – into which she then marries. At the end of the novel, her rival lovers return to the west country by train to seek a resolution, without realising that they are accompanied by the coffin of Elfride, who has died young. They arrive in time to see her interred in the crypt.

In *A Laodicean* (1881), Hardy dealt with the attraction and repulsion of the Middle Ages for modern Victorians. Paula Power, heiress to a railway magnate, has inherited the medieval De Stancy castle. Once again a young architect is central; George Somerset is engaged to restore the castle to a medieval form, though Paula is herself equivocal about medievalism. Somerset, whose name suggests a man rooted in provincial soil, is the novel's man of integrity; Paula represents the new "Power" and money of the railway.

It becomes clear that Paula's position is one typical in the nineteenth-century novel: how to give respectability to a fortune gained in engineering; how to look aristocratic while being bourgeois. As she says to Somerset, should one be more proud that one's father built a railway and a tunnel, or that one's ancestor built a castle? Because Paula has many fears about authenticity, she does not brush this problem off easily. When Somerset falls in love with her, she makes it clear that she could feel more wholehearted about the medievalist restoration of the castle

[21] *A Pair of Blue Eyes*, 389.

[22] On this see Millgate, *Thomas Hardy: A Biography Revisited*, 112–16.

[23] In later editions of *A Pair of Blue Eyes*, Elfride's *Kellyon Castle* becomes *King Arthur's Castle*.

and Somerset himself if she were truly a De Stancy. "I should love it, and adore every stone, and think feudalism the only true romance of life, if – ... If I were a De Stancy, and the castle the long home of my forefathers." Elsewhere she declares, "I want to be romantic and historical."[24] Inevitably, Paula equivocates about romance with Somerset, triangulating matters by dallying instead with William de Stancy, who is impoverished but the true heir to the name.

William de Stancy is not a true villain, but is manipulated by the man who is, his illegitimate son, the aptly named Dare. Somerset, convinced he has lost the romantic battle and that Paula has married de Stancy, goes to Normandy where he embarks on a tour of churches. But Paula has realised, at the last minute, that De Stancy is a fraud. She does not marry him but goes off in pursuit of Somerset, trying but failing to engineer a romantic meeting in a gothic church. Instead, bathetically, she happens on George's father, till now not seen in the narrative. Reunited nevertheless, Somerset and Paula return as husband and wife to England. But on their first night there, Dare sets fire to De Stancy castle, among other things destroying the ancestral paintings which to him represent the lineage that is his but denied him through his illegitimacy. When the blaze dies down, it proves that the castle's Norman walls have resisted the fire. It would be possible to rebuild. But Paula and Somerset instead decide to build a new home, leaving the ruins to be grown over with vines and become picturesque.

Symbolically liberated from medieval lineage, Paula and Somerset can go into their marriage without the weight of heritage but with a large fortune now apparently untrammelled by any commitment to the past. As Andrew Radford writes, *A Laodicean* is "No dirge for a dying past," and in it "Hardy judges the past represented by the highborn de Stancy as a fake desiccated potency, crude and clumsy in its endeavour to harness the modern spirit."[25] Even so the romance ends on a characteristically Hardyan bittersweet note as Paula admits to Somerset in the last line, "I wish my castle wasn't burnt; and I wish you were a De Stancy!" (431).

Paula's closing, wistful words leave the reader with ambivalence rather than an unequivocal endorsement of modernity. It is only in his late novels that Hardy manifests a more thoroughgoing scepticism about medievalism. The plot of *Tess of the D'Urbervilles* (1891) is motivated by the foolish dreams of medieval lineage which are encouraged in Jack Durbeyfield.[26] This leads to the disastrous contact with Alec D'Urberville, who controls that lineage, albeit falsely. The kind of lineage which is conferred on Elfride Swancourt and yearned for by Paula Power proves fatal to Tess and Alec.

An even darker view is taken in Hardy's final novel, *Jude the Obscure* (1895). The novel opens in the village of Marygreen and as in so many of Hardy's novels, the opening chapter features a church. This one is a new, neo-gothic church, but at the end of the chapter there is a glancing reference to its old and ruined medi-

---

[24] Hardy, *A Laodicean*, 92, 111.
[25] Radford, *Thomas Hardy and the Survivals of Time*, 103, 112.
[26] The novel involves yet another love triangle; Clark and Wasserman persuasively argue for the legend of Tristan and Isolde as a model for it in "*Tess of the d'Urbervilles* as Arthurian Romance."

eval predecessor, which at this point serves no obvious narrative purpose. Jude's struggle, in the early chapters, is not with the Middle Ages but with the classics and classical languages, as he wishes to enter the ancient university of Christminster. Once he is in Christminster itself, however, he is unable to break into the world to which his classical learning was supposed to give him access. Instead he subsists by working as a stonemason (like Stephen Smith's father in *A Pair of Blue Eyes*, and Hardy's own father). His job is to help restore the medieval fabric of the city (which most readers would have understood to represent Oxford). Jude is said, by the novel's strong extradiegetic narrating voice, not to realise:

> that mediævalism was as dead as a fern-leaf in a lump of coal; that other developments were shaping in the world around him, in which Gothic architecture and its associations had no place. The deadly animosity of contemporary logic and vision towards so much of what he held in reverence was not yet revealed to him.[27]

Here, medievalism is unequivocally rejected. But what is meant by the term shifts and changes in this novel. In this quotation it refers at least in part to the fabric of the university town and appears to be an argument against neo-gothic. But when Sue Bridehead tells Jude, "The mediaevalism of Christminster must go," she is referring not to architecture but to backward looking religious faith (185).

Jude fails to break into the world of Christminster and ultimately moves to Melchester where he recommences his studies, now turning his back on classicism and working in a medievalist direction under the dominating sign of Melchester's cathedral (a version of Salisbury). Here, he reads "Newman, Pusey, and many other modern lights," clearly showing that in the 1890s, as Hardy understood, the original sense of the term "medievalism" was still prevalent.

The neo-gothic church of Marygreen which was glancingly described in the first chapter appears again at the end. Sue marries in the church, her husband not Jude but his rival Phillotson. Sue and Jude also have their final, hopeless meeting there, where "[e]verything was new, except a few pieces of carving preserved from the wrecked old fabric ... [which] seemed akin to the perished people of that place who were his ancestors and Sue's" (484). It is important here that this is *not* a fully gothic image. Jude's and Sue's dead ancestors are not present, and the church only imitates that gothic past, housing its last few remnants. The grim image underlines the inefficacy of the medieval past by emphasising the simulation represented by neo-gothic, as the not-married couple meet in the not-medieval space.

In Hardy's novels, then, there is residual nostalgia for the remnants of the medieval past, particularly in the early work. Later in his novelistic career Hardy comes to regard medievalism with increasing ambivalence. As an architect he begins by being sceptical of gothic renovation; as a novelist he is ultimately sceptical of the power of the medieval past to achieve anything in the present. At a time when the word "medievalism" was itself still ambiguous, Hardy uses it more than any other novelist, focusing attention on the key distinction between what

---

[27] Hardy, *Jude the Obscure*, 101.

survives from the Middle Ages, and what is revived. In the novels the former is subject to the decay of time, and hence seems to require the latter. But renovation and reclamation are viewed increasingly as inauthentic in Hardy's world. In that world, by the 1890s and *Jude*, it seems best to leave the medieval past to decline into picturesque ruin. In particular, romance and sexuality are inevitably destroyed by any contact with the medieval past. A century earlier, medievalism and the gothic were intrinsically connected to romance and sexuality, even if the result threatened an unbridled version of both. In Hardy's boyhood in the 1840s, in their different ways such leading figures as Carlyle, Disraeli, and Newman claimed social, political, and spiritual efficacy for medievalism. In Hardy's midlife work of the 1890s that potential has long since been emptied out of medievalism. Even as the neo-gothic tide turns and ebbs, Hardy, who had grown up with the turn to the medieval past, anticipates the modernist rejection of that turn.

Medievalism in the Closet: Alan Hollinghurst

Alan Hollinghurst was known as the elegant chronicler of modern gay male life in a series of slender novels when he published *The Line of Beauty* in 2004. This substantial novel set the story of a young gay man in the Britain of Margaret Thatcher's day, collocating a private and secret world with an eventful public history. In the novel, innocence is lost in two separate spheres: the secret liberating hedonism of the gay world runs into the AIDS crisis and converges with the stifling political conservatism of the world of public affairs.

Seven years later, Hollinghurst published his next novel, *The Stranger's Child* (2011), a similarly substantial work claiming even more expansive narrative territory. It opens in 1913 at "Two Acres," an upper middle-class home just outside London. George Sawle, whose mother owns the house, returns from Cambridge for the weekend, bringing with him his friend and fellow student Cecil Valance. To the reader, it is quickly clear that they are lovers; unsurprisingly, given the period, this is kept secret and instead George's impressionable sixteen-year-old sister, Daphne, thinks she has established the foundations of a more conventional heterosexual relationship with Cecil. The book's first section ends with the revelation that Cecil, on departing, has written a poem in praise of "Two Acres" which everyone reads as addressed to Daphne.

The rest of the book is dominated by two parallel but mutually exclusive possibilities: the conventional love affair between Daphne and Cecil and the hidden one between Cecil and George. Ambiguity is perpetuated because by the mid-1920s, when the second section takes place, Cecil is dead, a victim of World War I at the age of 25. He is now famous as a war poet, characterised as an upper-class, second-rate Rupert Brooke. His poem "Two Acres" has become a minor classic, learnt by schoolchildren everywhere. Daphne now has some minor fame as its supposed addressee; we learn that she had become engaged to Cecil, then after his death married his brother, Dudley. Her brother George, to whom this and other poems were in reality covertly addressed, is now himself conventionally married. Cecil's gayness is barely known. A whole history of queerness has been suppressed but at this point only the reader knows this. An effigy of Cecil in full-dress uniform lies in the chapel at the family seat of Corley Court (the setting for the novel's second section), where it is emblematic of an official, straight history of masculine heroism and sacrifice.

It is through Corley Court that the theme of medievalism, muted but insistent, makes its appearance in the novel. Corley is a neo-gothic construction of the second half of the nineteenth century which Dudley Valance is busy modernising. Deploring what are referred to as "egregious grotesqueries of the Victorians," Dudley plans to have its gothic extravagances "boxed in."[28] When the novel then leaps to 1967 and its third section, Corley has become a school: another old stately home turned over to public purposes, it has indeed had most of its original features covered over and boxed in. But as one of the teachers – an assertive gay man named Peter Rowe – reflects, the covering over has actually preserved the neo-gothic origins (362).

In the novel's final sections the buried queer past is slowly brought to light. A far more diffident gay character, Paul Bryant, leaves his work as a bank clerk to write a biography of the long-dead war poet Cecil. Through his efforts, much about Cecil's own queerness and even his relationship with George is revealed. But the way that Paul goes about his work leads to resistance from the remaining family members, not all of whom choose to believe the queer narrative. Daphne herself, now an old woman, is both weary of but still invested in the mythology of herself as the addressee of a famous poem and one-time fiancée of a dead war poet. She and others persist with the straight story of the poet and hero, with its intrication of heterosexual love, tragedy, and classic English poetic production.

As the covering over of Corley's gothic ornament and the covering up of Cecil's and George's gayness suggest, throughout the novel there is a persistent relationship between queerness and medievalism. Queerness is repressed in the novel, while medievalism is a different kind of embarrassment that must also be hidden away. Cecil, in his guise as heroic poet, is containable within a known narrative. The truth about him is one of excess: he was unrestrained in all senses, priapic, apparently bisexual, he took all sexual opportunities (while Daphne lives for years on the story of her engagement to Cecil, it is known that he had offered marriage to another woman at the same time). Victorian medievalism, too, is regarded as excessive. Its grotesque ornamentation is contrasted to the cleaner lines of modernity – the lines that Dudley tries to achieve by the "boxing in" at Corley Court. Consequently, queerness and medievalism are imbricated. When one character in the 1920s section is pressed on his attitude to the St Pancras station hotel, he resists the obvious invitation to deplore Victorian monstrosity and says that when he first saw it, "I thought it was the most beautiful building on earth." He argues evasively that "there's room in the world for more than one kind of beauty" (141). In the context of this novel, this is as good as an admission of gayness; this character's evasiveness about St Pancras is also an evasiveness about his probable homosexuality. Correspondingly, it is unsurprising to find in the 1960s section that Peter Rowe is said to have been part of the campaign to save St Pancras.

[28] Hollinghurst, *The Stranger's Child*, 140.

In this novel then medievalism operates as a code for queerness. The buried queerness of the past – like the boxed-in parts of Corley Court – is nevertheless the authentic core of history that needs to be uncovered. The novel is most directly concerned with the Victorian interpretation of the medieval, and it uses Victorian medievalist ornamentation as a central metaphor. Knightliness and chivalry are constantly at issue, most obviously through the image of Cecil's effigy that keeps recurring through the novel – an image of the fallen chivalric knight, behind which is a different, homoerotic truth. But the novel also occasionally invokes a deeper medieval past. Dudley, third baronet at Corley Court and also a writer, lives in the shadow of his dead brother. He is given to spouting short, deeply sarcastic verses, which he labels "Skeltonics." At one point, as he unleashes some cruel rhymes on the death of a house guest, Dudley's young, uncomprehending son thinks to please his father by announcing, "Oh, Skeleton, Daddy" (242). He says more than he knows: skeletons, poets, and the medieval past are all in the closet in this novel, all boxed in. The dead medieval past is always a gothic presence in it, as Cecil's effigy keeps reminding us. But there are no simple oppositions, because male queerness, too, is made gothic. Characters dislike the biographer Paul Bryant's uncovering of the queer past because his is a kind of gothic book of Cecil. Bryant wants a newly queered past, less because it is liberatory than because – despite his own gayness – the queer past can be gothically salacious.

I am not suggesting here that medievalism is *the* key to *The Stranger's Child*. Ranging across the twentieth and early twenty-first centuries, in the modes of both chronicle and satire, the novel cannot be pinned to this single concern. Neither am I suggesting in this chapter that medievalism is a major strand of the contemporary literary novel. But the insistent presence of medievalism in one of the major novels of recent times by one of the acclaimed English novelists is an indicator of the way in which the medieval period can and does still turn up everywhere in contemporary culture, even in contexts which – like the modern, realist novel in English – would on the face of it appear to have nothing to do with the Middle Ages. To some extent the modern realist novel is founded on resistance to medievalism – growing out of the romance tradition, the novel was fashioned as a realistic alternative to that tradition and based on the everyday rather than the fantastic. Yet romance remains an animating principle and it is not surprising that traces of the earlier romance tradition frequently show up in novels. This is particularly the case in the nineteenth-century tradition, with its unbroken links to the romantic revival. As Ian Duncan points out, the beginning of Dickens's career coincides with the end of Scott's and Scott, as translator, scholar, poet, novelist and historian was entirely formed within the counter-revolutionary phase of the romantic revival. As Hollinghurst's earlier career suggests, the modern novelist need not reproduce nineteenth-century gothic and its allegiances; even *The Line of Beauty*, his most substantial novel to that point, avoids any comparison with the Dickensian polyphonic novel, suggesting affinities instead with modernism in its abrupt shifts and gaps. *The Stranger's Child* extends that technique with its leaps from one time period to another. But towards the end, Corley Court is seen by Daphne as "a vision out of some old romance" (504). It is as if, finally, the novelist confronts the romance heritage of his endeavour even though his novel aims to defeat conventional notions of romance. As a result, in this novel as in so many others, some of them the central texts of Western realism, we find an almost obsessive return to a Middle Ages that will not stay "boxed in."

Conclusion
Against a Synthesis: Medievalism, Cultural Studies, and Antidisciplinarity

A S WE SAW in the introductory chapter, the English adjective "medieval" was a relatively late arrival in the early nineteenth century, and when it came into widespread use it had to overcome the prejudice engendered by its predecessor "gothic." If "medieval," originally the neutral alternative to "gothic," had had a longer history, then in the 1840s the word "*neo*medievalism" might have been coined instead of "medievalism." Much might have been simplified thereby. Just as we understand the relation of neoclassicism to classicism, we might today have a terminology which drew a clear distinction between medievalism (meaning phenomena of the Middle Ages) and neomedievalisms, referring to recreations after the Middle Ages. A field called neomedievalism might have established itself in parallel with, even leading the way for, the field of neo-Victorian studies (the e-journal *Neo-Victorian Studies* was established in 2008). Alternatively, if *Mittelalter-Rezeption* had been adopted in English, there might have been a parallel field of medieval reception, in line with the rise in recent years of classical reception studies (a multivolume *Oxford History of Classical Reception in English Literature* is currently under way, with volume 3 appearing in 2012, while the *Classical Receptions Journal* was established in 2009[1]).

But these things did not happen. Instead, with the appearance of the concept of medievalism in the 1840s, an ambiguity (sometimes a creative one) was opened up; medievalism was able to be deployed as a pejorative term with a dual sense of time, medieval and modern. In turn, with the apparent authority of John Ruskin, the term "medievalism" entered scholarly discourse in the late 1970s to indicate "the study of responses to the Middle Ages at all periods since a sense of the mediaeval began to develop" (to cite T. A. Shippey and the *SiM* website once

---

[1] Hopkins and Martindale, eds., *The Oxford History of Classical Reception in English Literature*; see Hardwick, Editorial, which discusses the field and potential problems with the guiding notion of "reception" in ways that are also very pertinent to medievalism.

more). At the same time, in the German-speaking world the term *Mittelalter-Rezeption* was developed for much the same purpose.[2] The term "neomedievalism" was eventually coined in the 1870s but has not been influential until recently, chiefly in a specialised sense in which it indicates a new sub-branch of medievalism itself focusing on postmodern medievalisms.[3]

Like any new discipline, "medievalism" faced resistance. Sessions on medievalism were quickly accepted and integrated into the annual International Congress on Medieval Studies at Kalamazoo, Michigan, in the 1970s. Later, when the European equivalent in Leeds was inaugurated in 1994, medievalism became a feature there as well. Yet despite this relative openness to the new field on the part of conference directors, there was and remains resistance to medievalism's presence, even from within the constituencies of those conferences themselves. There are those who feel that the study of medieval influences in Tolkien's *The Lord of the Rings* has no place in medieval studies, and there was outrage both inside and outside the academy when J. K. Rowling's Harry Potter novels made their debut at Kalamazoo as examples of medievalism. "[Y]ou thought that the Middle Ages was all about jousting knights and damsels in distress," wrote one distressed journalist after the 2008 congress. Having heard papers on Tolkien, Harry Potter and "Managing Human Waste in French Farce," Charlotte Allen concluded that this is "definitely not your grandfather's Middle Ages."[4]

It was in Britain, however, that medievalism was most staunchly resisted. It is only recently that study of post-medieval reception – a relatively long-term feature of teaching in America and Australia – can be seen having an impact in teaching in Britain. For some, there is a sense that medievalism is essentially a pursuit of postcolonial nations which are forced to it because they do not have their own manuscripts and medieval artefacts to study.[5] There is an underlying sense in this attitude that on the one hand, there is the real thing, and then there are the simulacra of medievalism. In this respect, medievalism, in relation to medieval studies, faces very similar problems to those once confronted by cultural studies in relation to literary studies, when cultural studies forced the introduction of noncanonical, nontraditional, and nonliterary forms of culture into the curriculum. And it is to cultural studies, without a doubt, that the study of medievalism belongs, though this has been a delayed recognition. As Ute Berns and Andrew James Johnston write:

---

[2]   Gentry and Müller, "The Reception of the Middle Ages in Germany," 399.

[3]   See Robinson and Clements, "Living with Neomedievalism," and the discussion in the introduction to this book. Holsinger emphasised this term in his 2007 book *Neomedievalism, Neoconservatism, and the War on Terror*, but its use in this wider sense has not generally taken hold.

[4]   Allen, "A Dark Age for Medievalists." For academic reactions, I am relying on considerable anecdotal evidence I have gathered while co-ordinating the strand "Medievalism and Reception of the Middle Ages" for the Leeds International Medieval Congress from 2007 to 2010.

[5]   As was once said to me in a job interview, "I suppose you have to do medievalism in Australia, because you don't have any manuscripts." I did not get the job.

To a certain extent, medievalism is a typical offspring of Cultural Studies. From its very beginning, medievalism has focused strongly on popular images of the Middle Ages, on films and graphic novels, on computer games and forms of reenactment, but also on more elite phenomena such as Victorian re-creations of the medieval past as championed, for instance, by the Pre-Raphaelites. Especially in its early stages and in as much as it was concerned with popular themes, medievalism seemed to lack scholarly credentials and threatened to remain a rather marginal academic pursuit.[6]

By some measures, nevertheless, medievalism has certainly secured itself in the scholarly canon. The journal *Studies in Medievalism* continues to appear and to remain a power in the field, now under its third editor, while a newer journal, *post-medievalism: a journal of medieval cultural studies*, has in the past few years taken the discipline in new directions. The strand at the Leeds conference "Medievalism and Reception of the Middle Ages" has been a fixture for several years, and continues to attract excellent contributors. Medievalism has even made its debut at the Medieval Academy of America annual meeting. Both the material for new areas of interest within medievalism, and the scholars wishing to study it, seem inexhaustible. We have perhaps reached the defining point in the history of this discipline: that at which it threatens to take over the parent discipline. Berns and Johnston suggest that "medievalism has expanded into what has traditionally been seen as medieval studies proper" (98), while in the same journal issue Richard Utz asks the almost heretical question, "Could it be that medievalism and medieval studies might become coterminous at some future moment?"[7]

Nevertheless, whereas cultural studies has received broad acceptance and is effectively mainstream today, there remain serious doubts about medievalism *as a discipline*. Some of this has to do with fundamental confusions in the term "medievalism" itself, not least because while "medievalism" wants to see itself as distinct from medieval studies, some scholars still use the term as an exact synonym for "medieval studies." Adherents of medievalism studies generally see a necessary differentiation between the two domains of medieval studies and of post-medieval responses to the Middle Ages, the later reception of medieval thought, genres, and topoi.

To look at it another way, within *medieval studies* scholars called *medievalists* edit medieval texts, unearth medieval artefacts, and read medieval historiography; under the aegis of the new field of medievalism, however, scholars look at how such figures as Thomas Percy, Thomas Warton, Walter Scott, Dante Gabriel Rossetti, John Ruskin and Alfred Tennyson (and La Curne de Sainte-Palaye, Victor Hugo, the Grimms, Thomas Jefferson, Henry Adams) responded to, recreated and reprocessed aspects of the Middle Ages. The key criterion here (true for both German and English definitions) is the difference between what went on *in the*

---

[6] Berns and Johnston, "Medievalism: A Very Short Introduction," 97. See also the discussion of medieval studies and cultural studies in Joy and Seaman, "Introduction: Through a Glass, Darkly: Medieval Cultural Studies at the End of History," esp. 9–12.

[7] Utz, "Coming to Terms with Medievalism," 109.

Middle Ages and *after* the Middle Ages. The former is the preserve of medieval studies, the latter, of medievalism.

Describing *Mittelalter-Rezeption*, Francis Gentry and Ulrich Müller note that it followed from the work of Hans-Georg Gadamer and Hans Robert Jauss and a shift from *Wirkungsgeschichte* (history of actions) to *Rezeptionsgeschichte* (reception history). Under the terms of the latter, critics would usually examine all aspects of a work's reception, from the moment of its initial distribution. But, for reasons they do not explain, Gentry and Müller state that *Mittelalter-Rezeption* "refer[s] primarily to the later 'reception' and revision of medieval literature."[8] Their concern in short is with *post*-medieval reception. While they do not clarify why this should be, the obvious reason is that the reception of medieval works *in* the Middle Ages is already the domain of *Mediävistik* (medieval studies). Hence *Mittelalter-Rezeption* must be content with what goes on *after* the Middle Ages.

As a way of keeping apart two forms of study, this would only work if medieval studies was exclusively concerned with what happened to medieval texts and artefacts *in* the medieval period itself – leaving the rest to medievalism studies. Much of the time, medieval studies gives a good impression of doing just that. As a discipline, it has traditionally been obsessed with origins: the history of textual editing has been dominated by the quest for archetypes, for example, what the author wrote before the scribes got to it; criticism has been devoted to reconstructing the context in which literary writings made sense; the disciplines of codicology, diplomatics, palaeography all, in their different ways, examine origins. Many scholars have argued for the essential *difference* of the Middle Ages from modernity, its *alterity*; within this model medievalists seek to retrieve the culture of the Middle Ages in terms dictated by that alterity, and the later impact and reception of that culture has been correspondingly neglected.[9]

But the idea that medieval studies is or could be *purely* concerned with what went on in the Middle Ages, *wie es eigentlich ist*, in Ranke's celebrated formula, does not really stand up to scrutiny. The editions which aim to reconstruct originals are themselves postmedieval artefacts. Their originary purity is all too easily exposed as coloured by contemporary ideologies and ways of going about things. Successive editions of *Beowulf* may aim to give us the original poem as it really was – but we nevertheless continue to need new editions of *Beowulf*, which suggests at the very least that our Rankean ideas of "how things really were" keep changing. In order to give us what they purport to present as the original poem, editors must recreate a *post*medieval artefact. This is most dramatically visible when such a poet as Seamus Heaney translates the poem into a modern idiom, or when, in 1875, Ludwig Ettmüller edited *Beowulf* with the Christian content removed (on the grounds that this must be a scribal interpolation). But any edition or translation of *Beowulf* is a *post*medieval artefact; it cannot be anything else. The scholarship that constitutes medieval studies, and aims to retrieve the Middle Ages, is by definition postmedieval. The simple split, then, between that which is

[8]   Gentry and Müller, "The Reception of the Middle Ages in Germany," 399.
[9]   On the alterity of the Middle Ages see Jauss, "The Alterity and Modernity of Medieval Literature."

concerned with the medieval period itself, and that which is concerned with the postmedieval, is not internally coherent.

The consequences run through the "discipline" of medievalism studies and its attempts to define itself. Particular problems arise in relation to the place of medieval scholarship within medievalism and to illustrate these further I will look at that key period in any consideration of British medievalism, the 1760s and 1770s, when a host of medievalist and pseudomedievalist literary and scholarly works appeared, signalling the reaction against classicist literary taste and fresh enthusiasm for the Middle Ages which formed part of the Medieval, or Romantic, Revival.

In 1760–63, James Macpherson published three books of poetry purporting to be the work of ancient Gaelic bards, especially the legendary figure Ossian. "By the succession of these Bards, such poems were handed down from race to race," Macpherson (anonymously) wrote; "some in manuscript, but more by oral tradition."[10] In 1764, Horace Walpole published his novel *The Castle of Otranto*, also anonymously, claiming in a preface that the story was translated from the Italian of a sixteenth-century black-letter print "found in the library of an ancient catholic family in the north of England."[11] A few months later, a Northamptonshire vicar, Thomas Percy, published the *Reliques of Ancient English Poetry*, claiming that many of the poems in the collection had been found in an old manuscript he had rescued from the house of a friend in Shropshire. Towards the end of the same decade the poems of a medieval monk named Thomas Rowley began to appear, their discoverer, Thomas Chatterton, claiming that they came from manuscripts in an old chest found by his father in a church in Bristol. Then in 1775 Thomas Tyrwhitt published his edition of *The Canterbury Tales*, claiming to have arrived at a substantially new version of Chaucer's great work by consulting old manuscripts.[12]

Several conclusions are suggested by the close juxtaposition of these texts in time. Obviously their appearance testifies, broadly, to a new interest in old books, specifically manuscripts, a pursuit made suddenly more fruitful at this time by the opening of the British Museum in 1759 and the publication of catalogues to the manuscript collections now newly available to scholars. The texts point to new possibilities for the claiming of authority derived from the past and prior texts. But these prior texts, importantly, are not classical texts. Macpherson, Walpole, Percy, Chatterton, and Tyrwhitt all leave their readers feeling that they have been put in touch with something that is *British* and so belongs to them in a way that no classical text could. Readers are also encouraged to think that something precious has only just survived: the story that Percy told of how he rescued his famous folio manuscript from use as a firelighter happens (as far as we can tell)

---

[10] [McPherson,] *Fragments of Ancient Poetry, Collected in the Highlands of Scotland*, v–vi.

[11] Walpole, *The Castle of Otranto*, 3.

[12] On Percy see Groom, *The Making of Percy's Reliques*; for a succinct summary of Macpherson, Chatterton and the import of their historicist inventions, see Butler, "Romanticism in England," esp. 44–46.

to be true, but it fits in neatly with such fictions of rescue as Macpherson's notion that he had drawn forth great epics from the folk mind of Highland Scotland. Most of these productions, too, are resolutely non-metropolitan, drawing authority from their derivation outside London and metropolitan culture, in the margins of Britain. Macpherson's Ossian poems are the most extreme example, but Walpole, Chatterton and Percy also played with the idea of texts retrieved from centuries of undisturbed provincial obscurity: Percy prints ballads from the border region with Scotland, taken from a manuscript found near the borders with Wales; Walpole pretends to have "collected" his story in the north, and so on.[13]

There is one exception in this list to these general rules. To the modern eye Tyrwhitt's scholarly *Canterbury Tales* edition stands out from what are otherwise fictions and frauds. For whatever the artistic merits, and in some cases the genuine scholarliness, of their productions, Macpherson confected his poems, Percy embellished his, Chatterton forged his, and Walpole, of course, invented his novel. To a greater or lesser degree, each "editor/translator" was in truth an author. Correspondingly, the legitimating sources had to be obscured at the same time as they were declared: Percy jealously guarded his manuscript, so that no one could see what his ballads looked like before he repaired them; Chatterton took great pains to make his manuscripts look genuine; Walpole's originary black-letter print did not exist, other than as an elegant fiction no one was really supposed to believe. But Tyrwhitt's manuscripts, of course, did exist and could be viewed by an interested public, in libraries in Oxford and London. And Tyrwhitt was also distinguished from the antiquarians in that he concerned himself with canonical metropolitan culture: he was an Oxford scholar interested in the London laureate rather than the borderland bards.

This comparison, then, appears to demonstrate the difference between a nascent English medieval *studies* (in Tyrwhitt's edition) and, in the other texts, emergent medieval*ism*: that is, to invoke yet another definition, "the perception (and the continued existence, the impact) of the Middle Ages in all succeeding periods, the Middle Ages as seen from 1500 ... to the present."[14] Tyrwhitt's edition had a very respectable run as the standard text of the *Canterbury Tales* for seventy-five years and is now consistently celebrated as a founding document in modern Chaucer studies.[15] Self-evidently, it belongs in medieval studies. By contrast the most scholarly among the other works mentioned, Thomas Percy's *Reliques*, has long since joined medievalism, as a collection of attractive but essentially false documents about a romantic Middle Ages of minstrelsy that Percy invented.

In fact, however, this apparently simple opposition between medieval studies and medievalism as exemplified by the Tyrwhitt-Percy comparison is completely

---

[13] On the provincial character of antiquarianism in the period, see Butler, *Romantics, Rebels and Reactionaries*, 35.

[14] Calin, "Leslie Workman: A Speech of Thanks," 451.

[15] See Windeatt, "Thomas Tyrwhitt." Dane, however, contests Tyrwhitt's place as a founder, finding the unfinished edition of the *Canterbury Tales* Thomas Morell to be more innovative: *Who Is Buried in Chaucer's Tomb?* 121–28. See also Dane's review of *Editing Chaucer* (in which Windeatt's essay appears) in *Huntington Library Quarterly*.

misleading. In the first place, these scholars' eighteenth-century peers and their nineteenth-century successors certainly did not themselves see the distinction that I have just made. Any medievally inclined scholar in the century after its appearance would have had Tyrwhitt's work alongside Percy's on his shelf. It is true that scholars did complain about Percy's lack of fidelity to sources and thought him a bad editor, but the same scholars were just as likely to complain about Tyrwhitt's work and to find his edition "very objectionable" (as the noted scholar of Middle English, Frederic Madden, put it in 1855).[16]

Moreover Tyrwhitt, whose knowledge of classical and late medieval studies was extensive, does not himself appear to have drawn a line between medieval studies and medievalism. Around the same time as he was working on the glossary to his *Canterbury Tales* (which appeared in a supplementary volume in 1778), he must also have been working on his edition of Chatterton's works, which appeared in 1777 with a second edition the following year.[17] Obviously the foremost scholar of Chaucer manuscripts of his time did not imagine that Chatterton's poems were medieval. Yet after his important work on Chaucer he chose to turn to the forger, Chatterton, suggesting that the poet and the forger belonged, as far as he was concerned, in the same disciplinary domain.

In short, the allocation of Tyrwhitt to medieval studies and Percy to medievalism is a modern judgement, based on a *retrospective* understanding of their relative positions. "Judgement" is perhaps too strong a word for what has become an assumption, the ideology of which is now obscured: while Tyrwhitt was a scholar working on the "real" Middle Ages, Percy's work was not real scholarship and invented its Middle Ages, much as the editor part-invented most of his texts. Tyrwhitt was a textual editor, but Percy was, in effect, a forger. Not so great a forger as Chatterton, but a forger nevertheless who belongs with Chatterton, Macpherson, Walpole and other confecters of medievalism. The principal criterion separating Tyrwhitt from the rest, then, is the idea that he went out as a scholar to *discover* the Middle Ages, while the others *invented* their Middle Ages.

This is deeply problematic. It relies on a retrospective judgement which in effect sorts good medieval studies from bad: that which we still sanction as belonging in the lineage of modern medieval studies (Tyrwhitt) from the wrong turnings (Percy). This means that, in many cases, to say of a given textual object that it constitutes medievalism rather than medieval studies is essentially to say that it is cast out of the true lineage of medieval studies. Neither Tyrwhitt's *Canterbury Tales* nor Percy's *Reliques* conforms to modern standards of scholarship or editing. Yet the former is automatically sanctioned as belonging in the correct lineage

---

[16] Tyrwhitt's current lofty reputation is a product of the *late* nineteenth century and the respect accorded by such figures as Skeat. Thomas Wright, the next major editor of the *Canterbury Tales,* referred to "Tyrwhitt's entire ignorance of the grammar of the language of Chaucer" and his "want of philological knowledge." Wright, ed., *The Canterbury Tales of Geoffrey Chaucer,* 2:xxxiv, xxxvii; Madden's comment was made in a letter to Francis Child.

[17] [Tyrwhitt,] *Poems Supposed To Have Been Written at Bristol by Thomas Rowley.* See Tanya Caldwell, "Tyrwhitt, Thomas (1730–1786)," *ODNB,* http://www.oxforddnb.com/view/article/27959, accessed 25 February 2014.

of medieval studies, belonging in a tradition which eventually gives us modern academic study of the Middle Ages, while Percy's is in the excluded line of medieval studies, belonging in a tradition which gives us interesting frauds and fictions.

One consequence has been a longstanding uncertainty about where, or whether, such early scholarship belongs in the history of medievalism. Michael Alexander's *Medievalism*, for example, discusses Percy and Chatterton in a chapter on the 1760s, but not Tyrwhitt. This is because Alexander is avowedly concerned only with medievalism of the imaginative kind, which is also why he breaks off from a discussion of Warton's *History of English Poetry*. His narrative of late eighteenth-century medievalism then obliges him, however, to turn to the scholarship of Thomas Percy in the *Reliques of Ancient English Poetry*, before briefly considering the scholar Joseph Ritson.[18] The categories of creative and scholarly medievalism simply cannot be kept apart.

This is disabling for medievalism's claims on disciplinary status. In definitions given by advocates of medievalism, the distinction relies on the difference between examination of the Middle Ages themselves, and the study of the impact of the Middle Ages after the Middle Ages. Leslie Workman tirelessly promoted the idea that "medievalism" describes the "*process* of creating the Middle Ages" or, as he put it in another context, "the study not of the Middle Ages themselves but of the scholars, artists, and writers who ... constructed the idea of the Middle Ages that we inherited."[19] The clarity of this distinction lies in the apparently straightforward point that medievalism concerns itself with the *process* of creating the Middle Ages, while medieval studies is concerned with the medieval period itself.

The distinction breaks down, however, because of one striking problem. While medieval studies might be concerned with the medieval period, *all* such study of the Middle Ages (by definition) has gone on after the Middle Ages. So medieval studies is part of the "*process* of creating the Middle Ages" and is involved in "the perception (and the continued existence, the impact) of the Middle Ages in all succeeding periods." This would mean that medieval studies is indistinguishable from medievalism. When, in his second definition above, Leslie Workman includes *scholarship* in medievalism, he points to this inescapable conclusion.[20] Tyrwhitt's *Canterbury Tales*, for example, is quite obviously involved in the "process of creating the Middle Ages." Tyrwhitt came to Chaucer studies and left it changed, significantly altering the Chaucer canon and the way in which Chaucerian verse was pronounced. Hence the instability of any line drawn between, say, Tyrwhitt's *Canterbury Tales* and Percy's *Reliques*. They both set out to be medieval studies but are in fact both medievalism – because by the definitions given, all medieval studies is also medievalism.

<hr/>

18   Alexander, *Medievalism*, ch. 1; 16–19.
19   Workman, Editorial, 2; qtd Utz and Shippey, *Medievalism in the Modern World*, 5, emphasis theirs. Utz, "Speaking of Medievalism," 439.
20   Richard Utz points to changing definitions of medievalism in Workman's own usage, to the point that all scholarship was included under its umbrella. See "Resistance to (the new) Medievalism?" 156.

Britton J. Harwood has put this concisely: "Medievalism has to do with the use of the Middle Ages. Surely there is no form of study of the Middle Ages that is not also a medievalism; and of course there is no medievalism that is not also a form of study."[21] But the medieval studies/medievalism divide, though illusory, persists because of the unarticulated criterion separating "good" medieval studies from "bad." Implicitly, Tyrwhitt is treated not as if he were involved in the process of creating the Middle Ages (though he was) but as if he were only *discovering* what was already objectively there. Percy, by contrast, just made things up. It is only by the application of an occulted ideological criterion that the medieval studies sheep can be sorted from medievalism's goats. Strangely, then, even those recent scholars who focus on what appears to be the one straightforward, obvious and concentrated example of British medievalism – the works of the 1760s – can make no real distinction between medievalism and medieval studies.

This results in part from the way in which historically, as I have indicated earlier, medievalism studies has taken an anomaly as normative. *Studies in Medievalism* began – hardly surprisingly – with a focus on the great medieval revival of the late eighteenth century and the nineteenth; in this regard, the journal was under the influence of Alice Chandler's important study, *A Dream of Order* (1970). Chandler had written about Cobbett, Carlyle, Ruskin, the Pre-Raphaelites, and Morris. The first issue of *SiM* in 1979 (discussed in chapter 5) featured articles on Samuel Johnson's attitudes to the Middle Ages; Carlyle's *Past and Present*; Dante in Ruskin's thought; Morris's *Earthly Paradise*; *Tess of the d'Urbervilles* as Arthurian Romance. With the exception of Johnson, this is a highly "canonical" list of medievalisms, all of them falling chronologically into the Medieval Revival. Nothing here seriously asked the reader to know exactly what medievalism *was*, because these texts appeared to make it self-evident.

What needed to happen next, if *SiM* was to prove that "medievalism" was not simply coterminous with the Medieval Revival, was for far more wide-ranging material to appear. With admirable breadth, the journal thus proceeded in its first dozen years to offer issues on Medievalism in America, Twentieth-Century Medievalism, Medievalism in France, Dante in the Modern World, Modern Arthurian Literature, Medievalism in France 1500–1700, Architecture and Design, Inklings and Others, and German Medievalism. Of these issues, that on France from 1500 in particular broke with the usual chronology of the Medieval Revival.

These issues of the journal raised a separate problem, however, which was that the more one looked, the more medievalism there was. Medievalism certainly *had* to demonstrate that it was more than simply the Medieval Revival: otherwise there was no need for a new term, still less a discipline. But at the same time, if medievalism turned out to be present in all periods and genres, could it really claim to be a coherent disciplinary category? Was it not just a discourse that turned up in one form or another at all times after the Middle Ages? In *SiM*'s very first article, on Samuel Johnson's attitudes to the Middle Ages, the problem was posed. We tend to think of Johnson as a quintessentially eighteenth-century,

---

[21] Harwood, "The Political Use of Chaucer in Twentieth-Century America," 391.

Augustan figure, far removed from any interest in the Middle Ages. But of course, *everyone*, at some level, has an attitude to the Middle Ages. This is fine as a field for investigation, but immediately suggests the explosion of any useful category of "medievalism," if medievalism is simply everywhere and in all times – the viral past lurking in the body of culture throughout history.

A converse problem is raised by the relative silence of *SiM* on the place of scholarship in medievalism. At first, *SiM* avoided the problem discussed above of the supposed difference between scholarly and creative medievalisms by avoiding scholarship altogether. It was not until twelve years after the journal's founding that Kathryn Kerby-Fulton's "'Standing on Lewis's Shoulders': C.S. Lewis as Critic of Medieval Literature," appeared, the first article that unequivocally focused on a scholar.[22] There then followed Frank R. Jacoby's "Historical Method and Romantic Vision in Jacob Grimm's Writings" and D. R. Woolf's "The Dawn of the Artifact: The Antiquarian Impulse in England, 1500–1730."[23] But scholars, as opposed to artists, writers, and filmmakers, have never had a central place in *SiM*, despite the fact that as his definitions of medievalism evolved, Workman increasingly admitted scholarly work to the field. Even *SiM* 14 (2005), *Correspondences: Medievalism in Scholarship and the Arts*, restricted itself largely to scholars of the relatively distant past.

In one respect, Workman, who had initially been resistant to admitting scholarship to medievalism, *had* to change his position. How could J. B. de la Curne de Sainte-Palaye, Richard Hurd, Thomas Warton, Thomas Percy, Walter Scott, and a host of others *not* be brought into consideration? But if such figures are admitted, what then of such a figure as Tyrwhitt, who did *not* have a popular readership? Why has his work never been examined within the framework of medievalism? The problem is of course that if it were opened up to *all* medieval scholarship, medievalism studies would no longer be able to distinguish itself from medieval studies. When does medievalism stop and medieval studies begin? These are difficult questions and until recently have never really been posed, let alone answered.

The dilemmas raised are exemplified in two contrasting works, Norman Cantor's *Inventing the Middle Ages* (1991), his account of the lives of eminent medievalists of what he called the founding era of medieval studies, 1895–1965, and the three volumes edited by Helen Damico under the general title *Medieval Scholarship: Biographical Studies on the Formation of a Discipline* (1995–2000). Cantor argues that "the Middle Ages are the invention of the twentieth rather than the nineteenth century," proposing that nineteenth-century historians were "early pioneers" hampered by working with "a very narrow data base" and prone to the shortcomings of the Victorian mind: "its love of huge entities, vulgarly simple models, hastily generalized and overdetermined evolutionary schemes – that made it unsuitable for doing lasting work in interpreting the Middle Ages."[24]

---

[22] *SiM* 3 (1991): 257–78.
[23] *SiM* 3.4 (1991): 489–504; *SiM* 4 (1992): 5–35.
[24] Cantor, *Inventing the Middle Ages*, 36, 29.

Hence Cantor's governing concept of "inventing the Middle Ages," applied to twentieth-century scholars, is apparently meant positively. His inventors – such figures as Charles Homer Haskins, C. S. Lewis, Marc Bloch, Ernst Kantorowicz, and so on – were unequivocally scholars in medieval studies. Cantor's thesis is that for reasons of biography, biology and other personal dispositions, these medievalists created the Middle Ages in a certain image. The book was therefore scandalous to those who did not want to acknowledge that scholarship and invention could be so closely intertwined – that scholars were involved in the sub-activity of the process of the creation of the Middle Ages. In short, though it did not use this terminology, the book put medieval studies far too close to medievalism for many medievalists to be comfortable with it.

Conversely, *Inventing the Middle Ages* was quickly taken up by the medievalism camp. Leslie Workman himself had no difficulty with embracing it, as he had by then acknowledged that scholarship was part of medievalism. "I think not only that people want to hear more of the kind of thing that Norman Cantor told them about how the ideas of medieval scholars were shaped by their society and personal history," he said in an interview, "but how these things determined their thinking."[25] And as Richard Utz and Tom Shippey write in their introduction to *Medievalism in the Modern World*, Cantor's was "the first monograph to contend in a serious manner that the multitude of scholarly endeavors to recuperate the *Medium Aevum* had only resulted in so many (subjective) reinventions of that time period."[26]

Despite such clear acknowledgements that scholarship is one form of the process of creating the Middle Ages, there is still a tendency within medievalism studies to want to keep the two distinct. It is a peculiarity of some of Workman's own statements that they show a desire to *avoid* their own obvious ramification: that the two categories of medieval studies and medievalism will collapse into one another. He once commented, "I think medieval studies and medievalism are moving closer and will continue to do so," but immediately added in mitigation that they will not do so "to the point of becoming one and the same thing." Yet he acknowledged, of the volumes edited by Helen Damico, that they are "both medievalism and medieval studies."[27]

Damico's three volumes, with contributions ranging back to the founders of medieval studies in the sixteenth century, stand as an implicit riposte to Cantor's book, offering unspeculative, "objective" biographies as if to recuperate medieval studies from the medievalism towards which Cantor had dragged it. The biographies contained in the books are far more respectful of their subjects than Cantor, tending, in complete contrast with his work, to avoid the intrication of personal politics with scholarship. A comparison of their respective treatments of the German historian Percy Ernst Schramm illustrates the opposition. János Bak, writing on Schramm in the Damico volume, is quick to dissociate the scholar,

[25] "Speaking of Medievalism," 444.
[26] *Medievalism in the Modern World*, 5; see the similarly worded statement in Utz, "Resistance to (the New) Medievalism?," 155.
[27] "Speaking of Medievalism," 444, 445.

born into a wealthy and prominent Hamburg family in 1894, from Nazism: "Schramm supported Field Marshal Hindenburg and briefly even the National Socialists, but these political escapades did not color his historical studies."[28] Bak notes the fact that during World War II Schramm was a diarist in the German High Command but does not mention that he wrote a personal memoir of Hitler. Cantor, by contrast, revels in Schramm's Nazi associations, discussing him along with Ernst Kantorowicz in a chapter whose title, "The Nazi Twins," is obviously designed to be provocative. He discusses the memoir of Hitler at length and proposes that Schramm's work for the High Command "makes him a prominent Nazi accomplice and in effect a war criminal."[29]

Cantor's book was controversial – and highly successful – precisely because of its going-behind-the-scenes, its tabloid approach to respectable academic medievalists. What is happening here is an uneasy play: in effect, in the moment when medieval studies is contaminated by ideology, it becomes medievalism. Bak, by contrast, exemplifies the general approach in the Damico volumes, which is to keep the biographical-ideological material separate from the scholarship; that is, to use the investigation of scholarly biography to reinforce the purity of medieval studies. Cantor's book is suspect in the eyes of many medievalists precisely because of its flirtation with medievalism, via ideology and personal interest. Like the case of Tyrwhitt and Percy, then, this contrast displays the occulted criterion behind much discussion of medievalism: that which implies that medievalism is a form of medieval studies with its ideological predispositions on display. Conversely, an equally occulted conclusion is that a purer, disinterested medieval studies seems to be what we do *now;* medievalism is always a generation ago (as, in 1991, Cantor's own cut-off date of 1965 suggested).

One way of viewing medievalism in the realm of scholarship, then, is to see it as Kathleen Biddick and Clare Simmons have both done, as consisting of what in course of time has been rejected from medieval studies. This explains how older scholarship such as that of Hurd, Warton, and Percy, fits so easily into medievalism, while Tyrwhitt (who is still regarded as having a founding position in modern Chaucer editing) does not. This process of ejection from the canons of scholarship is ongoing: in the late eighteenth century, Warton's *History of English Poetry* was *the* crucial reference for late medieval poetry. Now, it is just medievalism. In the late nineteenth, Bishop Stubbs's *Constitutional History of England* was the bedrock of English historiography, indisputably a work of medieval studies. Now, of course, Stubbs's work is famous mostly for a thesis which no one supports. Its ideological motives exposed, his work has become medieval*ism.*

Hence what tends to happen over time is that medieval studies passes into medievalism; as it ceaselessly updates itself, medieval studies expels what it no longer wishes to recognise as part of itself. Kathleen Biddick argued something similar when she suggested that medievalism in the nineteenth century was "a

[28] Damico and Zavadil, eds., *Biographical Studies*, vol. 1, 247.
[29] *Inventing the Middle Ages*, 92; see Bak's rebuttal in Damico and Zavadil, eds., *Biographical Studies*, vol. 1, 249.

fabricated effect of this newly forming medieval studies ... its despised 'other,' its exteriority."[30] But Biddick then, somewhat ironically, goes on to wield this form of exclusion herself. A critique she offers of Steven Justice's *Writing and Rebellion* is explicitly along the lines that Justice himself lapses into medievalism. In her view, having described the creation, by William Morris, of an idealised "Gothic peasant" in his novel *A Dream of John Ball*, Justice then himself envisages a village "romantically along nineteenth-century lines," as a place which "enjoys the devotional 'integration' of Corpus Christi and is remarkably unmarred by anticlericalism and anti-Semitism ... Villagers beat their rounds on Rogation Days seemingly untroubled by their own litigious lawsuits over resources."[31] Here, medievalism is the ideologically tainted work that must be expelled from the purer medieval studies.

Biddick perhaps does not intend it, but she focuses the way in which medievalism is, once again, "bad medieval studies." If pursued, this would mean that modern scholarship marks itself out by pointing to its own exteriority, just as literary and political histories previously marked themselves out against Warton and Stubbs. This is a process that continues, so that medievalism studies risks being no more than a sifting through the *disjecta membra* of medieval studies. At the same time, medievalism, with its definitions that insist on its posteriority to the Middle Ages, conspires in the creation of a stable and static period, fixed in the past and irreducibly other to modernity.

These disciplinary internal inconsistencies suggest that the attempt to differentiate medieval studies from medievalism is compromised from the beginning. Recent scholars have shifted to the usage "medievalism studies," obviously by way of a parallel to medieval studies, which certainly works better than the deployment of the word "medievalism" alone, but still does not fully address the problem. What is the *stuff* of medievalism? By what criterion does the work of Thomas Percy fall into the domain of medievalism studies and that of Thomas Tyrhwhitt into medieval studies? As such scholars as Berns and Johnston, and Joy and Seaman, have recently made explicit, there is a clear affinity between the study of medievalism and cultural studies. It is time to examine this affinity a little more closely.

It is no accident that medievalism studies arose in the 1970s in the wake of the counter-culture of the 1960s and the early 1970s. In the English-speaking world, the counter-culture embodied significant medievalist impulses: hippies embraced the romantic Middle Ages of the kind seen in William Morris's pastoral romances (written in the 1890s, reprinted in the 1970s) and in the work of two men inspired by Morris, J. R. R. Tolkien and C. S. Lewis. This was the communitarian, pastoral and anti-industrial Middle Ages discussed elsewhere in this book, which took the fundamentally nostalgic form seen in Tolkien's Shire and the Society for Creative Anachronism. Gentry and Müller, too, point to a *Mittelalter-Nostalgie* which they argue was evident in Central Europe from the mid 1970s, and from which their

[30] *The Shock of Medievalism*, 1.
[31] Biddick, *The Shock of Medievalism*, 52.

own study of *Mittelalter-Rezeption* flowed. The effect that medievalism has on medieval studies – loosening up or exploding its canons of value and retrieving the neglected by-ways of medieval culture, by putting it under the lens of gender studies, by listening to the voices of the poor, the workers – is exactly that which cultural studies aimed to have on the traditional literary canon. This is why medievalism has attracted negative responses from those who seek reassurance in an older, more stable canon and the approaches that go with it: your grandfather's Middle Ages, in short, a period which comes with the reassurance of a loveable old man (not a woman), perhaps in a cardigan, smoking a pipe, telling reassuringly familiar stories.

The most fruitful way forward for "medievalism studies," correspondingly, would be to embrace its cultural studies identity. Apart from anything else, this would help allay the considerable anxieties medievalism creates around the issue of its own disciplinarity, and which are ultimately unresolveable. Cultural studies is usually characterised as an antidiscipline. As John Frow has written (and this is probably truer now than at the time he said it), this should be taken "with a grain of salt, as a self-validating claim." Nevertheless, he suggested:

> it remains true that it [cultural studies] doesn't have the sort of secure defini-
> tion of its object that would give it the thematic coherence and the sense of
> a progressive accumulation of knowledge that most established disciplines
> see, rightly or wrongly, as underlying their claim to produce and to control
> valid knowledges. Cultural studies exists in a state of productive uncertainty
> about its status as a discipline.[32]

In my view, this "productive uncertainty" would make a more acceptable alternative to the paralysing lack of self-definition that currently afflicts medievalism. The study of medievalism would be greatly advanced by the recognition that rather than existing as a separate and new discipline, it is simply one part of medieval studies – and an inescapable part of it. This would be resisted from within both medievalism studies and medieval studies: in the latter, by those who wish to maintain their grandfather's Middle Ages; in the former, by those who cherish the idea of a separate discipline. But these forms of resistance maintain the artificial boundary which has been used for at least a century to say that medieval studies can have nothing to do with anything after 1500.

A disciplinary shift of this kind emphatically should not mean that anything goes. Cultural studies, by origin at least, was polemical and medievalism studies could follow that example. I have suggested elsewhere in this book that medievalists need to be self-aware in their proprietorial attitude to their period. When someone describes his torture at the hands of a western state as "medieval," our first concern should not be historical accuracy. It is at times appropriate, nevertheless, for medievalists to follow Umberto Eco in his call to a gatekeeping role. In France, the extreme right-wing *Front National* persistently lays claim to the historical figure

---

[32] Frow, *Cultural Studies and Cultural Value*, 7.

of Joan of Arc. On May Day 2012 the party's leader, Marine Le Pen, held a rally on the Place de l'Opera in Paris in front of the statue of Joan of Arc in order to announce that she would vote neither for Nicolas Sarkozy nor François Hollande in the presidential run-off. The party's founder, Jean-Marie Le Pen, said, "Joan of Arc represents the most extraordinary destiny in human history ... the history of France."[33] The extreme right persistently appropriates medieval symbols and it is important to follow such figures as Eco, or Patrick Geary, in resisting such historical hijacking.[34]

As a paradigm for how things might look in an altered landscape with a conjoined medieval-medievalism studies, we could look to the field of Arthurian studies. This is a field which is fundamentally a part of medieval studies, given its basis in the twelfth-century material which first elaborated at length the chronicle and romance forms of the Arthur story. From those origins, the Arthur story went on to become one of the most prolifically disseminated fictions of the Middle Ages across Europe. At the same time, the Arthur story has an incredibly insistent and diverse postmedieval existence, to such an extent that it would be entirely artificial to draw a line between medieval and later manifestations of the Arthur story, as if one were authentic and the other simply medievalism. Some of the post-medieval material has achieved canonical importance in its own right – Spenser's *Faerie Queene*, Tennyson's *Idylls of the King*, Wagner's *Tristan*. Some texts that have fallen from view deserve far more attention than they get: the Purcell/Dryden dramatic opera, *King Arthur* (1691), or Swinburne's *Tristram of Lyonesse* (1882), far more sensually unrestrained than, but overshadowed by, Tennyson's *Idylls*.

Nevertheless, in much of Arthurian studies there is a tendency to see the medieval material as quite separate from, even more authentic than, the later material. But self-evidently, Arthurian material exists in one long continuum from the twelfth century until today. There is, evidently, no authentic Arthur story, but rather multiply disseminating and proliferating texts, medieval, early modern, modern, and postmodern, none of them able to claim primacy.

Another field, however, with even more compellingly impeccable credentials than Arthur in both medieval and cultural studies is Robin Hood studies. This has burgeoned in the past two decades, following the work of Rodney Hilton, Stephen Knight, Thomas Hahn, Helen Phillips, and others. The reason for the lack of sustained study of Robin Hood within medieval studies before that date was chiefly the absence of canonical literary or historical texts. Revived by Joseph Ritson as the subject of ballads in the late eighteenth century, by Walter Scott as a hero in the early nineteenth century and, since the early twentieth century, in countless novelistic and filmic appearances, the outlaw Robin Hood is one of the most recognisable figures of the English Middle Ages. The exemplary peculiarity of Robin Hood from a disciplinary point of view is that this quintessentially medieval figure has in fact hardly any *medieval* existence. From chronicle references and a line in *Piers Plowman*, we can infer the widespread knowledge of tales of Robin

---

[33] http://www.guardian.co.uk/world/2012/may/01/marine-le-pen-french-runoff
[34] See Geary, *The Myth of Nations*.

Hood in the Middle Ages. But of all the vast textual, archaeological and historical remains of Robin, hardly anything is actually medieval.

As a result, while Robin Hood as a figure is quintessentially medieval, almost all study of Robin Hood necessarily relates to postmedieval phenomena. Hence the marginality of Robin Hood to medieval studies until relatively recently: despite good medieval credentials, Robin Hood could only be studied as a piece of medievalism. It took the advent of cultural studies to revolutionise understanding of the outlaw figure. The character Robin Hood was, indeed, tailor-made for the left-wing British cultural studies that arose in the 1970s, as an outlaw and anti-authoritarian found only in the marginal texts of a noncanonical tradition. This work has been conducted chiefly by medievalists. But it is not, and should not be regarded as, a closed shop: some of the notable work in the field of Robin Hood studies has been conducted, for example, by the independent writer and film-maker, Michael Eaton.

Hence today Robin Hood studies, once dominated by discussions of Robin's authenticity or otherwise, can be taken as exemplary of a medievalist cultural studies. With its volumes of essays, its key monographs and its regular conferences, Robin Hood studies is a paradigm of how "medievalism" might work. It is a field founded on the Middle Ages, yet necessarily unconfined by traditional medieval period boundaries. Today it is large-scale, but internally coherent and limited; it brings the medieval period into engagement with the post-medieval, and it draws on cultural studies methodologies to do so. Robin Hood studies has in fact developed the disciplinary coherence that "medievalism" as such cannot achieve.

Bold Robin Hood points the way to one possible disciplinary future. In a context of pressure on the humanities and the assumption that the Middle Ages is less and less relevant, there should instead be a recognition of an extended medieval studies, a cultural studies which naturally incorporates the operations of the medieval in the modern. A new drive to capaciousness is indeed evident in various places in medieval studies. The insights provided by Kathleen Davis, or Bruce Holsinger, and many others show that there is no longer any reason to lock up the study of the medieval as something pertaining only to the period before 1500 and that the medievalist should understand the present from the point of view of a deep history. "When medieval studies include the ongoing legacies of the European Middle Ages," writes Michelle Warren, "and when postcolonial studies include global histories that extend to the European Middle Ages and beyond, we will all be better equipped to identify the broadest painful truths of collective violence as well as the poignant idiosyncrasies of individual actions."[35]

It might seem ironic to be recommending such an expanded medieval studies at the very moment when medievalism studies appears to be fracturing from within (as "neomedievalism" makes its debut) and moving beyond the purview of medievalists. But medievalism studies has plenty of room for this kind of diversification. Just as the scholars who call themselves "medievalists"

---

[35] Warren, "Medievalism and the Making of Nations," 297.

do not attempt to specialise in all areas of a millennium-long period, specialists in the extraordinarily diverse field of medievalism can also specialise while acknowledging the enormous diversity of the field of medievalism studies and its multifold possibilities.

Afterword

APERFORMANCE OF Lavinia Greenlaw's *A Double Sorrow* – her "version," rather than a translation, of *Troilus and Criseyde* – took place in February 2014 and was the last thing of a medievalist kind I saw in the very last stages of writing this book. Or rather, it was the point at which I drew the line, deciding that some end, however arbitrary, must be put to the unstoppable flow of medievalisms which quickly becomes apparent to anyone who chooses to work on them.

Running slightly late for the performance at London's Southbank Centre, and having no idea what to expect, we arrived at the venue a little out of breath to find no signage and no directions to the now imminent performance. Eventually, more by process of elimination than anything else, we found our way to a side corridor of the centre, pushing through a roped-off entrance, walking past young men and women limbering up for a dance class in a long corridor and then, when there was almost nowhere further to go, finding a sign for *A Double Sorrow*.

This seemed typical of Chaucer's obliqueness and marginality in his own city. One has to go Kent to find Chaucer's medievalist traces, which are suddenly ubiquitous. In Canterbury, the city that Chaucer's pilgrims do not even reach, Chaucer's name is everywhere, as if guaranteeing that yes, this really *is* a medieval place.[1] Even the cafe of Turner Contemporary, the art gallery on the beach at Margate, serves Chaucerian fish and chips. But in Bardic London, already gearing up for the quatercentenary of Shakespeare's death in 2016, and where a new playhouse had just opened next to the Globe Theatre, Chaucer's is a shadowy presence, more appropriate to a customs official than a major poet.

So here he was, right out on the edges of the Southbank Centre, in what felt like the basement, in a bare room with a starkly simple production of his poem – no stage, just some candles, which are lit and then extinguished in the course of the performance. A cellist; three actors, Greenlaw herself in the role of a narrator. And yet, as we settled into the performance, as the actors shifted into words that were occasionally familiar, mostly just a little oblique to one's memories of *Troilus and Criseyde*, "As sure of where we're going as if climbing stairs. / Not noticing how one step leads to another / And step by step we're heading somewhere," there came the gradual sense that something significant was happening.[2] Translations of

---

[1]   On Chaucer's continuing presence at Canterbury see Barr, *Transporting Chaucer.*
[2]   Greenlaw, *A Double Sorrow*, 20.

Chaucer have rarely been successful; with few exceptions, they have been rejected medievalisms. In recent times Simon Armitage has had much more success by looking a little aside from Chaucer, with his versions of *Sir Gawain and the Green Knight* and the *Alliterative Morte Arthure*. Still, after Heaney and *Beowulf*, after Armitage, surrounded by Greenlaw's words, it was possible to think that there is something going on in Middle English literature. Is it that late Middle English has now become sufficiently estranged for it to be timely, today, to make it familiar again in new shapes? Do we get these translations and new versions when we need to claim something back, something that is otherwise slipping from view? Greenlaw's version of *Troilus* might have been an experiment out at the edge of the Southbank Centre but it is also a major book with Faber, an example of a major poet doing something with Chaucer beyond a quick sale, fast food, half-remembered, and in any case spurious, geographical connections. As Troilus's laughter echoed from the eighth sphere, anyway, and the last chords from the cello died away, I walked away thinking there was some future in all of this, some future for the Middle Ages.

Appendix I
The Survey of Reenactors

Participation was invited in the survey in June 2012. Responses were received from 67 reenactors from the UK, US, and continental Europe. Questions elicited responses on the topic of personae adopted and on the participants' attitudes to the Middle Ages, before and after their involvement. Participants commented on the sources they used for information on the Middle Ages.

Length of Involvement

	Number	Percentage
Less than 5 years	7	11%
5–10 years	17	26%
11–20 years	26	39%
21–30 years	12	18%
31–40 years	3	4.5%
More than 40 years	1	1.5%

Country of Origin

Country	Number	Percentage
United Kingdom	54	82%
of which: England	32	48%
Scotland	3	4.5%
Wales	2	3%
Not Specified	17	26%
USA	9	14%
Canada	2	3%
The Netherlands	1	1%

Gender

Gender	Number	Percentage
Male	35	53%
Female	31	47%

Age

Age	Overall		Male		Female	
Under 15	0	0%	0	0%	0	0%
15–20	0	0%	0	0%	0	0%
21–30	8	12%	6	17%	2	6%
31–40	13	20%	5	14%	8	26%
41–50	24	36%	15	43%	9	29%
51–60	14	21%	5	14.5%	9	29%
61–70	7	11%	4	11.5%	3	10%
Over 70	0	0%	0	0%	0	0%

Employment (*some participants selected more than one option*)

Level of Employment	Number	Percentage
FT Employed	9	14%
PT Employed	2	3%
Self-Employed	14	21%
Professional	24	36%
Military	1	2%
Student	2	3%
Not Currently Employed	3	5%
House-Spouse	4	6%
Retired	7	11%

Educational Background (*highest level recorded*)

Educational Level	Number	Percentage
School	8	12%
FE	17	26%
Undergraduate	27	41%
Postgraduate	11	17%
Military	3	4%

Periods Chosen (*a number of participants recorded more than one*)

(a) General

Period of Middle Ages	Number	Percentage
Early (500–1066)	47	71%
High (1066–1300)	4	6%
Late (1300–1500)	17	26%
Post (1500 onwards)	5	8%

(b) Specific – based on the period definitions and specific dates given by participants (NB: not all gave specifics)

Period	Number	Percentage
9th Century	1	1.5%
10th Century	6	9%
13th Century	2	3%
14th Century	6	9%
15th Century	6	9%
16th Century	3	4.5%
16th Century (India)	1	1.5%
17th Century	1	1.5%
Anglo-Saxon/Saxon	8	12%
Anglo-Danish	1	1.5%
Viking	17	26%
Hiberno-Norse	1	1.5%
Dark Ages	7	11%
Wars of the Roses	2	3%
Tudor	1	1.5%

Sources Used (*all participants selected more than one option*)

Source	Number	Percentage
Reading Fiction	27	41%
TV/Film Drama	28	42%
Read Historical/Factual Works	65	98%
Internet	59	89%
Documentary TV/Film	59	89%

Other Sources Used (*based on recurring responses*)

Source	Number	Percentage
Talking to other re-enactors/archaeologists/historians	33	50%
Visiting museums and historical sites	16	24%
Academic study	3	4.5%
Attending re-enactments	6	9%
Reading archaeological reports	8	12%
Membership of Academic Societies	1	1.5%

Appendix II
Key Moments in Medievalism

Date	Religion/Society/Politics	Literature and Scholarship	Art/Architecture/Music
1534	Act of Supremacy; Dissolution of monasteries in Britain	1540s: Leland tours monastic libraries	
1558	Death of Queen Mary: end of English Catholicism		
1570	Wars of Religion, till end of century in France	First reference in English to "Midle Age," Foxe, *Actes and Monuments*, 2nd edn.	
1589		Spenser, *Faerie Queen*, 1st edn	
1643		Jean Bolland commences *Acta Sanctorum* publishing project	
1648	Thirty Years' War concluded with Treaty of Westphalia		
1660	Civil Wars in Britain		
1663		Colbert establishes *Académie des inscriptions*	
1681		Mabillon, *De Re Diplomatica*	
1688	"Glorious Revolution" in Britain; end of Stuart rule, succession of William and Mary		
1691			Dryden/Purcell opera, *King Arthur*
1700		Dryden, *Fables, Ancient and Modern*	
1701		Re-establishment of *Académie des inscriptions*	
1703		Hickes begins publication of his *Thesaurus*	
1723		Muratori, *Rerum italicarum scriptores* (1723–38, 1751)	

1724–5		Hearne's edition of *Robert of Gloucester's Chronicle* appears; first edition of the Cotton text of *Mandeville's Travels* appears	
1754			Walpole completes Strawberry Hill
1759	British Museum opened	La Curne de Sainte-Palaye, *Mémoires sur l'ancienne chevalerie*	
1760		James Macpherson begins publishing his "translations" from Ossian	
1763	Seven Years War ends, Britain consolidates gains		
1764		Walpole, *Castle of Otranto*	
1765		Percy, *Reliques of Ancient English Poetry*, 1st edn.	
1774		Warton, *History of English Poetry*, vol. 1; La Curne de Sainte-Palaye, *Histoire littéraire des troubadours*	
1775		Tyrwhitt, *Canterbury Tales*	
1777	American independence	Warton, "The Grave of King Arthur"	
1780	Gordon Riots in Britain		
1781		Death of La Curne de Sainte-Palaye; last completed volume of Warton, *History of English Poetry*	
1789	French Revolution		
1790		Burke, *Reflections on the Revolution in France*	
1798		Wordsworth and Coleridge, *Lyrical Ballads*, 1st edn.; Scott, translation of Goethe's *Der Erlkönig*	
1801		Schiller, *Die Jungrau von Orleans*	
1802	Napoleon makes himself emperor of France	Ritson, *Ancient Engleish Metrical Romanceës*; Scott, *Minstrelsy of the Scottish Border*	
1804		Schiller, *Wilhelm Tell*	F. von Schlegel lectures on Gothic architecture
1809			Schinkel paints *Gotische Klosterruine und Baumgruppen*; in Vienna, Overbeck and Pforr found "Nazarenes"

1813		Whitaker edits *Piers Plowman*, first edition in 250 years	
1815	Fall of Napoleon	Scott, *The Lord of the Isles*	
1816		First new editions of Malory's *Morte Darthur* in nearly 200 years	
1817		First recorded use of word "mediaeval," Fosbroke, *British Monachism*	
1819	Peterloo massacre	Scott, *Ivanhoe*; Keats, "La Belle Dame Sans Merci"; Grimm, *Deutsche Grammatik*, 1st edn.	Rickman, *An Attempt to Discriminate the Styles of Gothic Architecture*, 2nd edn.
1820		Keats, *Lamia, Isabella, The Eve of St Agnes, and other Poems*	Carl Blechen enters Berlin academy
1822		Digby, *The Broad Stone of Honour*, 1st edn.	Prevalence of "Commissioners' Gothic"
1829	Catholic emancipation in Britain		
1831		Hugo, *Notre Dame de Paris*	
1833	Oxford Movement: first of Tracts appears	English version of *Notre Dame de Paris* (*The Hunchback of Notre-Dame*)	
1834	Westminster Palace burns down	Mérimée made inspector-general of historic monuments in France	
1835		Bulwer Lytton, *Rienzi: Last of the Tribunes*; Lönnrot, first version of *Kalevala*	Redesign of Westminster by Barry and Pugin begins
1836			Pugin, *Contrasts*, 1st edn.
1837	Accession of Q. Victoria		
1839	Chartism begins; Eglinton Tournament	Madden edits *Sir Gawain and the Green Knight*	Pugin's St Chad's, Birmingham, commenced
1840		"Willibald Alexis," *Der Roland von Berlin*; Browning, *Sordello*	Germany: Recommencement of building of Cologne cathedral; Wagner, *Rienzi*
1841	Newman, Tract XC		Pugin, *True Principles of Christian or Pointed Architecture*; *Contrasts*, 2nd edn.
1842			Australia: Robert Willson made Catholic bishop of Hobart

1843		Carlyle, *Past and Present*; Bulwer Lytton, *Last of the Barons*; Manners, *Plea for National Holy-Days*; France: Mérimée, *Monuments historiques*	Pugin, *Apology for the Revival of Christian Architecture in England*
1844		First recorded use of word "mediaevalism," in *The British Churchman*; France: Commission des monuments historiques established; Abbé Migne commences *Patrologia latina*	France: Viollet-le-Duc begins restorations of La Sainte-Chapelle and Notre-Dame in Paris
1845	Newman converts to Catholicism	Disraeli, *Sybil, or the Two Nations*	Cambridge Camden Society moves to London, becomes Ecclesiological Society
1846			
1847			
1848	Revolutions in Europe; Marx and Engels, *Communist Manifesto*; France: Louis-Napoleon becomes president		Rossetti, Millais, Holman Hunt, est. Pre-Raphaelite Brotherhood
1849		Charlotte Guest's translation of *Mabinogion* appears; Lönnrot, final version of *Kalevala*	Ruskin, *Seven Lamps of Architecture*, 1st edn.; Schlegel, English transl. of "An Essay on Gothic Architecture"; Millais exhibits *Isabella*
1850			
1851			Great Exhibition, London, includes Pugin's Mediaeval Court; Madox Brown completes *Chaucer at the Court of Edward III*
1852	Second Empire established in France		
1853		Ruskin, *The Stones of Venice*	
1854		Ruskin, *Lectures on Architecture*	Viollet-le-Duc, *Dictionnaire raisonné de l'architecture française*
1857		Founding of Rolls Series of historical publications	Morris, Rossetti, and Burne-Jones paint the Oxford Union
1858		Morris, *The Defence of Guinevere and Other Poems*	Wardell emigrates to Australia
1859		Tennyson, *Idylls of the King*, first version	A. Waterhouse designs Manchester Assize Courts building

1861		Founding of Morris, Marshall, Faulkener & Co presages Arts and Crafts movement
1864	Furnivall establishes Early English Text Society	
1865		George Gilbert Scott begins designs for Midland Grand Hotel, St Pancras
1870	Unification of Germany; Franco-Prussian War	
1875	Establishment of *Monumenta Germaniae Historica* and *Société des anciens textes français*	
1877		A. Waterhouse completes Manchester town hall; founding of SPAB
1882	Swinburne, *Tristram of Lyonesse*; death of Rossetti	Wagner's last opera, *Parsifal*
1883		Death of Wagner
1885	Tennyson completes *Idylls of the King*	
1888	Morris, *A Dream of John Ball*	J. W. Waterhouse paints *Lady of Shalott*
1892	Death of Tennyson	US: Commencement of St John the Divine, New York
1896	Death of Morris	
1897		Australia: Consecration of Wardell's St Patrick's, Melbourne
1898	Huysmans, *La Cathédrale*	
1900	Death of Ruskin	John Rylands Library, Manchester, opens
1901	Death of Queen Victoria	
1903		Giles Gilbert Scott wins Liverpool cathedral competition
1906	Everyman's Library established, includes Guest's *Mabinogion*, Malory, *Morte Darthur*	Cram becomes university architect at Princeton, consolidates Collegiate Gothic

Bibliography

Aberth, John. *A Knight at the Movies: Medieval History on Film*. London: Routledge, 2003

Adams, Henry. *Mont-Saint-Michel and Chartres*, intro. and notes by Raymond Carney. 1904; New York: Penguin, 1986

A Few Words to Church Builders, 3rd edn. Cambridge, 1844

"A Glance at the Exhibition," *Chambers's Edinburgh Journal* ns no. 387, Saturday 31 May, 1851, 337–40

Agnew, Vanessa. "Introduction: What Is Reenactment?" *Criticism* 46 (2004): 327–39

——. "History's Affective Turn: Historical Reenactment and its Work in the Present," *Rethinking History: The Journal of Theory and Practice* 11 (2007): 299–312

Alexander, Michael. *Medievalism: The Middle Ages in Modern England*. New Haven: Yale University Press, 2007

Allen, Charlotte. "A Dark Age for Medievalists," *Weekly Standard*, 2 June 2008, volume 13, issue 36; http://www.weeklystandard.com/Content/Public/Articles/000/000/015/146etleh.asp (accessed 26 August 2014)

Anderson, David. "A Language to Translate Into: The Pre-Elizabethan Idiom of Pound's Later Cavalcanti Translations," *SiM* 2, no. 1 (1982): 9–18

Andrews, Brian. *Australian Gothic: The Gothic Revival in Australian Architecture from the 1840s to the 1950s*. Melbourne: Miegunyah Press at Melbourne University Press, 2001

——. *Creating a Gothic Paradise: Pugin at the Antipodes*. Hobart: Tasmanian Museum & Art Gallery, 2002

Anstruther, Ian. *The Knight and the Umbrella: An Account of The Eglinton Tournament 1839*. London: Geoffrey Bles, 1963

"Architectural Drawings," *Athenaeum* 1071, 6 May 1848, 465

Armitage, Simon, trans. *The Death of King Arthur*. London: Faber and Faber, 2012

——. *Sir Gawain and the Green Knight: A New Verse Translation*. New York: W.W. Norton, 2007

Bale, John, and John Leland. *The laboryouse iourney [and] serche of Iohan Leylande, for Englandes antiquitees...* London: S. Mierdman, 1549, STC 15445

Banham, Joanna, and Jennifer Harris, eds. *William Morris and the Middle Ages: A Collection of Essays*. Manchester: Manchester University Press, 1984

Barr, Helen. *Transporting Chaucer*. Manchester: Manchester University Press, 2014.

——. "Religious Practice in Chaucer's *Prioress's Tale:* Rabbit and/or Duck?" *SAC* 32 (2010): 39–66

Baudrillard, Jean. "The Orders of Simulacra," trans. Philip Beitchman, in Jean Baudrillard, *Simulations*, trans. Paul Foss, Paul Patton, and Philip Beitchman. New York: Semiotext(e), 1983, 83–159

Benjamin, Walter. "Paris, the Capital of the Nineteenth Century, <Exposé of 1935>," *The Arcades Project*, trans. Howard Eiland and Kevin McLaughlin. Cambridge MA and London: Belknap Press, 1999, 1–13

——. "The Work of Art in the Age of Mechanical Reproduction," *Illuminations*, ed. with intro. by Hannah Arendt, trans. Harry Zohn. London: Fontana, 1973, 211–44

Bennett, Josephine Waters. *The Rediscovery of Sir John Mandeville*. 1954; New York: Kraus Reprint, 1971.

Beregi, Tamas. "Nostalgia for a Golden Age: Arthurian Legends in Twentieth-Century Visual Culture," Unpublished PhD dissertation, University of Manchester, 2007

Bernard-Griffiths, Simone, Pierre Glaudes, and Bertrand Vibert, eds. *La fabrique du moyen âge: La réception de la civilisation médiévale dans la littérature française du XIX siècle*. Paris: H. Champion, 2006

Bernau, Anke, and Bettina Bildhauer, eds. *Medieval Film*. Manchester: Manchester University Press, 2009

Berns, Ute, and Andrew James Johnston. "Medievalism: A Very Short Introduction," *European Journal of English Studies* 15 (2011): 97–100

Bessborough, The Earl of, ed. *Lady Charlotte Guest: Extracts from her Journal 1833–1852*. London: John Murray, 1950

Biddick, Kathleen. *The Shock of Medievalism*. Durham NC and London: Duke University Press, 1998

Bidney, Martin. "Dante Retailored for the Nineteenth Century: His Place in Ruskin's Thought," *SiM* 1, no.1 (1979): 33–44

Bildhauer, Bettina. *Filming the Middle Ages*. London: Reaktion Books, 2011

"Billy Bragg and BNP clash over St George's Day," *The Guardian*, 24 April 2010; http://www.guardian.co.uk/politics/2010/apr/24/billy-bragg-barnbrook-st-george (accessed 7 September 2011)

Birnbaum, Dieter, ed. *Rezeption deutscher Dichtung des Mittelalters*. Greifswald: Ernst-Moritz-Arndt Universität, 1982

Blond, Phillip. *Red Tory: How [the] Left and Right have Broken Britain and How We Can Fix It*. London: Faber and Faber, 2010

Boldrini, Lucia, ed. *Medieval Joyce*. Amsterdam and New York: Rodopi, 2002

Boos, Florence S., ed. *History and Community: Essays in Victorian Medievalism*. New York: Garland, 1992

——. "The Medieval Tales of William Morris' *The Earthly Paradise*," *SiM* 1, no.1 (1979): 45–54

Bourdieu, Pierre. *The Field of Cultural Production: Essays on Art and Literature*, ed. and intro. Randal Johnson. Cambridge: Polity Press, 1993

Brantlinger, Patrick. "What is 'Sensational' about the 'Sensational Novel'?" *Nineteenth Century Fiction* 37 (1982): 1–28

Bronte, Charlotte. *Villette*, ed. Herbert Rosengarten and Margaret Smith. Oxford: Clarendon Press, 1984

Bryden, Inga. *Reinventing King Arthur: The Arthurian Legends in Victorian Culture.* Aldershot: Ashgate, 2005

Bulwer Lytton, Sir Edward. *The Last of the Barons,* 2 vols. 1843; Edinburgh and London: William Blackwood and Sons, 1861

Bump, Jerome. "Hopkins's Imagery and Medievalist Poetics," *Victorian Poetry* 15 (1977): 99–119

——. "Hopkins, Pater, and Medievalism," *Victorian Newsletter* 50 (1976): 10–15

Busby, Keith. "An Eighteenth-Century Plea on Behalf of the Medieval Romances: La Curne de Sainte-Palaye's *Memoire concernant la lecture des anciens romans de chevalerie,*" *SiM* 3 (1987): 55–69

Butler, Marilyn. "Romanticism in England," in Roy Porter and Mikulas Teich, eds. *Romanticism in National Context.* Cambridge: Cambridge University Press, 1988, 37–67

——. *Romantics, Rebels and Reactionaries: English Literature and its Background 1760–1830.* Oxford: Oxford University Press, 1981

C.B. "On Mediaeval Art, as Exemplified in the Great Exhibition of 1851," *Gentleman's Magazine* (December 1851), 579–85

Calin, William. "Leslie Workman: A Speech of Thanks," in Utz and Shippey, eds. *Medievalism in the Modern World,* 451–52

Camber, Rebecca. "Top lawyer, his lover and a sex session that led to bloodshed at the Hilton," *Daily Mail,* Wednesday 23 June 2010, p. 21

Camden, William. "Certaine Poemes, or Poesies, Epigrammes, Rythmes, and Epitaphs of the English Nation in former Times," in *Remaines of a greater worke, concerning Britaine...* London, 1605, STC 4521

Camille, Michael. *The Gargoyles of Notre-Dame: Medievalism and the Monsters of Modernity.* Chicago: Chicago University Press, 2009

Cantor, Norman. *Inventing the Middle Ages: The Lives, Works, and Ideas of the Great Medievalists of the Twentieth Century.* New York: William Morrow, 1991

Caselli, Daniela. *Beckett's Dantes.* Manchester: Manchester University Press, 2005

Chakrabarty, Dipesh. "Historicism and Its Supplements: A Note on a Predicament Shared by Medieval and Postcolonial Studies," in Davis and Altschul, *Medievalisms in the Postcolonial World,* 109–19

——. *Provincializing Europe: Postcolonial Thought and Historical Difference.* Princeton and Oxford: Princeton University Press, 2000

Chandler, Alice. *A Dream of Order: The Medieval Ideal in Nineteenth-Century English Literature.* 1970; London: Routledge & Kegan Paul, 1971

Chibnall, Marjorie. *The Debate on the Norman Conquest.* Manchester: Manchester University Press, 1999

Clark, Susan L. and Julian C. Wasserman. "*Tess of the d'Urbervilles* as Arthurian Romance," *SiM* 1, no.1 (1979): 55–64

Cole, Andrew, and D. Vance Smith, eds. *The Legitimacy of the Middle Ages: On the Unwritten History of Theory.* Durham NC and London: Duke University Press, 2010

Colley, Linda. *Britons: Forging the Nation 1707–1837.* New Haven: Yale University Press, 1992

Collier, Paul. *The Bottom Billion: Why the Poorest Countries Are Failing and What Can Be Done about It*. Oxford: Oxford University Press, 2007

Collins, Wilkie. *No Name*, ed. Mark Ford. 1862; London: Penguin, 1994

Cram, Ralph Adams. *Walled Towns*. 1919; Boston: Marshall Jones, 1920

Cramer, Michael A. *Medieval Fantasy as Performance: The Society for Creative Anachronism and the Current Middle Ages*. Lanham MD: Scarecrow Press, 2010

Crane, Ronald S. "The Vogue of *Guy of Warwick* from the Close of the Middle Ages to the Romantic Revival," *PMLA* 30 (1915): 125–94

D'Arcens, Louise, ed. *The Cambridge Companion to Medievalism*, forthcoming.

——. *Old Songs in the Timeless Land: Medievalism in Australian Literature 1840–1910*. Turnhout: Brepols, 2011

——. "Laughing in the Face of the Past: Satire and Nostalgia in Medieval Heritage Tourism," *postmedieval* 2 (2011): 155–70

Dakyns, Janine. *The Middle Ages in French Literature*. London: Oxford University Press, 1973

Damico, Helen, with Donald Fennema and Karmen Lenz, eds. *Medieval Scholarship: Biographical Studies in the Formation of a Discipline, vol. 2: Literature and Philology*. New York and London: Garland, 1998

——, and Joseph B. Zavadil, eds. *Medieval Scholarship: Biographical Studies in the Formation of a Discipline*. New York and London: Garland, 1995

Dane, Joseph A. *Who Is Buried in Chaucer's Tomb? Studies in the Reception of Chaucer's Book*. East Lansing: Michigan State University Press, 1998

——. Review of Paul G. Ruggiers, *Editing Chaucer: The Great Tradition* (Norman, OK: Pilgrim Books, 1984), *Huntington Library Quarterly* 54 (1991): 283–300

Davis, Alex. *Renaissance Historical Fiction: Sidney, Deloney, Nashe*. Cambridge: D. S. Brewer, 2011

——. *Chivalry and Romance in the English Renaissance*. Cambridge: D. S. Brewer, 2003

Davis, Kathleen, *Periodization and Sovereignty: How Ideas of Feudalism and Secularization Govern the Politics of Time*. Philadelphia: University of Pennsylvania Press, 2008

Davis, Kathleen, and Nadia Altschul. "Introduction: The Idea of 'The Middle Ages' Outside Europe," in Davis and Altschul, eds. *Medievalisms in the Postcolonial World*, 1–24

——, and Nadia Altschul, eds. *Medievalisms in the Postcolonial World: The Idea of "The Middle Ages" Outside Europe*. Baltimore: Johns Hopkins University Press, 2009

De Groot, Jerome. *Consuming History: Historians and Heritage in Contemporary Popular Culture*. Oxford and New York: Routledge, 2009

De la Bretèque, François Amy. *L'Imaginaire médiéval dans le cinéma occidental*. Paris: Champion, 2004

Defoe, Daniel. *Robinson Crusoe*, ed. Angus Ross. Harmondsworth: Penguin, 1965

Dellheim, Charles. "Interpreting Victorian Medievalism," in Boos, ed. *History and Community*, 39–58

——. *The Face of the Past: The Preservation of the Medieval Inheritance in Victorian England*. Cambridge: Cambridge University Press, 1982

Dickens, Charles. *The Old Curiosity Shop*, ed. Elizabeth M. Brennan. Oxford: Oxford University Press, 2008
——. *Great Expectations*, ed. Margaret Cardwell. Oxford: Clarendon Press, 1993
Digby, Kenelm Henry. *The Broad Stone of Honour*, 5 vols. London: Bernard Quaritch, 1877, 1876
——. *The Broad Stone of Honour*. London: Rivington, 1823
Dinshaw, Carolyn. "All Kinds of Time," *Studies in the Age of Chaucer* 35 (2013): 3–25
——. *How Soon is Now?: Medieval Texts, Amateur Readers, and the Queerness of Time*. Durham NC and London: Duke University Press, 2012
——. "Temporalities," in Paul Strohm, ed. *Oxford Twenty-First Century Approaches to Literature: Middle English*. Oxford: Oxford University Press, 2007, 107–23
——. *Getting Medieval: Sexualities and Communities, Pre- and Postmodern*. Durham NC and London: Duke University Press, 1999
Dinzelbacher, Peter, ed. *Sachwörterbuch der Mediävistik*. Stuttgart: Alfred Kröner Verlag, 1992
Disraeli, Benjamin. *Sybil, or, the Two Nations*, ed. with an intro. and notes by Sheila M. Smith. Oxford: Oxford University Press, 1981
Dodsworth, M. "Twentieth-Century Lit 1930–1998," in *An Outline of English Literature*, ed. Pat Rogers. Oxford: Oxford University Press, 1998, 392–449
Duckworth, Melanie. "Medievalism and the Language of Belonging in Selected Works of Les Murray, Randolph Stow, Francis Webb, Kevin Hart." Unpublished PhD dissertation, University of Leeds, 2009
Duff, David. *Romance and Revolution: Shelley and the Politics of a Genre*. Cambridge: Cambridge University Press, 1994
Duncan, Ian. "*Waverley* (Walter Scott, 1814)," in *The Novel, Volume 2: Forms and Themes*, ed. Franco Moretti. Princeton and Oxford: Princeton University Press, 2006, 173–80
——. *Modern Romance and Transformations of the Novel: The Gothic, Scott, Dickens*. Cambridge: Cambridge University Press, 1992
During, Simon. *Exit Capitalism: Literary Culture, Theory, and Post-Secular Modernity*. London and New York: Routledge, 2010
——. "Mimic Toil: Eighteenth-Century Preconditions for the Modern Historical Reenactment," *Rethinking History: The Journal of Theory and Practice*, 11 (2007): 313–33
E.T. "A Visit to Tintagel," *Once a Week* 4:98 (11 May 1861), 553–57
Echard, Siân. *Printing the Middle Ages*. Philadelphia: University of Pennsylvania Press, 2008
Eco, Umberto. *Faith in Fakes: Travels in Hyperreality*, trans. William Weaver. 1986; London Vintage, 1998
Elliott, Ralph. "Hardy and the Middle Ages," *The Thomas Hardy Journal* 6 (1990): 97–108
Emery, Elizabeth. "Postcolonial Gothic: The Medievalism of America's 'National' Cathedrals," in Davis and Altschul, eds. *Medievalisms in the Postcolonial World*, 237–64
——. "Medievalism and the Middle Ages," *SiM* 17 (2009): 77–85

——. *Romancing the Cathedral: Gothic Architecture in Fin-de-Siècle French Culture.* Albany: State University of New York Press, 2001

Erisman, Wendy Elizabeth. "Forward into the Past: The Poetics and Politics of Community in Two Historical Re-Creation Groups." Unpublished PhD dissertation, University of Texas at Austin, 1998

Fabian, Johannes. *Time and the Other: How Anthropology Makes its Object.* 1983; New York: Columbia University Press, 2002

"False Reports about the Vicar of Leeds," *The Hull Packet and East Riding Times,* no. 3399, 22 February 1850

Farrelly, Elizabeth. "Icon sets the tone for everything but music." *Sydney Morning Herald,* 11 November 2006; http://www.smh.com.au/news/national/icon-sets-the-tone-for-everything-but-music/2006/11/10/1162661901881.html?page=fullpage#contentSwap1 (accessed 26 August 2014)

Fellows, Jennifer. "*Bevis redivivus*: The Printed Editions of *Sir Bevis of Hampton,*" in *Romance Reading on the Book: Essays on Medieval Narrative presented to Maldwyn Mills,* ed. Fellows, Rosalind Field, Gillian Rogers and Judith Weiss. Cardiff: University of Wales Press, 1996, 251–68

Ferguson, Niall. *Civilization: The West and the Rest.* New York: Penguin, 2011

Ferguson, Wallace, *The Renaissance in Historical Thought.* Boston: Houghton Mifflin, 1948

Finke, Laurie A., and Martin B. Shichtman. *Cinematic Illuminations: The Middle Ages on Film.* Baltimore: Johns Hopkins University Press, 2010

Fisher, Susan. "Choosing a Persona," in Hilary Powers, ed., *The Known World Handbook.* Milpitas CA: Society for Creative Anachronism, 1985, 98–100

Fosbrooke [Fosbroke], Thomas Dudley. *British Monachism, or, Manners and Customs of the Monks and Nuns of England...* new [2nd] edn. 2 vols. London, 1817

Frantzen, Allen J. *Bloody Good: Chivalry, Sacrifice, and the Great War.* Chicago and London: University of Chicago Press, 2004

——. *Desire for Origins: New Language, Old English, and Teaching the Tradition.* New Brunswick and London: Rutgers University Press, 1990

Freedman, Paul, and Gabrielle M. Spiegel. "Medievalisms Old and New: The Rediscovery of Alterity in North American Medieval Studies," *AHR* 103 (1998): 677–704

Friedrichs, Jörg. "The Meaning of New Medievalism," *European Journal of International Relations* 7 (2001): 475–501

Frow, John. *Cultural Studies and Cultural Value.* Oxford: Clarendon Press, 1995

Fugelso, Karl. Editorial note, *SiM* 17 (2009): xi

Gamer, Michael. *Romanticism and the Gothic: Genre, Reception, and Canon Formation.* Cambridge: Cambridge University Press, 2000

Ganim, John. "Cosmopolitanism, Sovereignty, and Medievalism," *ALS: Australian Literary Studies* 26 (2011): 6–20

——. "Medieval Film *Noir*: Anatomy of a Metaphor," in Anke Bernau and Bettina Bildhauer eds. *Medieval Film.* Manchester: Manchester University Press, 2009, 182–202

——. *Medievalism and Orientalism: Three Essays on Literature, Architecture and Cultural Identity.* New York: Palgrave, 2005

——. "Native Studies: Orientalism and Medievalism," in J. J. Cohen, ed., *The Post-colonial Middle Ages*. New York: Palgrave, 2000, 123–34

Gaskell, Elizabeth. *Mary Barton*, ed. Thomas Recchio. Norton Critical Edition. New York and London: Norton, 2008

Geary, Patrick J. *The Myth of Nations: The Medieval Origins of Europe*. Princeton NJ: Princeton University Press, 2002

Gentry, Francis G., and Ulrich Müller. "The Reception of the Middle Ages in Germany: An Overview," *SiM* 3, no. 4 (Spring 1991): 399–422

Geoffrey of Monmouth. *The History of the Kings of Britain*, trans. Lewis Thorpe. Harmondsworth: Penguin, 1966

Gikandi, Simon. "Africa and the Signs of Medievalism," in Davis and Altschul, eds., *Medievalisms in the Postcolonial World*, 369–82

Girouard, Mark. *The Return to Camelot: Chivalry and the English Gentleman*. New Haven and London: Yale University Press, 1981

Gordon, George. "Medium Aevum and the Middle Age," *SPE Tract* 19 (1925): 3–28

Gossman, Lionel. *Medievalism and the Ideologies of the Enlightenment: The World and Work of La Curne de Sainte-Palaye*. Baltimore: Johns Hopkins Press, 1968

Greenlaw, Lavinia. *A Double Sorrow: Troilus and Criseyde*. London: Faber and Faber, 2014

Grewell, Cory Lowell. "Neomedievalism: An Eleventh Little Middle Ages?" *SiM* 19 (2010): 34–43

Griffin, Susan M. "The Yellow Mask, the Black Robe, and the Woman in White: Wilkie Collins, Anti-Catholic Discourse, and the Sensation Novel," *Narrative* 12.1 (2004): 55–73

Groom, Nick. *The Making of Percy's Reliques*. Oxford: Oxford University Press, 1999

——, Joanne Parker, and Corinna Wagner, eds. *The Oxford Handbook to Victorian Medievalism*, forthcoming

Hadjadj, Dany. "'Moyen Âge' à l' épreuve des dictionnaires," in Bernard-Griffiths et al., eds., *La Fabrique du moyen age*, 45–56

Hamilton, Adina. "A New Sort of Castle in the Air: Medievalist Communities in Contemporary Australia," in Trigg, ed. *Medievalism and the Gothic in Australian Culture*, 205–22

Hand-Book for Travellers in France. London: John Murray, 1843

Hardwick, Lorna. Editorial, *Classical Receptions Journal* 1 (2009): 1–3

Hardy, Thomas. *Jude the Obscure*, intro. J. Hillis Miller. New York, London, and Toronto: Alfred A. Knopf, 1992

——. *A Pair of Blue Eyes*, ed. Pamela Dalziel. London: Penguin, 2005

——. *A Laodicean*, ed. Jane Gatewood. Oxford and New York, 1991

Harty, Kevin. *Cinema Arthuriana*. New York: Garland, 1991

Harwood, Britton J. "The Political Use of Chaucer in Twentieth-Century America," in Utz and Shippey, eds. *Medievalism in the Modern World*, 379–92

Havely, Nick, ed. *Dante's Modern Afterlife*. London: Macmillan, 1998

Haweis, Mrs H. R. *Chaucer for Schools*. London: Chatto & Windus, Piccadilly, 1881

——. *Chaucer for Children: A Golden Key*. London: Chatto & Windus, Piccadilly, 1877

Haydock, Nickolas. *Movie Medievalism: The Imaginary Middle Ages*. Jefferson, NC: McFarland, 2008

Higson, Andrew, "'Medievalism', the Period Film and the British Past in Contemporary Cinema," in Bernau and Bildhauer, eds., *Medieval Film*.

Hill, Christopher. "The Norman Yoke," in Hill, *Puritanism and Revolution: Studies in the Interpretation of the English Revolution of the 17th Century*. London: Secker and Warburg, 1958, 50–122

Hill, Rosemary. *God's Architect: Pugin and the Building of Romantic Britain*. London: Allen Lane, 2007

Hollinghurst, Alan. *The Stranger's Child*. London: Picador, 2011

Holsinger, Bruce. *Neomedievalism, Neoconservatism, and the War on Terror*. Chicago: Prickly Paradigm, 2007

——. *The Premodern Condition: Medievalism and the Making of Theory*. Chicago and London: University of Chicago Press, 2005

——, and Ethan Knapp. "The Marxist Premodern," *Journal of Medieval and Early Modern Studies* 34, no. 2 (2004), 463–71

Hooper, John, and Luke Harding. "Muslim leaders demand apology for Pope's 'medieval' remarks," *The Guardian*, Saturday 16 September 2006; http://www.guardian.co.uk/world/2006/sep/16/catholicism.religion (accessed 26 August 2014)

Hopkins, David, and Charles Martindale. *The Oxford History of Classical Reception in English Literature: Volume 3 (1660–1790)*. Oxford: Oxford University Press, 2012

Huysmans, J.-K. *The Cathedral*, trans. Clara Bell and Brendan King. 1898; Sawtry: Dedalus Books, 2011

Jackson, Aaron Isaac. "Authoring the Century: J.R.R. Tolkien, the Great War and Modernism," *English* 59, issue 224 (2010): 44–69

Jacoby, Frank R. "Historical Method and Romantic Vision in Jacob Grimm's Writings," *SiM* 3, no. 4 (1991): 489–504

Jann, Rosemary. "The Condition of England Past and Present: Thomas Carlyle and the Middle Ages," *SiM* 1, no.1 (1979): 15–31

Jauss, Hans Robert. "The Alterity and Modernity of Medieval Literature," *NLH* 10 (1979): 181–227

Jewel, John. *Certaine sermons preached before the Queenes Maiestie*. London: Christopher Barker, 1583, STC 14596

Johnston, Arthur. *Enchanted Ground: The Study of Medieval Romance in the Eighteenth Century*. London: Athlone Press, 1964

Johnston, Judith. *George Eliot and the Discourses of Medievalism*. Turnhout: Brepols, 2006

Jones, Chris. *Strange Likeness: The Use of Old English in Twentieth-Century Poetry*. Oxford: Oxford University Press, 2006

Joy, Eileen, Myra Seaman, Kimberly K. Bell, and Mary K. Ramsey, eds. *Cultural Studies of the Modern Middle Ages*. New York: Palgrave Macmillan, 2007

Knight, Henry Gally. *An Architectural Tour in Normandy*. London: John Murray, 1836

Knight, Stephen. *Robin Hood: A Complete Study of the English Outlaw*. Oxford: Blackwell, 1994

Koerner, Lisbet. "Nazi Medievalist Art and the Politics of Memory," *SiM* 5 (1994 [for 1993]): 48–75

Koselleck, Reinhart. *The Practice of Conceptual History: Timing History, Spacing*

Concepts, trans. Todd Samuel Presner and others. Stanford CA: Stanford University Press, 2002

Kreutziger-Herr, Annette. "Imagining Medieval Music: A Short History," *SiM* 14 (2005): 81–109

Kühnel, Jürgen, Hans-Dieter Mück, and Ulrich Müller, eds. *Mittelalter-Rezeption: Gesammelte Vorträge des Salzburger Symposions "Die Rezeption Mittelalterlicher Dichter und ihrer Werke in Literatur, Bildender Kunst und Musik des 19. und 20. Jahrhunderts."* Göppingen: Kümmerle Verlag, 1979

Kuskin, William. "At Hector's Tomb: Fifteenth-Century Literary History and Shakespeare's *Troilus and Cressida*," in Sarah A. Kelen, ed. *Renaissance Retrospections: Tudor Views of the Middle Ages.* Kalamazoo: Medieval Institute Publications, 2013, 141–73

Labbie, Erin Felicia. *Lacan's Medievalism.* Minneapolis: University of Minnesota Press, 2006

Lears, T. J. Jackson. *No Place of Grace: Antimodernism and the Transformation of American Culture 1880–1920.* New York: Pantheon Books, 1981

Letters of Dante Gabriel Rossetti, ed. Oswald Doughty and John Robert Wahl, vol. 1. Oxford: Clarendon Press, 1965

Lindley, Arthur "The Ahistoricism of Medieval Film," http://tlweb.latrobe.edu.au/humanities/screeningthepast/firstrelease/fir598/ALfr3a.htm (accessed 23 October 2013)

MacCannell, Dean. *The Tourist: A New Theory of the Leisure Class*, with a new foreword by Lucy R. Lippard and a new epilogue by the author. 1976; Berkeley: University of California Press, 1989

Madden, Frederic, Letter to Francis Child, 16 November 1855, Harvard University, Houghton Library, MS Am 1922 (185)

Manners, Lord John. *A Plea for National Holy-Days.* London: Painter, 1843

Martinelli, Renzo. *Barbarossa* (film), 2009

Marx, Karl, and Friedrich Engels. *Manifesto of the Communist Party*, trans. Samuel Moore, in Karl Marx, *The Revolutions of 1848: Political Writings vol. 1*, ed. and intro. David Fernbach. London: Penguin, 1973, 62–98

Matthews, David. "Said in Jest: Who's Laughing at the Middle Ages (and When?)" *postmedieval* 5.2 (2014): 126–39

——. "From Mediaeval to Mediaevalism: A New Semantic History," *Review of English Studies* 62 (2011): 695–715

——. "Whatever Happened to Your Heroes?: Bevis of Hampton and Guy of Warwick after the Middle Ages," in *The Making of the Middle Ages: Liverpool Essays*, ed. Marios Costambeys, Andrew Hamer, and Martin Heale. Liverpool: Liverpool University Press, 2007, 54–70

——. "The Further Travels of Sir John: Mandeville, Chaucer, and the Canon of Middle English," in *Travel and Travellers from Bede to Dampier*, ed. Geraldine Barnes. Newcastle: Cambridge Scholars Press, 2005, 159–76.

——. "Infantilising the Father: Chaucer Translations and Moral Regulation," *Studies in the Age of Chaucer* 22 (2000): 93–114

McPherson, James. *Fragments of Ancient Poetry, Collected in the Highlands of Scotland and Translated from the Galic or Erse Language.* Edinburgh, 1760

Millgate, Michael. *Thomas Hardy: A Biography Revisited.* Oxford: Oxford University Press, 2004

Milner, John. "On the Rise and Progress of the Pointed Arch," in *Essays on Gothic Architecture by the Rev. T. Warton, Rev. J. Bentham, Captain Grose, and the Rev. J. Milner,* 2nd edn. London, 1802

——. *A Dissertation on the Modern Style of Altering Antient Cathedrals, as exemplified in the Cathedral of Salisbury.* London, 1798

Mommsen, Theodore E. "Petrarch's Conception of the Dark Ages," *Speculum* 17 (1942): 226–42

Moore, R. I. *The War on Heresy: Faith and Power in Medieval Europe.* London: Profile, 2012

Moreland, Kim. *The Medievalist Impulse in American Literature: Twain, Adams, Fitzgerald, and Hemingway.* Charlottesville and London: University Press of Virginia, 1996

Morgan, Gwendolyn A. "Medievalism, Authority, and the Academy," *SiM* 17 (2009): 55–67

Morris, William. *The Earthly Paradise: A Poem.* London: F. S. Ellis, 1868–70; http://morrisedition.lib.uiowa.edu/eptexts.html

——. "Gothic Architecture," in *News from Nowhere and Other Writings,* ed. with intro. and notes by Clive Wilmer. London: Penguin, 2004

Oberg, Charlotte H. "Ralph Adams Cram: Last Knight of the Gothic Quest," in Boos, ed., *History and Community,* 169–208

Odard. "A Sentimental Journey through Normandy," *Bentley's Miscellany* 21 (1847), 395–412

"October Term at Oxford, 1870," *The Graphic,* no. 49, 5 November 1870, p. 446

"Oxford Tutors—What Are They?" *The Examiner,* issue 2516, 19 April 1856, 242–43

Ortenberg, Veronica. *In Search of the Holy Grail: The Quest for the Middle Ages.* London: Hambledon Continuum, 2006

Parins, Marylyn Jackson. *Malory: The Critical Heritage.* London and New York: Routledge, 1988

Parish, H. L. *Monks, Miracles and Magic: Reformation Representations of the Medieval Church.* London: Routledge, 2005

Partner, Nancy F. "Foreword: Medieval Presentism before the Present," in Joy et al., eds. *Cultural Studies of the Modern Middle Ages,* xi–xiii

Peacham, Henry. *The Compleat Gentleman.* London, 1622

Peck, Jeffrey M. "'In the Beginning was the Word': Germany and the Origins of German Studies," in R. Howard Bloch and Stephen G. Nichols, eds. *Medievalism and the Modernist Temper.* Baltimore: Johns Hopkins University Press, 1996, 127–47

Penn, Thomas. "A Man for this Season," *The Guardian,* 20 October 2012, 44.

Proust, Marcel. *In Search of Lost Time I: Swann's Way.* trans. C. K. Scott Moncrieff and Terence Kilmartin, rev. by D. J. Enright. London: Vintage Books, 2005

Pugh, Tison, and Angela Jane Weisl. *Medievalisms: Making the Past in the Present.* London and New York: Routledge, 2013.

——. "'It's prolly fulla dirty stories': Masturbatory Allegory and Queer Medievalism in John Kennedy Toole's *A Confederacy of Dunces,*" *SiM* 15 (2007): 77–100

Puttenham, George. *The Arte of English Poesie.* London, 1589

Pykett, Lyn. *Wilkie Collins.* Oxford: Oxford University Press, 2005

Raban, Jonathan. "Crankish." Review of *Red Tory: How Left and Right Have Broken Britain and How We Can Fix It,* by Phillip Blond. *LRB* 32.8, 22 April 2010, 22–23

Radford, Andrew. *Thomas Hardy and the Survivals of Time.* Aldershot: Ashgate, 2003

Randles, Sarah. "Rebuilding the Middle Ages: Medievalism in Australian Architecture," in Trigg, ed. *Medievalism and the Gothic in Australian Culture,* 147–69

Richmond, Velma Bourgeois. *The Legend of Guy of Warwick.* New York and London: Garland, 1996

Rickman, Thomas. *An Attempt to Discriminate the Styles of Architecture, from the Conquest to the Reformation.* London, 1817

Rigby, S. H. "Historical Materialism: Social Structure and Social Change in the Middle Ages," *Journal of Medieval and Early Modern Studies* 34 (2004): 473–522

Rigney, Ann. *The Afterlives of Walter Scott: Memory on the Move.* Oxford: Oxford University Press, 2012

Robichaud, Paul. *Making the Past Present: David Jones, the Middle Ages, & Modernism.* Washington DC: Catholic University of America Press, 2007

Robinson, Carol L., and Pamela Clements. "Living with Neomedievalism," *SiM* 18 (2009): 55–75

Robinson, Fred C. "*Medieval,* the *Middle Ages,*" in *The Tomb of Beowulf and other Essays on Old English.* Oxford: Blackwells, 1993, 304–15

Rogers, Shannon L. "Medievalism in the Last Novels of Thomas Hardy: New Wine in Old Bottles," *English Literature in Transition, 1880–1920* 42 (1999): 298–316

Rouse, Robert Allen, and Cory James Rushton. "Arthurian Geography," in Elizabeth Archibald and Ad Putter, eds. *The Cambridge Companion to the Arthurian Legend.* Cambridge: Cambridge University Press, 2009, 218–34

Rusbridger, Alan. "Can we, together, lift one village out of the Middle Ages?" *The Guardian,* Saturday 20 October 2007; http://www.guardian.co.uk/katine/2007/oct/20/about (accessed 26 August 2014)

Ruskin, John. "Traffic," in *The Political Economy of Art; Unto this Last; Sesame and Lilies; The Crown of Wild Olive.* London: Macmillan, 1912, 322–44; Originally published in *The Crown of Wild Olive: Three Lectures on Work, Traffic and War.* London, 1866

——. *The Seven Lamps of Architecture.* London: Smith, Elder & Co., 1849; 2nd edn. London: Smith, Elder, and Co., 1855

——. "The Nature of Gothic," in *The Stones of Venice,* vol. 2. London: Smith, Elder & Co., 1853

Sahlins, Marshall. *Culture and Practical Reason.* Chicago: University of Chicago Press, 1976

Salih, Sarah. "Julian in Norwich: Heritage and Iconography," in Salih and Denise N. Baker, eds. *Julian of Norwich's Legacy: Medieval Mysticism and Post-Medieval Reception.* New York: Palgrave Macmillan, 2009, 153–72

Samuel, Raphael. *Theatres of Memory, vol. 1: Past and Present in Contemporary Culture.* London: Verso, 1994

Schlegel, Friedrich von. *The Aesthetic and Miscellaneous Works of Frederick von Schlegel,* trans. E. J. Millington. London: Henry G. Bohn, 1860

Schofield, Hugh. "France's new medieval castle," BBC News, 30 June 2010, http://www.bbc.co.uk/news/10440300 (accessed 20 September 2012)

Scott, Sir Walter. *Ivanhoe*, ed. with an intro. by A. N. Wilson. Harmondsworth: Penguin, 1982

Selden, John. *The historie of tithes...* London, 1618, STC 22172.3

Shakespeare, William, and John Fletcher. *Henry VIII (All is True)*, ed. Gordon McMullan. London: Arden Shakespeare, 2000

Shelston, Alan, ed. *Thomas Carlyle: Selected Writings*. London: Penguin, 1971

Shippey, T. A. "Medievalisms and Why They Matter," *SiM* 17 (2009): 45–54

——. *J. R. R. Tolkien: Author of the Century*. London: HarperCollins, 2000

Simmons, Clare A. "Medievalism: Its Linguistic History in Nineteenth-Century Britain," *SiM* 17 (2009): 28–35

Simpson, James. *Under the Hammer: Iconoclasm in the Anglo-American Tradition*. Oxford: Oxford University Press, 2010

——. *The Oxford English Literary History, vol. 2: Reform and Cultural Revolution*. Oxford: Oxford University Press, 2002

——. "The Rule of Medieval Imagination," in Jeremy Dimmick, Simpson, and Nicolette Zeeman, eds. *Images, Idolatry, and Iconoclasm in Late Medieval England: Textuality and Visual Image*. Oxford: Oxford University Press, 2002, 4–24

Smith, R. J. *The Gothic Bequest: Medieval Institutions in British Thought, 1688–1833*. Cambridge: Cambridge University Press, 1987

Spooner, Catherine. *Contemporary Gothic*. London: Reaktion, 2006

Stanley, E. G. "The Early Middle Ages = The Dark Ages = The Heroic Age of England and in English," in *The Middle Ages after the Middle Ages*, ed. Marie-Françoise Alamichel and Derek Brewer. Cambridge: D.S. Brewer, 1997, 43–77

Stevenson, William. *A Supplement to the First Edition of Mr Bentham's History and Antiquities of the Cathedral and Conventual Church of Ely*. Norwich, 1817

Struther, William. *A looking glasse for princes and people Delivered in a sermon of thanksgiving for the birth of the hopefull Prince Charles...* Edinburgh, 1632, STC 23369

Sutherland, John. "Waverley Street," *TLS* 5694, 18 May 2012, 3–4

Swinburne, Algernon. *Tristram of Lyonesse and other Poems*. London: Chatto & Windus, 1882

Tambling, Jeremy. *Going Astray: Dickens and London*. London: Longman, 2008

Taylor, Beverly, and Elisabeth Brewer. *The Return of King Arthur: British and American Arthurian Literature since 1800*. Cambridge: D. S. Brewer, 1983

"The New Protestant Leadership," *Manchester Guardian*, 16 September 1854, p. 6

"The Russian Epidemic," *The Graphic*, no. 479, 1 February 1879, 98

Thompson, E. P. *The Making of the English Working Class*. 1963; Harmondsworth: Penguin, 1968

Thorpe, Adam. *Hodd*. London: Jonathan Cape, 2009

"Tintagel Castle," *Leisure Hour* 1218, 1 May 1875, 280–82

"Tintagel Castle," *Sharpe's London Magazine of Entertainment and Instruction* 4 (January 1854), 173–74

Tolkien, J. R. R. *Tree and Leaf*. London: Unwin Books, 1964

——. "*Beowulf*: The Monsters and the Critics," *Proceedings of the British Academy* 22 (1937): 245–95

——. *The Book of Lost Tales, Parts I and II*, ed. Christopher Tolkien. London: George Allen & Unwin, 1983, 1984

Tomarken, Edward. "'The Fictions of Romantic Chivalry: Samuel Johnson's Attitudes to the Middle Ages," *SiM* 1, no.1 (1979): 5–13

Townsend, Mark. "Revealed: full horror of Gitmo inmate's beatings," *The Observer*, 22 February 2009, p. 6; http://www.guardian.co.uk/world/2009/feb/22/binyam-mohamed-injuries

Trigg, Stephanie, and Thomas A. Prendergast. *Medievalism and its Discontents*. Forthcoming

Trigg, Stephanie. *Shame and Honor: A Vulgar History of the Order of the Garter*. Philadelphia: University of Pennsylvania Press, 2012

——, ed. *Medievalism and the Gothic in Australian Culture*. Making the Middle Ages 8. Turnhout: Brepols, 2005

——. "Walking through Cathedrals: Scholars, Pilgrims, and Medieval Tourists," *New Medieval Literatures* 7 (2005): 9–33

——. "Once and Future Medievalism," *antiTHESIS* Forum, vol. 3; http://pandora.nla.gov.au/pan/66374/20070301-0000/www.english.unimelb.edu.au/antithesis/new2005/forum-3/index.html (accessed 26 August 2014)

——. Review of James Gallant, *The Year's Work in Medievalism: 1995* 10 (1999), in *Prolepsis: The Heidelberg Review of English Studies* 9 (September 2001); http://www.rzuser.uni-heidelberg.de/~ps9/prolepsis/01_06_tri.html (accessed 26 August 2014)

Turner, Sharon. *The History of the Anglo-Saxons*. London, 1799

Tyrwhitt, Thomas. *Poems Supposed To Have Been Written at Bristol by Thomas Rowley, and Others*. London: T. Payne, 1777.

Upton, Dell. "'Authentic' Anxieties" in Nezar AlSayyad, ed. *Consuming Tradition, Manufacturing Heritage: Global Norms and Urban Forms in the Age of Tourism*. London: Routledge, 2001, 298–306

Utz, Richard. "Coming to Terms with Medievalism," *European Journal of English Studies* 15 (2011): 101–13

——. "'There Are Places We Remember': Situating the Medieval Past in Postmedieval Cultural Memories," *Transfiguration: Nordisk Tidsskrift for Kunst og Kristendom* 6.2 (2004): 89–108

——. "Resistance to (the New) Medievalism? Comparative Deliberations on (National) Philology, *Mediävalismus*, and *Mittelalter-Rezeption* in Germany and North America," in Roger Dahood, ed. *The Future of the Middle Ages and the Renaissance: Problems, Trends, and Opportunities for Research* (Turnhout: Brepols, 1998), 151–70

Utz, Richard, and Tom Shippey, eds. *Medievalism in the Modern World: Essays in Honour of Leslie Workman*. Turnhout, Brepols, 1998

Utzig, Maj. Nicholas. "(Re)casting the Past: The Cloisters and Medievalism," *Year's Work in Medievalism* 27 (2012) http://ejournals.library.gatech.edu/medievalism/index.php/studies (accessed 26 August 2014)

Verduin, Kathleen. "Grace of Action: Dante in the Life of Longfellow," *Dante Studies* 128 (2010): 17–44

——. "Dante's Inferno, Jonathan Edwards, and New England Calvinism," *Dante Studies* 123 (2005): 133–61

——. "Sayers, Sex, and Dante," *Dante Studies* 111 (1993): 223–33

——. "Lawrence and the Middle Ages," *D. H. Lawrence Review* 18 (1986): 169–81

Voss, Jürgen. *Das Mittelalter im Historischen Denken Frankreichs*. Munich: Wilhelm Fink Verlag, 1972

Walpole, Horace. *The Castle of Otranto: A Gothic Story*, ed. W. S. Lewis. Oxford and New York: Oxford University Press, 1982

Wapnewski, Peter. *Mittelalter-Rezeption: Ein Symposion*. Stuttgart: Metzler, 1986

Warren, Michelle R. "Medievalism and the Making of Nations," in Davis and Altschul, eds. *Medievalisms in the Postcolonial World*, 286–98

Warton, Thomas. "The Grave of King Arthur," 1777; http://spenserians.cath.vt.edu/ TextRecord.php?action=GET&textsid=34908 (accessed 26 August 2014)

Waters, Chris. "Marxism, Medievalism and Popular Culture" in Boos, ed. *History and Community*, 137–68

Webb, Igor. "The Bradford Wool Exchange: Industrial Capitalism and the Popularity of Gothic," *Victorian Studies* 20 (1976): 45–68

Wedgwood, Alexandra. "The New Palace of Westminster," in Paul Atterbury and Clive Wainwright, eds., *Pugin: A Gothic Passion*. New Haven and London: Yale University Press, 1994

Williams, Raymond. *Marxism and Literature*. Oxford: Oxford University Press, 1977

Windeatt, B. A. "Thomas Tyrwhitt," in Paul G. Ruggiers, ed., *Editing Chaucer: The Great Tradition*. Norman, OK: Pilgrim Books, 1984, 117–43

Woodward, Will, and Rebecca Smithers. "Clarke dismisses medieval historians," *The Guardian*, 9 May 2003; http://www.guardian.co.uk/uk/2003/may/09/highereducation.politics (accessed 25 August 2014)

Woolf, D. R. "The Dawn of the Artifact: The Antiquarian Impulse in England, 1500–1730," *SiM* 4 (1992): 5–35

Workman, Leslie. "Editorial," *SiM* 7 (1995): 2

——. "Medievalism and Romanticism," *Poetica* 39–40 (1994): 1–40

Wright, Thomas, ed. *The Canterbury Tales of Geoffrey Chaucer: A New Text with Illustrative Notes*, 3 vols. London: Percy Society, 1847–51

Index

Medievalism

I
Anglo-Saxon Culture and the Modern Imagination
edited by David Clark and Nicholas Perkins

II
Medievalist Enlightenment: From Charles Perrault to Jean-Jacques Rousseau
Alicia C. Montoya

III
Memory and Myths of the Norman Conquest
Siobhan Brownlie

IV
Comic Medievalism: Laughing at the Middle Ages
Louise D'Arcens

V
Medievalism: Key Critical Terms
edited by Elizabeth Emery and Richard Utz

VI
Medievalism: A Critical History
David Matthews

VII
Chivalry and the Medieval Past
edited by Katie Stevenson and Barbara Gribling

VIII
Georgian Gothic: Medievalist Architecture, Furniture and Interiors, 1730–1840
Peter N. Lindfield

Lightning Source UK Ltd.
Milton Keynes UK
UKOW06f2004220617

303813UK00001B/101/P